Andy Murray

CHAMPION

Andy Murray

CHAMPION

The Full Extraordinary Story

MARK HODGKINSON

SIMON &
SCHUSTER

London · New York · Sydney · Toronto · New Delhi

A CBS COMPANY

First published in Great Britain by Simon & Schuster UK Ltd, 2012
A CBS COMPANY

Copyright © 2012 by Mark Hodgkinson

1 3 5 7 9 10 8 6 4 2

Simon & Schuster UK Ltd
1st Floor
222 Gray's Inn Road
London
WC1X 8HB

www.simonandschuster.co.uk

Simon & Schuster Australia, Sydney
Simon & Schuster India, New Delhi

A CIP catalogue for this book is available
from the British Library.

Hardback ISBN 978-1-47112-652-9
Trade paperback ISBN 978-1-47112-653-6
Ebook ISBN 978-1-47112-655-0

Typeset by M Rules
Printed and bound by CPI Group (UK) Ltd, Croydon, CR0 4YY

For Amy and Molly

Contents

Prologue

Prologue

Andy Murray was looking in the bathroom mirror. He has never been a vain man, and at almost any other moment in his life, he would have laughed at what was, even by his standards, a spectacularly bad hair day. Over the years, the New York tennis set, presided over by Anna Wintour, the editor-in-chief of American Vogue, had grown accustomed to Roger Federer's perfect hair; here was some Scottish grunge. Playing in the wind on the Arthur Ashe Stadium had at first left Murray with what *Sports Illustrated* magazine would later describe as a 'nutty professor' look; then the Scot had been transformed, gust by gust, and tuft by tuft, into what the writer S.L. Price called 'tennis pro drawn by Dr Zeus'. The wind was not finished with Murray. By the time Murray walked off the court for a loo break to prepare for the fifth set of the US Open final, Price noted that, with 'the whole hairy mess nearly standing on end', the tennis player appeared to be scared to death.

And who would have blamed Murray for having doubts in his head as he closed the bathroom door behind him? His hair, as entertaining as it was for those waiting for the match to resume, was no concern of his.

It was close to 8pm, New York time, on Monday 10th September 2012 (or 1am in Dunblane), and Murray knew the next hour – maybe it would not even be a full hour, perhaps it would be a little longer – could determine the rest of his life, on and off the court. When Murray had led by two sets to love, it had seemed as though he was on his way to winning his first grand slam title, and so becoming Britain's first male grand slam singles champion since Fred Perry in 1936. But that was to forget that Murray's tennis life has always been about the struggle, and there was no reason to imagine that this was going to be any different. For the next two sets, Novak Djokovic played eyes-out tennis, swinging hard at his ground-strokes, peacocking between points a little as if the court was his, and then throwing his racket at the ball once again. While in the opening stages, Djokovic had gone splat so often that one of the American television networks started an on-screen tally, his rubbery legs were now doing what he asked of them; he was sliding around the hard court in a manner that no one else attempts outside of the clay-court season. Murray's legs, meanwhile, had gone the other way. 'My legs are made of jelly,' he cried out, a line which sounded as though it had been taken from the pages of a children's bedtime story. The whole momentum and psychology of the final was shifting, and when Djokovic levelled the final at two sets apiece, the defending champion appeared to be well-placed.

Jelly-legged Murray had lost grand slam finals before. Four

of them. Three to Federer, and one to Djokovic. But this would have been different, on a whole new level of emotional pain; lose a grand slam final from two sets up and you want to crawl into your racket bag, get into the foetal position and zip yourself up from the inside, never to be seen again.

Murray had never questioned himself as much before a big occasion as he had before playing Djokovic for this title. Sitting in the locker-room before a ball was struck – a locker-room which was far too quiet for his liking – he could not help himself thinking back to past failures. About his semi-final with Djokovic in that year's Australian Open when he had led by two sets to one, only for the Serbian to come through in five, and he also recalled that summer's Wimbledon final, when he had taken the opening set against Federer, but had then lost in four. Murray's coach, Ivan Lendl, made the runner-up's speech after his first four grand slam finals, and then turned his career around in his fifth. More than anything, Murray didn't want to become the first man in tennis's professional era to lose his first five slam finals. Lendl had told him to enjoy the match, said that Murray had worked his whole life to give himself this opportunity. That was the problem, Murray replied; how could he have fun out there when he had put so much into this? Fun wasn't having Djokovic, who had seemed out of this match, come back from two sets down.

When players walk off for a pee, they are accompanied by one of the line-judges. This is not because the United States Tennis Association are worried that their competitors will get lost and wander down the wrong corridor, but to prevent the players being intercepted by their coach, a friend, or anyone else with a message to pass on. So there was nothing that Lendl, the rest of Murray's staff, his mother Judy or his girl-friend Kim Sears could do. Sir Alex Ferguson, the manager of Manchester United Football Club, who was sitting in Murray's guest box, was equally powerless. As was another knight of the realm at Flushing Meadows that afternoon and evening, Sir Sean Connery. The Hollywood actor Kevin Spacey, who had met Murray earlier in the tournament, couldn't do anything but fiddle with his tartan tie. This was all on Murray. Only he could dispel the negativity in his head. At that moment, he was not thinking too much about past finals, just about what had happened over the last four hours, and what he was going to do next. So he stood there in front of the mirror, his hair on end, and said to himself: 'For one set, just give it everything you've got. You don't want to come off this court with any regrets. Don't get down on yourself. Fight.'

1

The Worst Tennis Nation on Earth

Jane Henman, as far as anyone has ever established, never received hate mail. Judy Murray's greatest crime, it is sometimes said, is that she is not Tim Henman's mother – prim, still, silent, and in the background. That she is not a Home Counties tennis mum, cloaked in Laura Ashley and upper-middle-class discretion. That she doesn't follow dress codes.

You occasionally still hear people talking about the incident, during the 2006 Wimbledon Championships, when Mrs Murray had difficulty gaining access to the Members' Enclosure at the All England Club because she was wearing jeans. Andy Murray had just won a third-round match against Andy Roddick, for what was then the biggest win of his career at the grand slams, but this, alas, was a breach of the no-denim rule.

A couple of days later, Judy wrote a newspaper column about how Wimbledon was 'a bit too formal for me – I am not the floral dress type.'

When Jane Henman gave rare interviews to promote the range of ladies' tennis wear she had designed, she would decline to discuss her son's career – for the journalist getting her to acknowledge that Tim was actually her child, it must have felt like a significant victory. As much as she could, Jane Henman withdrew from Tim's story. However, there is no doubt that tennis parents are more visible than any other athletes' mothers and fathers; the television director knows where to find them, in their offspring's guest box beside the court, going through what Judy Murray has called a cross between seasickness and heart attack.

And Judy has never been one to sit on her hands or on her voice. There have been times when Murray has been playing in front of 23,000 New Yorkers in the US Open's Arthur Ashe Stadium, or before a 15,000-capacity crowd on Wimbledon's Centre Court, and, for someone on the other side of the court, it has still been possible to hear her above the rest of the crowd. Ivan Lendl pleaded with her once: if you're going to sit behind me again, you're going to have to bring me ear-plugs.

Judy Murray has been called the Tiger Mum of British tennis. She has also been called far worse. Opening the morning post is sometimes to wonder what vitriol the Royal Mail has delivered today, whether there will be another letter telling her what a terrible person she is. How awful she is. That they find her cries of 'C'monnnnn', or how she bares her teeth, shakes her fist or otherwise encourages her youngest son when he is playing tennis matches, nothing less than repellent.

It is not as if tennis had never seen a strong mother before. Gloria Connors would urge little Jimmy 'to play like a crazed animal', and 'to knock the ball down my throat, and he learned to do this because he found out that if I had the chance I would knock it down his'. Ivan Lendl's mother, Olga, was fierce. When Ivan was a boy, the story goes that Olga would strike him with her left hand if he talked back, until she broke her wristwatch with one of the blows, and she then had to remember to hit him with her right. An old issue of *Sports Illustrated* magazine tells the tale of Ivan's initial refusal to eat his carrots and peas; Olga set a timer for ten minutes and left the room – he knew then to clear his plate.

Those two were truly tennis matriarchs. And yet it can sometimes feel as though Judy Murray, who never tried to turn Murray into a street-hustler of a tennis player, and who certainly never struck her son, has become the most controversial mother in the sport's history. Perhaps that is because Connors and Lendl were playing in a gentler age, before the invention of 'trolls' and the internet message-board. To scroll through the comments beneath an article about Judy is to be shocked by the anger. 'I know I'm not hugely popular,' she has said. You would think, from the reaction she gets, that she was in the same nightmare parenting premier league as Jelena Dokic's father, Damir, who once threatened to assassinate the Australian ambassador to Serbia with a grenade-launcher. Or Jim Pierce, Mary's father, whose rap-sheet included calling out during one of her matches, 'Go on, Mary, kill the bitch,' and punching her bodyguard. Ever since ladies started flashing their ankles at Victorian garden parties, British tennis has had its scandals and its controversies, but Andy Murray is surely the first player on the main tour to have found himself defending his mother from an opponent's verbal attack.

On one of the rare occasions that Murray spent a 90-second change of ends trash-talking with an opponent, it was because Juan Martin Del Potro, who was a year and a bit off winning the US Open, had brought Judy into the argument. Murray and the Argentine were playing a night match at the clay-court Rome Masters in 2008, and Murray was unhappy with Del Potro for not apologising after appearing to deliberately aim the ball at his head. Del Potro's response was to say that Murray and his mother had not changed from the junior days, 'were always the same'; the South American seemed to be implying that he was still hearing too much of Judy.

Tennis does seated arguments better than any other sport, and the two young men sat there on their chairs, raging for a minute and a half. No one could recall Murray previously looking so angry on a tennis court, and the umpire asked him to calm down. 'I've had a lot of bad things said about me before, and that didn't really bother me. But I think when people start talking about your family, you're naturally not going to take that well. Someone saying something about your mother who is one of the nicest ladies you're ever going to meet? I don't think that's cool.'

Once Scotland's national coach, and now Britain's Fed Cup

captain (the women's team competition), Judy has wondered whether there is sexism at play across the international tennis world. Richard Williams started plotting Venus and Serena's tennis lives before they were born – his wife was not sure whether she wanted any more children, but he, hoping to raise tennis champions, hid her birth-control pills. He taught them how to play the game, and he is still on the scene. People don't tell him to back off. Rafa Nadal has had only one coach, his uncle Toni, and the family is celebrated for its closeness ('Sicilian, just without the malice or guns,' said the writer who collaborated with him on his memoirs). Novak Djokovic's father, Srdjan, turned up at the US Open one year wearing a T-shirt with a large image of his son's face on the front, and he just about got away with it; had Judy tried the same trick, there would have been letters. Lots of them.

Does modern tennis have one rule for the males in players' families and another for the females? It has never been properly explained how Judy is supposed to have pulled off this 'control freakery', what with her living in Scotland, her other commitments, and travelling to only a small number of tournaments a year. And with Murray living in England and spending most of the year out there on the tennis road, either playing events or killing his lungs during training blocks in Miami. While Judy and Murray naturally still talk to each other about tennis, much of the time they have the conversations you would expect any mother and son to have. There are paparazzi shots on file of Judy shopping with Murray just after he had moved house, and carrying loo roll and a new ironing board; you can bet that they didn't fill the silences by breaking down Roger Federer's backhand.

The criticism has been wounding, no doubt, even though Judy, as a former tennis correspondent for Scottish broadsheet the *Herald*, knows how the media game works. She was understandably unhappy when, during Wimbledon one summer, she picked up the newspaper she was writing for at the time, and saw that the front page was puffing a debate on the features pages about whether she was too pushy for her son's own good, how her tennis elbows were sharpened to a point that could take his opponents' eyes out. She didn't contribute many more columns for the paper after that.

When the former Wimbledon champion Boris Becker accused Judy of smothering Murray to the extent that she was potentially harming his chances of winning a grand slam title – in some quarters, this was reported as Becker calling him 'a mummy's boy' – she retorted that the German knew nothing about her family.

There is only one person who has divided opinion more sharply in British tennis than Andy Murray and that's his mother. For years, her critics have shouted so loudly that it has been tricky to hear much recognition and praise for the positive role she has played in British tennis. Of how she raised two boys from Dunblane in Stirlingshire – a part of the world where the climate is not conducive to playing tennis – who have gone on to play the sport at the highest level. You have Judy's permission to call her a pushy tennis mother, she once said, but only if you mean that she pushed for Andy and Jamie to have the best opportunities to further their tennis. Not if you mean that she forced them into playing a sport they did not love. Because she didn't.

Murray once said that his mother is the only person who 'gets' him. One Christmas, he gave Judy a card in which he thanked her for 'always believing in me, always supporting me, always letting me make my own decisions. But, most of all, I want to thank you for being the best Mum in the world.' There were tears. Murray affectionately scolded her: 'What are you crying for, stupid woman?'

For the first time since his acrimonious 'defection' from America to Russia, Alex Bogomolov Junior was to play the US Open. Anna Kournikova's former hitting-partner had kept the Junior in his name, but he was Moscow's now. And 'Red Alex' was not going to be allowed to slope in and out, to make a quiet return hidden away on one of the outside courts at Flushing Meadows; he had been drawn to play Andy Murray in the first round, and that meant a show court.

When Bogomolov jumped over the old Iron Curtain at the end of the 2011 season, with all the glee that Fred Perry used to hurdle the net after winning matches, it had not gone down well with the United States Tennis Association, and they had been insistent that he write them out a cheque for tens of thousands of dollars as repayment for their support. Though he initially considered taking the matter to court – it was his belief that the USTA had not given him any help since his teens, or even picked up the phone and called him – he paid up.

Across the American tennis scene, there was some sympathy for Bogomolov, who was born in Russia, and whose father Alex Senior had been a Soviet tennis coach (he had worked with Russia's former world number one Yevgeny Kafelnikov and Ukraine's Andrei Medvedev, a former French Open finalist), but who had lived in the States from childhood. Alex Junior, though he had shown early promise, hadn't had an easy senior career. He had served a short suspension after he was found to have a banned substance in his system. He had been through a public divorce from Ashley Harkleroad, an American tennis player who would pose for *Playboy* magazine, and a wrist injury almost ended it all. For a while, he needed coaching dollars to survive. After he recovered from the wrist injury, started to mobilise and moved up the rankings again, Moscow made contact, and American Davis Cup captain Jim Courier informed Bogomolov he had no future in his team. Wanting the best for his new family – he had recently become a father for the first time with a new partner – he opted to play for the country of his birth.

There had never been any confusion over Murray's nationality, where he came from, or who he would be playing for in years to come. Once in a while at Wimbledon, a player beats someone they are not supposed to, goes deeper still into the draw, has a career breakthrough, and then the full story emerges of how he or she made it from whatever tennis 'backwater' they are from, all the way to the wrought-iron gates of the All England Club.

But it is no less remarkable for the small city of Dunblane, just off the M9 motorway heading to the Scottish Highlands, and a few hundred miles north of Wimbledon's Centre Court, to have produced a player of great international standing. World-class British tennis players are rare enough. However, Scotland had never previously had a man in the world's tennis elite. The world was cruel and it laughed at British tennis, at how Britain had failed to produce a male grand slam singles champion since Perry was in flannels and Brylcreem. And Scottish tennis was even taking hits from *Monty Python's Flying Circus*; there is a sketch about a tennis-playing blancmange which comes close to winning Wimbledon by ensuring its opponents are from Scotland, 'well known as the worst tennis nation on earth'.

The Scottish climate is not the weather you need for producing tennis players. Plus, as Judy once noted, Scottish children have been deep-frying their bodies in chip fat. It is a short drive from Dunblane to the William Wallace monument in Stirling. And, for kids from that part of the world, William Wallace probably has as much relevance to their daily lives as another man immortalised by a statue, Fred Perry. You don't expect tennis players who know the words to 'Flower of Scotland'.

About the only family north of Hadrian's Wall with any great tennis pedigree were the Erskines. Judy Erskine's parents, Roy and Shirley, enjoyed their tennis. Roy, who had played football for Hibernian, Stirling Albion and Cowdenbeath, was a half-decent tennis player and, to this day, he still thinks he invented topspin. Watching his grandson's matches when he is at home in Dunblane, Roy can find himself shouting at the television screen, imploring Murray: 'You shouldn't be playing like that.' But he knows that, when they go to watch Murray play live, he has to control himself.

Judy was the dominant force of Scottish women's tennis – the tartan Chris Evert, if you like – winning 64 Scottish girls' and ladies' titles (so both Bogomolov and Murray have one parent who had been heavily involved in tennis). But life was not so easy when she left Scotland to scuffle around the lower levels of the international tennis circuit. The tent she was sleeping in at a French campsite, where she was staying for a tournament nearby, collapsed around her during a thunderstorm. Even with the money her parents were wiring her from Scotland, which she picked up from post-offices, she often did not have the funds to fly between tournaments, and so bought bus tickets instead. This was a backpacker's tour of Europe, just with tennis skirts and rackets stuffed into her bag. Judy was a good sport – she once lost in the first round of a tournament to Mariana Simionescu, and then stayed in the locker room to provide cover so the Romanian could enjoy a cigarette without having to deal with her boyfriend Bjorn Borg's disapproval.

The day that Judy's playing career effectively ended was when the teenager had her purse pinched while riding a bus in Barcelona. Inside the purse had been her passport, some money which her parents had just wired to her, and her airline tickets. On her return to Scotland, her father told her she should think seriously whether it was wise to continue. He was concerned for her safety, and also wondered whether this was really heading anywhere. So she learnt some shorthand and typing, and found secretarial work, first in a glass factory and then for an insurance firm. A job as a trainee manager at a department store followed, before she worked for a while as a travelling saleswoman for a firm which made sweets and chocolates. She studied French and business at Edinburgh University, and met and married Willie Murray, a retail manager.

Such was the pain that Judy experienced when she gave birth to a son, Jamie, on 13 February 1986 ('He was a very big baby with a very big head, it was horrendous and I thought, "Oh, I'll never do that again,"' she is quoted as telling the *Los Angeles Times*), that there was some doubt whether she and Willie would ever have a second child. But she must have quickly changed her mind, as Andy arrived just 15 months later, born on 15 May 1987 in Queen Mother's Hospital in Glasgow. Years later, Stephen Bierley, then the tennis correspondent for the *Guardian*, wrote that Judy 'should be held personally responsible for the ills of British tennis; she stopped producing children after she had Andy'.

With the two young boys she had 'produced', she sometimes struggled with what she called 'the frustration of an active person suddenly surrounded by mashed vegetables'. As the boys grew, she found that tennis – or at least a version of it – would burn off some of their energy. Murray's tennis life began when he was a toddler; he started by hitting balloons and sponge balls around the house and the garden.

Judy wasn't starting the long march to Wimbledon's Centre Court or to the US Open's Arthur Ashe Stadium; she was just trying to improve their co-ordination and movement so they would get the most out of any sport they played (as the years have passed, she became so convinced that the games she devised for her sons had helped them, and also convinced they could benefit others, that she pulled them all together and put them on an iPad app).

The boys graduated to swingball, which involved striking a small ball that was attached to a string on a pole in the back yard. Judy still remembers Andy's first racket – a 16-inch psychedelic Slazenger which had a bright metallic frame and multi-coloured strings. Initially, Judy thought that Murray had poor hand-to-eye co-ordination. 'My mum, my first tennis coach, will tell you that when I started playing tennis she thought I was useless. Mum used to spend hours throwing balls for me to hit. She says I kept missing whereas my brother, Jamie, could do it right away. It wasn't until I was about seven that I started to become noticeably better. I had bad concentration, bad co-ordination and a temper. It was not a good combination,' Murray recalled in his 2008 autobiography, *Hitting Back*.

An explanation for Murray's high tennis IQ, for his understanding of strategies and how to construct a point, and for the variety in his game, can be found in his tennis upbringing, which was in contrast to how his idol Andre Agassi had been introduced to the sport. Murray loved Agassi when he was a tennis punk. He forgave him his sins (eyeliner, shaving his legs,

Barbra Streisand). And Murray kept on loving Agassi as he transformed himself into a tennis gentleman who finished matches by bowing to all sides of the stadium, and became, at least in Streisand's head, a Zen master. To Murray's mind, Agassi was the first tennis player to have become a worldwide icon. John McEnroe, Murray thought, had been popular in America and in Europe, but not so much in Asia. Agassi's name meant something in every country of the world.

Murray's adoration was such that, to watch the Las Vegan win his first US Open title in 1994, the seven-year-old sat in front of the television wearing Agassi's signature 'hot lava' look – cut-off denim shorts, neon pink and purple cycling shorts and a baseball cap with a long blond ponytail clipped on to the back (it was only years later, with the publication of his book, that we discovered that Agassi's hair had been fake). The outfit, which had cost Murray eight pounds at a local market, was several sizes too big for him, and his mother remembers how ridiculous he looked.

On his first trip to Wimbledon, earlier that year, Murray had been less interested in using a ticket to a show court than in stalking out the practice courts for three days in the hope of getting Agassi's autograph; the disappointment he felt when he went home with a blank pad – he was too small for his hero to have noticed him – is the reason that he now tries to sign as many programmes, body parts and giant tennis balls as he can. The young Murray copied what he could from Agassi's game, and years later, one could detect certain similarities between the way that both hit their double-handed backhands or prepared for their forehands. The pair are two of the best returners of serve that the sport has ever seen.

Even when the adult Murray joined the main tour, and had the chance to meet Agassi for the first time at the pre-Wimbledon tournament at Queen's Club in 2006, he still felt a bit like the little boy dressed from head to toe in Nike; for the first time in his life he was nervous before a practice session, and, palms sweating, he forgot his water bottle. Perhaps Murray saw something of himself in Agassi. Judy has noted that both her son and Agassi are Taureans, 'so stubborn and perfectionists, and both have had dodgy mullets'.

For all that, Murray and Agassi could hardly have had more different starts to tennis. Agassi's early tennis life centred around a ball machine which became known as 'the dragon'; his father Mike, a former boxer who carried salt and pepper in his trouser pockets in case he needed to temporarily blind someone in a fight outside a Las Vegas casino, would have Andre in front of that machine, hitting balls, for hours. Murray, though, learnt the game through regularly playing points and then matches, not through drills.

It was Murray who decided that he should start competing. Murray was born, to borrow the phrase Ivan Lendl once used about himself, a competitive bastard. Murray would fling a Monopoly board in the air if he landed on Park Lane – to keep the peace, he was sometimes allowed to win. He was five, so not much bigger than his mid-sized racket, when he announced to his mother that he wanted to play, and she can recall his exact words: 'a proper match in a proper tournament.'

Since he could already serve over-arm, keep score, hit double-handed ground-strokes and use topspin and slice, she could see no harm in it.

Within three years – so when he was eight – Murray was playing in the Dunblane third team in the local league, when everyone else was at least a half-century older than him, though that did not stop him from sidling up to his doubles partner, a respected architect, to say: 'You're standing a bit close to the net – you should stand back a bit as you might get lobbed if I decide to serve and volley.' A number of other players in the Central District League did not like playing against an eight-year-old and proposed the introduction of a minimum age – effectively a ban on Andy Murray – but the motion did not pass.

Looking back on all those hours they played on the artificial grass courts at Dunblane Sports Club, just a couple of hundred yards from the family home, Judy believes she gave Murray a tactical rather than a technical base. There was no scheming on her part; it was just Murray trying to get the better of his mother and to do that he had to be clever. From an early age, Murray would analyse other players' games – opponents he might never encounter, but who just happened to be on court at the club or at a tournament – and work out in his mind how he would go about beating them.

Judy kept on taking her boys to the tennis courts because they enjoyed it, but also because she often did not have the money for a babysitter. When Judy could not take them with her, the boys' grandmother Shirley allowed Jamie and Andy to play with foam balls in her house, once she had removed all ornaments from the sitting-room. They praised Shirley for the shortbread she baked, and teased her about her slow driving when she ferried them to training at the indoor tennis centre on campus at the University of Stirling.

The Murray brothers were extremely fortunate, considering how many indoor courts there were in Scotland, to be able to spend ten minutes in the car – or 15 if Gran was driving – and to find themselves at a facility where they could practise with a roof over their heads. All that tennis in the Stirling hall helped Murray in future years – he is behind only Roger Federer on the list of the best indoor players of his generation.

Funny to think that, in his early years on the tour, Murray would be likened to Kevin the Teenager, the character created by comedian Harry Enfield which brilliantly captured adolescent angst. When he was at home with his mother, he rarely, if ever, went into angry Kevin mode. He cannot recall ever slamming a door in her face. Not once did Murray tell his mother: 'I hate you.' Perhaps, though, some of the blame for his fruity on-court language is hers. When they played doubles together, she would occasionally curse under her breath at a biffed shot (or so he has recalled). And, on long journeys travelling back and forth between home and tournaments, they would listen to cassettes of Billy Connolly, a Scottish comic who, to use the American tennis vernacular, is forever 'dropping f-bombs'.

For all the help that Judy gave her son, what she refused to do was to intervene in any of his tennis squabbles. That would have been the behaviour of a pushy tennis parent. Judy has some horror stories to tell of her days taking her sons to junior tennis tournaments. Junior tennis often isn't for the faint-hearted parent. There was the time she saw a father outside an indoor tennis hall, with his hands around his 12-year-old daughter's throat. She had just lost. Or the parents spewing at, or ignoring, their children after defeats. There were parents who tried to intimidate or distract their children's opponents, with tricks including cheering when the other child makes a mistake, calling balls out from the sidelines, or clapping when a shot landed close to the lines so that the opponent would be too scared to disagree.

Murray soon learnt that he was going to have to fight his own tennis battles. Judy remembers the day when a six-year-old Murray was playing in Wrexham – it was his first tournament outside Scotland – and on match point, when a drop-shot bounced three times on his opponent's side of the court, the young Scot walked to the net to shake hands. But, without an umpire and with no one watching, Murray's opponent was able to run in and hit a winner into the undefended court. Murray was so shocked that he did not win another point. The match had been an education.

Judy has a good recall of an under-12 doubles match that Murray was playing, when the father of one of the opponents was applauding Murray's double-faults. 'Andy ended up hitting a ball towards him, as if to say, "Will you just shut up?" I've never got into arguments with other parents. It's not worth it. Some parents send on bottles of water with notes taped to the side saying things like, "hit it to the backhand". I've seen parents reading newspapers from behind the court during matches, with instructions written in big bold letters on the back pages. There are parents who have devised coded signals, so if they scratch their right ear that means serve to the forehand, and if they scratch their left ear that means serving to the backhand.'

Judy has never been one of those tennis parents – they can be even worse than stage mums in this regard – who lives vicariously through their children; she had not achieved everything she wanted as a tennis player, but that was not why her sons had ended up in the sport. 'It's important to know why the child is playing, as it has to be because they love tennis. Sadly, you do get instances of parents who are living their dreams through their children. The parents didn't get as far as they wanted when they were playing, so they will try to get the kids to win the tournaments for them. I'm always getting asked if I was a pushy parent. I'll admit I often had to push to make things happen, but I never had to push my kids because they always wanted to play,' Judy once said in an interview with the *Daily Telegraph*.

Perhaps because her own father had always waved her out of the door with the words 'see and win', encouragement which inadvertently made her more fearful of losing, she has always tried to keep it light with her sons. As light as the best sponge-cake. If the uninitiated were to read the timeline for her personal Twitter account – she reports back on every profite-role, Battenburg or Death By Chocolate that crosses her plate – they might guess that she was a professional cake tester and not the mother of two tennis players. She has never wanted to control her sons' lives, the thinking being that if they don't take their own decisions, and don't take responsibility for the mistakes they make, they will never learn.

One thing that Judy pushed for, and made happen, was the chance to play against other talented juniors from across Britain. For her sons, and the other Scottish juniors, to test themselves, they had to leave Scotland, and travel south to play in English tournaments. Almost every weekend Judy was at the wheel, taking her troupe around the country. Turning up to these tournaments full of English boys, Andy and Jamie would have been forgiven for feeling like outsiders; the Scots, who had come in a mini-bus decorated with Saltires, were on cross-border tennis raids. Judy got to know Britain's motorways better than she could ever had imagined she would. Soon, the Murrays would grow out of taking on only the English.

There is a point in any tennis parent's life – well, in most, anyway – when they realise they have taken their child as far as they can. Or that they have become an embarrassment. When Andy was 11, Judy realised her son was reaching the age when being coached by your mother would not be considered 'cool' (her word, or possibly his).

Initially, Judy asked Leon Smith to have a couple of hits with her son. Many years later, Smith would go on to become the head of both men's and women's tennis at the Lawn Tennis Association. Back then, Smith was in his early twenties, and had an ear-ring and a sense of fun. Murray immediately took to him and it developed into a six-year relationship.

The first trip Smith and Murray took together was to Florida, when he played in the 12-and-under singles competition at the Orange Bowl in Florida, which is regarded as the unofficial world championships. Smith watched Murray use lobs and drop-shots to win the final, and then sat on the plane home thinking, 'We're dealing with one of the world's best talents.' That same season, Murray also won the British 14-and-under championships (when he still had two years left in that age group), and that was the time when Judy first thought that her son might have something special.

Murray never did have the opportunity to win the club championships at Dunblane Sports Club. Judy had given her son the best possible start in tennis. Murray had the option of trying to make a life for himself in football, just as his maternal grandfather had done, but he declined the offer of a six-week trial with the Glasgow Rangers School of Excellence for young players. He chose tennis. 'Bats above boots,' Mum said.

On the opening page of Agassi's book, *Open*, he writes that he 'hated tennis with a dark and secret passion'. Not once has Murray ever come close to echoing his idol's thoughts and that, surely, is Judy's greatest achievement.

Like all brothers, the Murrays have fallen out, with arguments settled either verbally or, sometimes during their childhood, with Chinese burns and clenched fists. The only difference is that Andy and Jamie have sometimes got into their tangles in public, with the cameras and the tape-recorders rolling.

There was the occasion when Jamie travelled with Britain's Davis Cup team to Buenos Aires for a tie against Argentina. If Andy had made the trip to South America in 2008, Jamie felt that Britain would have had half a chance on a clay court against Argentina. But Andy had withdrawn from the tie just days before, as a prevention against injury, and in a press conference Jamie spoke of his anger and disaffection: 'It kind of affects the way I feel about him.' Or there was the time when Andy and Jamie lost in the second round of the doubles competition at the 2008 Beijing Olympics, and Jamie bolted so quickly that he left his rackets and the rest of his kit on the court.

If Andy ever wants a reminder of the intensity of his childhood rivalry with his brother, he only has to look at the fingernail, which has never grown back properly after being thumped by Jamie. Andy, aged ten, had just beaten Jamie for the first time, in the final of an under-12s tournament in Solihull, and throughout the long mini-bus journey back to Dunblane, he kept on taunting his sibling. Jamie, an easy-going boy who was usually slow to anger, had heard enough and brought his fist crashing down on the ring finger of Andy's left hand. Judy, who had been at the wheel, had to stop the bus. She cleaned up the bus and carried on up the motorway, but the next morning she was on the phone making an emergency doctor's appointment as Andy's finger had swollen up with pus, and the nail was about to drop off. Someone who has closely examined the nail has described it as looking indented, purple and stunted.

The impression should not be formed, though, that brotherly love has always been in short supply. As grown men playing for prize-money, ranking points and glory, Andy has often felt more nervous partnering Jamie on a doubles court than he has when playing singles, as he puts extra pressure on himself to help his brother succeed. And he took as much pleasure from watching his brother flirt his way to the mixed doubles title with Serbia's Jelena Jankovic at the 2007 Wimbledon Championships as he has from any of his own triumphs. Andy cried that day, and took offence when someone asked him on live radio whether he was jealous that his brother had gained an invite to Wimbledon's Champions' Dinner before he had.

Andy found himself 'welling up big time' after he and Jamie won their first doubles title together on the main tour, at a tournament in Valencia in the autumn of 2010. When Andy sobbed after the 2012 Wimbledon final, Jamie was on Twitter playing the part of proud older brother: 'My brother is a champion. He may not have won. But he is a champion.'

As they grew older, and started to play professional tennis, it was undoubtedly a blessing that right-handed Andy was making a career in singles and lefty Jamie in doubles. Andy and Jamie have never had to go through what Serena and Venus Williams have throughout their careers – chatting over breakfast bowls of Cheerios and then, later that day, slugging it out against each other on a tennis court while the world is watching. While Andy and Jamie have played the same tournaments, they have been on different draw sheets. If Andy and

Jamie clash on the schedules at grand slams, when Andy is playing singles and Jamie doubles at the same time, Judy does not prioritise her more famous son over the other; she tries to watch the same number of their matches.

As young boys, and then as young teens, they were constantly trying to outdo each other. That was the making of Murray. Without Jamie, Andy may never have had a future in tennis. Andy was always a competitive boy. But Jamie made Andy even more determined to succeed on the tennis court. Whatever Jamie was doing, Andy wanted to do, and he wanted to do it better. Andy remembers that Jamie was more intelligent and better academically than he was. Jamie was also faster around a running track. Judy's friends would tell her that Jamie was the better looking of the boys. 'Was Jamie nicer than you?' the *Guardian* once asked Andy, to which he replied: 'Probably, yeah. Yeah.' But Andy thought he could beat Jamie on the tennis court. That was where he would compete against his brother. Andy did not just want to beat Jamie, who at one stage was the second best junior player in the world; he wanted to crush him.

'I think Andy has a lot to thank Jamie for. Jamie was just a bit older, and a bit better, and Andy was always striving to keep up,' Judy has said. Even when the brothers did not play against each other, Andy never missed an opportunity to score points against Jamie. 'The first overseas tournament Andy went to, he was nine and Jamie went as well. It was an under-11 tournament in France, and Andy got to the semi-final and lost in three long sets to Gael Monfils (who would go on to become an elite player in the senior game), and Jamie got to the final and beat Monfils, one and love. 'And the whole way back home, Andy was saying, "you only won because I tired him out for you,"' Judy recalled in an interview with the *New York Times*. 'It was hilarious.'

The non-aficionados of men's tennis would not recognise Willie Murray if he was sitting having a pint in the Dog and Fox in Wimbledon Village or at the next table of the food court at Flushing Meadows. As the area manager of a chain of shops in Scotland, Andy and Jamie's father has not always found it easy to take the time off to watch his sons play international tennis tournaments, though on occasion his younger son has paid for him to travel to the grand slams. Judy, as the boys' first coach, and with her experience in the sport, has been much more closely involved with their tennis. And when Willie does come to watch Murray playing tennis, he tends to sit on the back row of the box, and he looks calm on the outside, so the television networks are not as interested in him. Inside, though, he will be experiencing the same as his ex-wife: nausea and heart-attack. 'I'm like a swan. I'll appear calm on top, but underneath my legs will be going like the clappers. Emotion takes over when I see Andy walk out to play really big matches,' he once told the *Mail on Sunday*. 'I well up.'

Judy's long and often unsociable hours in her job as Scotland's national coach – she worked most weekends – had an impact on her marriage. 'I was away a lot and then obviously you're coaching till quite late into the evening. Your domestic life gets hit for six. You're not eating at the same times, holidays become difficult.'

Willie has spoken endearingly of Andy and Jamie as 'two little guys from Dunblane' who took on the tennis world. One of the hardest things he ever did was telling his sons, still very young, that Judy was leaving home (they were separated for a few years before divorcing when Andy and Jamie were in their teens). 'It ripped me apart to have to hurt them by telling them what I did,' Willie has said of the initial break-up. 'They were distraught. They are very different personalities, but they took the news in much the same way, and I remember they were very upset. I worked full-time, but I cooked when they came home from school. I did the washing and ironing. I wouldn't say I was a single parent, because Judy stayed in Dunblane and she was around. She still took them to tennis, but I was the one in the family home with the boys.'

Murray has recalled being caught in the middle of his parents' arguments: 'My parents didn't speak too much and they didn't get on too well together. They are just two different people. I stayed with my mother for two nights, then I felt as though I should stay with my father for two nights. At Christmas, I didn't know how long to spend with each of them. I would get stuck in the middle of their arguments. I would get really upset, and one of the things I would have loved to have more than anything was a family that worked better together, although I love my mother and father to bits.'

Armchair psychologists have often speculated whether Murray's anger on a tennis court has something to do with his parents' divorce. 'It could be,' he has said of that theory. 'When I was younger and went on court, and was away from the arguments my parents were having, I could just go out and play.'

Divorce or not, one suspects that Andy Murray would always have been a cussed, emotional character on a tennis court, unlike Jamie, who everyone always felt was a little too nice for tennis. One lesson that Willie wanted to instil in Murray – whose middle name Barron translates from the old English as 'young warrior' – was to never allow anyone, whatever their age or position, to take advantage of him. 'He was always strict with me. If someone was trying to wind you up or take the mickey out of you, he told me to give them some stick back. If they were going to do it, you were going to come back with something. I played football a lot with his friends, five-a-side and seven-a-side, and playing football with forty-year-old men, although they're not the fittest. They'll kick you a little bit and try to sort you out.'

Willie tells the story of the time they went on holiday, to a place where there was always a tennis tournament on, and Murray started beating a boy some six years older, and a foot taller. When the older boy tried to preserve his dignity by cheating over the line-calls, Murray got angry, and, if Willie's memory serves him right, 'then it all kicked off'. 'That was an early indicator of Andy's competitive will to win,' Willie told the *Mail on Sunday*. 'He wouldn't let anyone climb all over him, and he wasn't afraid of any reputation – and he carried that with him into professional tennis.'

The worst day of Judy Murray's life was 13 March 1996. Everyone else in Dunblane, if asked, would give the same date. Dunblane is usually described as a small town. Technically, it's a cathedral city. It feels more like a village, and everyone in Dunblane knows someone who had a son or daughter in the primary school that day.

When Judy heard there had been a shooting – it was only later that the full story emerged, of how Thomas Hamilton had killed 16 children and a teacher, Gwen Mayor, before turning a handgun on himself – she jumped into her car and sped towards the school. 'I can remember slamming on my horn and swearing at the top of my voice while shouting, "Get out of the way." Eventually I had to stop the car and pull over. You couldn't get near the school for all the police vehicles and other cars that lined the road. I ran towards the school gates. You couldn't get near those either,' Judy wrote in Murray's autobiography.

It is one of the rare occasions that Judy or her son have spoken or written about the mass murder, mostly because they do not want to dwell on the events that day, but also because, you would imagine, they do not want to take ownership of a tragedy that affected all of Dunblane. The only time that Andy has volunteered to speak about the tragedy – on all other occasions he was either responding to enquiries, or he was having to discuss it with his ghost-writer for his book – was after he won the junior US Open in 2004. He dedicated his victory to the victims and to the people of Dunblane, as well as to the victims of the terrorist attack on a school in Beslan in Russia in 2004: 'I found it hard to watch those children coming out of the Russian school. I watched it on television and felt so much sorrow for them.'

Judy waited outside the gates of the primary school with the other parents. When the parents of Mrs Major's class were asked to come forward, Judy felt such a surge of relief that she almost collapsed on to the tarmac. Almost immediately, she felt guilty as one of the women she had been talking to had a daughter in that class.

When Hamilton had opened fire, eight-year-old Andy and ten-year-old Jamie had been walking towards the school gymnasium for a PE lesson. They diverted to the headteacher's office, where they hid under the desk. Andy does not have a clear memory, only what he calls 'patchy impressions'; what he does remember is, in the hours after the massacre, sitting in a classroom singing songs. 'The weirdest thing was that we knew the guy,' Andy has written. 'He had been in my mum's car. It's obviously weird to think you had a murderer in your car, sitting next to your mum. That is probably another reason why I don't want to look back at it. It is just so uncomfortable to think that it is someone we knew from the Boys Club.' He has admitted that it was hard to get used to the idea that someone he knew turned out to be a murderer, and that he too could have been one of his victims.

For days and weeks, Dunblane was unusually quiet. And

for years it was primarily known as the place where Hamilton, a former scout leader, had committed the most horrific of crimes. Some years later, Andy and Jamie moved away, not because they were trying to escape the memories, but because they were never going to have much of a future in tennis if they stayed in Dunblane. Andy, once he had returned from training in Spain, bought a penthouse apartment near the river in south London, and then a house in Surrey's footballers-and-commuters belt, while Jamie lived in a flat in south-west London. But the rest of the family stayed put. Their father Willie continued to live in the town, as did Judy and her parents. Andy and Jamie's uncle, Niall Erskine, has an optometrist business in the town. Andy's tennis, and Jamie's too, has gone a long way to changing how people look at the town, casting Dunblane in a more positive light. Even as a teenager, Murray was aware that Dunblane was 'known around the world for the wrong reasons', and spoke of his desire to change that.

Like the Murrays, the rest of Dunblane do not much want to talk about the crime. 'Of course nobody will ever forget what happened here, but it's lovely that people now think of something else when they hear of Dunblane,' one resident has said, and it felt as though he was speaking for the whole city.

Any list of the most influential figures in Andy Murray's tennis education must include Rafa Nadal, one of the greatest players of all time. It was when no one outside Majorca knew Nadal's name that he had a life-changing conversation with his

Scottish friend. Life-changing for Murray, that is, as Nadal already seemed to be on his way.

Murray was 15 years old, and Britain and Nadal's Spain had been competing in the European under-16 team championships in Andorra. Spain beat Britain in the final, and Murray went off to play a friendly game of racketball with Nadal, and when that was over – no one can remember who won – they started chatting. Though Nadal's English was far from fluent and everything was delivered with a Majorcan accent, he had a large enough vocabulary to be able to communicate to Murray the benefits he was gaining from training in Majorca with Carlos Moya, also a native of the island, and a player of the class to have held the world number one ranking and the French Open title.

For a while, Murray had been thinking that he was in danger of falling behind his European peer-group. Most days, there was not time for more than two good hours of practice, once he had finished his schoolwork, had been driven to and from the centre in Stirling, and had arranged courts and sparring partners. And when he was on court, the available hitting-partners did not extend much beyond his brother, his mother and whichever county-level players were in the mood that day. Tim Henman and Greg Rusedski certainly never passed through Dunblane or Stirling looking for juniors to share a practice court with. The conversation with Nadal had confirmed in Murray's mind: he had to leave Scotland if he was to make the most of his talent. 'Rafa's out in the sun all day,' Murray said to his mother when he returned home. 'He hardly goes to school and he's playing four and a half hours a day. I'm playing four and a half hours a week. It's not enough.'

There was another reason for Murray to move abroad: to escape what he regarded as the catty, negative British tennis scene. Murray can remember playing tournaments when he felt as though some of the British players were willing him to lose. If they were not going to make it as tennis players, they did not want anyone else making a success of themselves either.

After what had happened to her other son, Judy was concerned how leaving home would affect Murray. When Jamie was 12, he had gone to the Lawn Tennis Association's boarding-school-style academy in Cambridge, but after just a few months he had returned home, disenchanted with tennis. Andy has recalled training with Jamie, soon after his return from East Anglia, and thinking that his brother looked fraught and unhappy. During the same practice session, Judy walked to the back of the court, and tearfully said to Andy: 'I can't believe what they've done to him.' Andy thought that the LTA had 'ruined' his brother, and he carried that anger around with him for years. While the Murrays considered sending Andy to the United States – possibly even to the Nick Bollettieri Academy in Florida, which Andre Agassi regarded as *Lord of the Flies* with forehands – as it was English-speaking, they believed that he would be too far away from home. So Europe it was, and they settled on the Sanchez-Casal Academy, just a short drive from Barcelona's airport.

A Spanish tennis education would not be cheap. The annual

boarding fees were £25,000, with competition expenses on top of that. Though Sport England, Tennis Scotland and the LTA all contributed, and Judy found a couple of private sponsors, Murray's move would mean family sacrifices.

Before Murray left, his father gave him this advice: 'Don't take s— from anyone.' As if that was ever going to happen. Willie's pep-talk was akin to John McEnroe's father imploring his son to express himself more forcefully when talking to umpires. The first time that Emilio Sanchez, one of the founders and a former doubles world number one, saw Murray, he thought he was wasting his time. Murray had recently gone through a growth spurt. 'Andy was tall and skinny, bandy-legged, he walked a bit slow, sloping with his shoulders. He didn't look like a tennis player. I thought he must have been talked up by his mother.' But then they stepped on court, and Sanchez realised that this skinny kid from Scotland had some talent. Murray beat Sanchez in straight sets, and the Spaniard was so impressed that he put the Briton in a squad of players aged between 19 and 26, with a spread of world rankings from 200 to 700.

A typical day for Murray at the academy – he would spend around 18 months there – involved three hours of tennis in the morning, an hour in the gym, lunch and the shortest of siestas, a couple of hours of school, an hour and a half of match play, and then another hour of school. There was the risk, when Murray went to the academy, that he would end up with no academic qualifications to fall back on; so if he failed to make a career in tennis, he would have nothing. Though he

was supposed to be studying English, Maths, French and col-
loquial Spanish, he felt as though the schoolwork was holding
him back with his tennis; the books came a very distant second
behind the rackets.

Pato Alvarez, a Colombian in his late sixties who was known
around those parts as 'El Guru del Tenis', had Murray working
hard, putting the clay-court miles into the boy's legs. It was not
unusual for elite tennis players to drop into the academy looking for some juniors to practise with. When they did, Murray
more than held his own. Murray split sets with Moya, and beat
Guillermo Coria, the 2004 French Open finalist, two days in
a row; here was encouragement that he was not too far off
their level. Never mind that Murray was not picking up much
Spanish.

Murray once complained that he had been allocated the
worst bungalow in the complex. It was a small wooden hut
painted chemical yellow, with a bunk bed, a flower-print sofa
and a Ukrainian stranger for a room-mate. But he had only
himself to blame for the mess, with the floor covered in
around a week's worth of empty food packets, dirty tennis kit,
discarded rackets and used tennis balls. There was more debris
on the sofa. When Judy came to visit, she brought news from
home, and several bags of Milkybar Buttons and chocolate
digestive biscuits (that was what Murray had meant when he
had requested 'normal food'). She often struggled to fully open
the door of the bungalow, such was the build-up of litter.

Murray liked the place. Here he could develop his game
away from the British tennis mainstream. He felt that no one

here was willing him to fail, or actively trying to bring him down. There was a good international crowd, all committed to reaching the top, but not wanting to step on anyone to get there. Murray was happy to keep his life low key. In that hut, it felt as though he could escape the gathering comparisons with Henman, and the rest of the attention he regarded as absurd. In Catalonia, no one could reach Murray. Or at least no one that Murray didn't want to speak to.

Some in Britain did not share the Murray family's view that Andy was doing the right thing by basing himself in Barcelona, and by playing Futures events, the lowest level of professional tennis, in Spain rather than in Britain. Tony Pickard, a former British Davis Cup captain, and Stefan Edberg's ex-coach, bumped into Judy Murray at a tournament and told her it looked as though her son was scared of his British contemporaries. 'What's Andy doing playing in Spain and not in British Futures events? He should be back here in Britain, competing at home. It shows fear that he's leaving his country. He will lose locker-room respect if he goes on avoiding British players.'

But it was not as if Britain's best male players at the time, Tim Henman and Greg Rusedski, had come through the LTA's system either. Henman was not a product of the LTA, and Rusedski, when he changed nationalities, arrived fully formed from Canada, with a fast serve, a Union Flag bandana and a professed love of Arsenal Football Club and James Bond.

On top of the tennis, Murray enjoyed being a budget flight away from home; for the first time in his life, he felt independent. Whenever he returned home, his parents were 'always telling me what to do', but in Barcelona he was his own man. He didn't abuse that freedom with late nights of beer, tapas and tequila along Las Ramblas ('going to bars isn't my scene'). Any free time he had was spent sleeping in the bunk, at the city's English-language cinema or watching DVDs with friends.

Murray appreciated the financial commitment that his family had made to allow him to train in Spain, and that he was not there to have fun. If this was about having fun, he should board the first plane back to Scotland. For several long months, he did have to stay in Scotland. That was when, in 2003, the cause of the pain he had been playing through was diagnosed as a bipartite patella, or split kneecap. As Murray was still growing, they could not operate, and so all he could do was rest his right knee, work on his upper-body strength, shoot some pool, take Spanish classes, and mope. 'That was the worst period of Andy's tennis career,' Judy has said, but when her son returned to the sport it was not long before he was alerting the wider tennis world to his potential.

When Murray returned to Spain after a trip to the 2004 US Open, he told his friends that he had won the boys' singles title – thinking that they might not have noticed – but he did not want to be treated like a superstar. Or for there to be any fuss. But, whether Murray liked it or not, the sporting world was starting to make a fuss over him. That December, he was put on the shortlist for the BBC Young Sports Personality of the Year award. Murray won, but the day was not without its dramas – he almost missed the ceremony after locking himself in his hotel loo.

Eight years after winning the boys' tournament, and four years after playing in the senior final against Roger Federer, Andy Murray was being spoken of as the man to beat at Flushing Meadows. He came to the US Open as the Olympic singles champion, a title Federer or Novak Djokovic have never won. And just three of the so-called Fab Four of men's tennis would be at the tournament, as Rafa Nadal, who had withdrawn from the London Olympics because of a knee injury, was also in no shape to fling himself around New York.

Of all the British athletes to have won a gold medal at a home Olympics, Murray was the first to find himself pitched back into a major competition. In the preparation week before the US Open, Murray had some time to himself, which he spent strolling around the streets of Manhattan. That was a rare chance to reflect on the Olympics and to consider what was ahead of him. He knew that, as the tournament drew closer, many of the preview packages on television, radio and in the international press would centre around him. For the past few years, every time he started a grand slam, it had been dressed up as his best chance yet to win that major, but this time there was no arguing with that assessment. By winning the Olympics, beating Djokovic in the semi-finals and then marmalising Federer in the gold-medal match, he had shown he was more than capable of performing when it mattered. Murray's lifetime dream was to

win a slam. Murray's pre-US Open mental state could perhaps have been analysed by looking at his other dreams. He
had dreamt that he had won the Wimbledon final against
Federer, when he had actually lost it, and then the reverse for
the Olympic final; it was a relief, when he woke, that he did
not have to be content with a silver.

When the draw is made for a grand slam, tennis players will
tell you that they look no further than their first match.
Whether you believe that or not is up to you, but it is hard to
imagine that Murray was unaware he had a projected semi-
final with Federer and a potential final with Djokovic. Even so,
Murray would not have been mentally fast-forwarding
through the fortnight. This was still only the first Monday, it
was a hot and steamy afternoon, and he had what was potentially an awkward match.

In the early rounds of a grand slam tournament, there is
almost nothing to gain, and everything to lose, for the top
seeds. By the time the US Open rolled around, men's tennis
was in what some were calling a post-Rosol world. Lukas
Rosol was the Czech player who had achieved one of the
greatest shocks in tennis history – if not the greatest – by
beating Nadal in the second round of that summer's
Wimbledon Championships. The thinking was that Rosol's
victory would have encouraged many of the 'lesser' players in
the locker-room to consider that they actually had a prayer of
achieving the previously unthinkable, taking down one of the
big four before the middle weekend of a slam. But Murray
must have appreciated that if he lost to Alex Bogomolov

Junior, then ranked number 73 in the world, that would be more shocking than when Rosol had skewered Nadal.

Murray had prior knowledge of how horrible it felt to lose to Bogomolov. In the spring of 2011, when he was in a post-Australian Open funk, still feeling sore after his defeat to Djokovic in Melbourne, he had drawn the then American and played one of the most excruciating matches of his life. The danger for Murray, for his coach Ivan Lendl, and for anyone else in the Arthur Ashe Stadium who wished Murray well, was that Bogomolov would draw on that memory. There was also the unknown of how Bogomolov would react to playing the US Open for the first time as a Russian, and the possibility that the crowd could provoke him into brilliance. Still, this wasn't Paris. Try turning up to Roland Garros, the first year after renouncing French citizenship, and see what sort of reception you get. A Parisian tennis crowd is never slow to hiss, to whistle or to boo. To draw some horns on a decent journey-man pro, so someone who usually goes quietly about their business is turned into the devil. While the New Yorkers can be loud, and sometimes a little too enthusiastic with their support of American players, they are not often cruel, not even to former Americans. When Bogomolov Junior walked out into the stadium, hot-dogs and paper cups of beers did not rain down from the sky.

While the match had been pushed back by two hours because of rain, the humidity had not cleared, and Murray and Bogomolov were breathing in warm, heavy air. Though Murray had left for North America soon after winning a gold medal, he had not played a great deal of tennis during the hard-court swing, known as the US Open Series, which leads up to New York. Having pulled out of a third-round match against Canada's Milos Raonic at the Toronto Masters to avoid further aggravating a knee injury, he lost at the same stage of the Cincinnati Masters to France's Jeremy Chardy.

The transition from English grass courts, and the Wimbledon double-header of the Championships and the London Games, to playing on North American hard courts is not just about the surface; your body must adjust to the climate. You have to remember how to sweat again. Murray had not played enough tennis in the heat of North America that summer to be fully prepared for this. He also had not taken on enough water, which would leave him cramping.

There was an alarming start for Murray when he was broken in his first two service games of the US Open, and throughout the match he looked like a very different player to the one who, just a few weeks earlier, had pulverised Federer in the Olympic final. Anyone who did not see a ball of Murray versus Bogomolov Junior, just the result, a 6-2, 6-4, 6-1 victory for the Briton, would be forgiven for thinking that this had been straightforward.

Still, Murray's next encounter, with Croatia's Ivan Dodig, would take place out of the heat of the day. American television had chosen it as a night match, which was good news for Murray, but not so good for Dodig; the Scot has always loved New York City after dark.

2

The Coach That Everybody Cares About

Anyone who thinks that every modern tennis player commutes to work by Learjet ought to acquaint themselves with Ivan Dodig; he has both competed at the US Open and slept under bridges (though never in the same season).

A Croat in his late twenties, he had arrived in the second round of the US Open, to play the third seed Andy Murray, with a ranking the wrong side of 100 and one of the sport's most remarkable back-stories. Sleeping rough is part of British tennis culture, but only when it involves camping overnight in south-west London for Centre Court tickets, and for one night only, kept warm by supermarket booze and a sense of hope. For Dodig, sleeping rough was how he had survived financially in the years before he could even have imagined playing someone like Murray on a floodlit show court at Flushing Meadows. Some players dream of winning grand slams, others of earning enough money to afford a hotel room.

It's the same sport being played at the US Open and at the entry-level professional tournaments, but they are two very different worlds. Competing at venues where the crowd sometimes didn't make double figures, Dodig had slept in train stations, bus stations, on the back seat of his old car, or under bridges. Dodig is from Medjugorje, a small hill-top settlement in Bosnia Herzegovina where the Virgin Mary is said to have repeatedly appeared to people since the 1980s. One wonders whether Dodig or his family and friends ever joined the pilgrims walking up Medjugorje's Apparition Hill to ask for a heavier forehand or a higher first-serve percentage.

After the Bosnian War and the break-up of Yugoslavia, funding tennis players had not been near the top of anyone's list of priorities, and if Dodig wanted to travel from one tournament to the next, he needed to win a few rounds, and save money by living like a tramp. By 2012, Dodig had risen high enough to be familiar with room service menus and hotel laundry bags. But Dodig was not the only Ivan that Murray knew who had slept in train stations during his career. The other was Ivan Lendl, who had gone on to win eight grand slam titles, and who was now his coach.

Ivan Lendl tells some of the dirtiest jokes in tennis. People on the tour often remark on that; what they won't then do is repeat any of his jokes. Meet the man once described as 'an equal opportunities offender', whose locker-room gags were said by John McEnroe to have been 'dubious at best'. Lendl could make Jilly Cooper blush.

Political correctness seems to be as foreign to Lendl as smiling when Andy Murray is on the match court; Annabel Croft, a former British player and now a television analyst, had that confirmed for her during the US Open. It was while Croft and her colleagues for Sky Sports were on the air – the studio was at the end of a line of practice courts, closest to the court which Murray was repeat-booking – that someone noticed that Lendl had carried an iron and ironing-board into shot. On the side of the iron, Lendl had written 'Annabel'. When they met later on in the green room, Lendl made a point of showing her what he had done. 'I didn't mind,' she had said. 'Lendl's mad, quirky, totally eccentric. He really made me laugh.'

To get his other kicks, Lendl launched tennis balls at Murray during training. Lendl the player had been known for drilling the ball at opponents in matches – he felt it was a legitimate tactic, and he also took some pleasure from causing mischief – and now, in his fifties, he was still doing it. A direct hit from Lendl stings like a paintball shot. Lendl would inflict pain, and then expect a laugh.

Lendl has not always had them chuckling in America. When he was winning US Open titles in the 1980s, he was seen as sour, robotic and humourless – he had all the charm of an Ostrava tower-block. He was about as much fun as communism. To mark Lendl's achievement of winning the 1986

US Open, *Sports Illustrated* put him on the cover with the headline 'The Champion That Nobody Cares About'. The copy inside was not much gentler either, with Lendl – who had moved to America just a few years earlier – accused of 'clearing the stadium like a bomb threat'. 'This was his second straight US Open title, and the fifth consecutive year he has reached the finals. In that time he has won 32 of 35 matches, and almost as many fans. In the early rounds of the Open a certain "Lendl Factor" emerged. As soon as his matches were announced, multitudes would abandon the stadium and the outer courts would jam up. Lendl may someday empty entire cities.' Another magazine writer who spent time with him reported: 'In a sport that had exploded in the 1970s on the gunpowder of personality, Lendl had none.'

Lendl thinks he was always funny, just that the public and media had been slow to realise. Were people aware that he used to roller-skate around the practice court in his back yard? Maybe the problem during the Cold War was that he was delivering his lines with a thick Czech accent. Or perhaps, back then, the jokes were just not very amusing. As Richard Hinds, of the *Melbourne Age*, has recalled of Lendl the touring professional: 'Occasionally you would see a picture of Lendl walking his German Shepherds or read about his wicked sense of humour. But when he tried to tell a joke at a press conference it would fall so flat you figured he should have let the dogs do the talking.' Sometimes the joke was on Lendl, such as when a friend arranged for an actor dressed as a traffic cop to knock on his door and arrest him for failing to pay a speeding ticket.

Lendl's immediate response was to cry out: 'Get me my lawyer.' The friend told *Sports Illustrated*: 'Sweat was pouring off him; he was stuttering. We had to tell him it was a joke. We were afraid he was going to break down.'

When the news broke, on New Year's Eve 2011, that Lendl would be re-engaging with tennis, one satirical website ran a story about his appointment as Murray's new 'misery coach'. So, who had Murray hired, Mr Sour Face from behind the old Iron Curtain, the player who had once threatened to kill the sport off in America, or the funniest man in tennis? Both, perhaps. There have always been two Lendls: the man dedicated to his task like no other, whether that be playing or coaching, and the man who uses humour to relieve any social awkwardness, to score points (he will be the only one keeping score) and also as a way of showing affection. The harder he was hitting the ball at Murray, the more jokes he was telling him, the more he was in fact showing how fond he was of the Scot. Lendl was surprised at how Murray laughed hard, and kept on laughing. 'Andy's sense of humour is almost as sick as mine. That's helped our relationship. You don't have to tiptoe around if you want to tell a bad joke.'

Of course, professional tennis is not a Will Ferrell movie. Murray did not imagine he was going to giggle all the way to his first grand slam.

Murray's decision to hire Lendl was not without risk. For all Lendl's achievements as a player – in addition to his eight slams, he had held the world number one ranking, and had an enraged Jimmy Connors giving him the finger – he was a rookie as a coach. In a 15-year self-imposed exile from tennis, he had spent much of his time helping three of his five daughters with their golf, as well as working on his own swing. Did he now know more about golf than he did about tennis? Plus, having the unsmiling Lendl in his corner was bound to draw more international attention to his efforts to become Britain's first male champion since tennis's 'dinosaur ball' age. Lendl would become 'The Coach That Everybody Cares About'. It would, in Lendl's words, up the ante.

When Murray announced he was linking up with Lendl, his rivals were in established, long-term coaching relationships. Rafa Nadal has only ever had one coach – his uncle Toni. All of Novak Djokovic's grand slam titles had come while he was working with Marian Vajda. And when the 2012 tennis season began, Roger Federer was settled with Paul Annacone, Pete Sampras's former coach. Murray, still very much the fourth member of the quartet, was the one who had to try something new. A few saw this as a desperate move by a player who was running out of options. Since becoming a professional tennis player, Murray had had guidance from a number of different characters – Leon Smith, Pato Alvarez, Mark Petchey, Brad Gilbert, Alex Corretja, Miles Maclagan and Darren Cahill. So what could Lendl possibly do any differently?

And if Murray was risking some of his personal credibility on this new venture, then Lendl was also going to have some skin in the game. Lendl was the joint most successful former player – the other being Jimmy Connors, who worked with Andy Roddick for a while – to coach at the highest level. He didn't have to do this, to take the chance that the partnership could go badly wrong. Lendl said he had already turned down a number of other offers from players. But he was intrigued by Murray.

Time magazine once described Andy Murray's tennis as 'a concerto of arrhythmic disharmony'. His mother Judy put it more simply: 'He messes people about.' In an era of baseline bashing and slashing – when most are incapable of doing anything more imaginative than wellying their forehand – Murray is different.

From an early age, he knew all this: a tennis court's geometry and how to use angles and impart spin; how to infuriate opponents with 'junk' or deliberately low-grade shots; how to slow a rally down; how to then speed it up; a fondness for drop-shots. Andy Roddick once remarked when you played Murray it could feel as though you were playing points in reverse, because of his habit of taking the pace off the ball at the beginning of the point. So Murray had introduced himself to the tennis world as a counter-puncher – he would soak up whatever his opponent was throwing at him before waiting for his moment to strike. The elite didn't like it, and Murray was soon bamboozling those who just couldn't work out how to deal with his intelligent, creative game. The problem, though, was this: Murray had become so good at playing defensive tennis, at allowing his opponent to make the first move, that he was reluctant to be proactive in rallies. Winning a grand slam is hard enough already without trying to do it playing defensive tennis.

The ten months that Murray spent with Mark Petchey, from June 2005 until April 2006, was the time he went from an Andrew to an Andy – he used the back-page of the *Sun* one morning to say that his friends and family had always called him Andy, so could the press and public please do the same. Those ten months also saw Murray thrill and torment Wimbledon, become a top-100 player, compete in a first ATP final, and win a first senior title. But Murray and Petchey couldn't always agree on how Murray should be playing. Petchey would have liked to have seen Murray being more assertive and aggressive. Murray wasn't so sure.

Before Petchey came on the scene, Murray was making an impression on senior tennis. In March 2005, the 17-year-old had become the youngest-ever British player to compete in the Davis Cup when he appeared in a doubles rubber in a tie against Israel in Tel Aviv (as the team bus later overtook the media shuttle on the way back to the hotel, Murray turned and bounced on his seat, shaking his fist in triumph).

A month later, Murray made his first appearance on the ATP Tour, and to listen to the self-recriminations that followed 'a terrible, terrible match' was to begin to appreciate the ambitions he had for himself. With Murray living at the Sanchez-Casal Academy outside the city, the clay-court event at the Real Club de Tenis Barcelona was effectively his home tournament. The night before the wild card played Jan Hernych of the Czech Republic, his mother Judy had sent him this scouting report about the then world number 79: 'Your granny volleys better than he does.' This had been enormously frustrating and hugely encouraging: if Hernych could reach the top 100, there was no reason why he couldn't too.

Not long afterwards, it started to get 'nasty' between Murray and Pato Alvarez, his Colombian coach from the academy, who had once worked with the Romanian Ilie Nastase. Realistically, this alliance between a South American man in his sixties and a Scottish teenager was never going to last long, but it had become personal. 'Off the court we were arguing a lot,' Murray said at a press conference. 'We weren't having so much fun. There were a lot of problems. The last week we were together, it got a bit nasty. He was saying bad things about my tennis and bad things about me. I didn't really need someone that negative in my corner.'

One thing Petchey had in his favour was that he was half Alvarez's age, so would be willing and able to run and lift weights with Murray, as well as compete at pool and darts. Another was that, when Murray had been recuperating for several months in 2004 after being diagnosed with a split kneecap, he had spent much of his time watching tennis on Sky television, which meant he had been listening to the Essex-born Petchey, himself a former top-100 player. To Murray's mind, Petchey, who was then also working for the Lawn Tennis Association, sounded as though he knew what he was talking about.

Their first tournament together was the pre-Wimbledon tournament at Queen's Club in the summer of 2005, though at that stage Petchey was just helping out, and was still employed by the LTA as their head of men's national training.

The tennis that Murray played at Queen's would lead to Petchey resigning from his job at the governing body. At the time, other coaches had been telling Petchey that he was mad to want to work with Murray as, 'he'll never do anything, he's very soft'. Clothing manufacturers were reluctant to sponsor Murray because they felt that he did not have enough power in his racket-arm. Petchey, though, saw something in Murray.

People tend to have a better recall of Murray's third-round defeat at Queen's than of the two matches which preceded it, when he beat Spain's Santiago Ventura and America's Taylor Dent for his first victories on the ATP Tour. It was not just Murray's tennis which made his match against Sweden's Thomas Johansson, a former Australian Open champion, score so highly on the Pimm's-ometer; there were medical mini-dramas to add to the narrative. The first time Murray collapsed on to the grass, after falling awkwardly, he screamed so loudly that all of West Kensington put their drinks down. The crowd had barely had time to pick them up again when Murray toppled to the floor once again. For five minutes, he lay face down in the turf, and when he eventually pulled himself to his feet, he chose not to wipe the grass and mud from his face, giving him the appearance of a rugby forward who had just resurfaced from the bottom of a ruck.

London's grass courts have seen too many 'Brave Brits' over the years, but as the tennis-literate members returned to the bar they appreciated that this match – Murray had come within two points of victory – was not to be filed away under 'heroic cameo', an entertaining effort from a player who was never to be heard from again. So Tim Henman had been right before Queen's when he had told Murray, still sore from losing in the semi-finals of the boys' singles at the French Open the week before: 'Who cares about the juniors?'

The interest in Murray was such that he was invited on to breakfast television (he declined – too early) and had to change his mobile telephone number. But Murray's summer, the soundtrack to which was the Black Eyed Peas track 'Let's Get It Started', which he would listen to on his headphones as he walked on court, had much more to give.

Who could have imagined that Petchey would walk around the All England Club wearing a baseball cap promoting the *Sun* newspaper, that Murray would become friends with James Bond (tennis enthusiast Sir Sean Connery), or that the teenager would go deeper into the draw at the Wimbledon Championships than Henman or Greg Rusedski? Or that Murray would find himself politely declining John McEnroe's offer of part-time coaching, as he thought, rightly, that the New Yorker would struggle to fit him in around his other commitments, and because the Scot was sure in his mind that he needed full-time assistance? Or that Petchey would suggest that Murray could go on to be bigger than Wayne Rooney?

The All England Club certainly got value from the wild card they gave Murray, who at the time was ranked outside the world's top 300, who arrived for practice wearing a replica Barcelona football shirt, and who played with a nerveless ease which only teenagers, not yet knowing any better, are truly capable of. Murray was an All England Club innocent, still excited by the attendants offering him towels in the locker-room and the fact that, had he chosen to, he could have sat there all day drinking unlimited Sprite. Or the fact that, though he was staying a few minutes' walk from the club, in a rented flat up in Wimbledon Village, people kept asking him whether he wanted to be driven down the hill in one of the tournament's official cars.

Murray's senior grand slam career began on the old Court Two, which is known as 'The Graveyard of Champions', not because Fred Perry and others were buried under the baseline, but because, for whatever reason, seeded players had tended to fare worse there than on any other lawn at the club. The most famous of all the upsets had been when George Bastl, an unknown from Switzerland, had beaten Pete Sampras in the second round in 2002, and the American, who had won seven Wimbledons, never played in the tournament again.

Bastl had not done much in the three years that followed, but after qualifying for the 2005 Championships he found himself paired in the first round with Murray. That morning, Murray had got himself in the mood for Wimbledon, which styles itself as tennis at an English summer's garden party, by switching on the television and turning up MTV to full volume. There had been concerns about his ankle injury from Queen's, but he was moving freely among the tombstones of Wimbledons past. The reward for Murray's straight-sets victory was having to sign so many autographs that Venus Williams was kept waiting for Court Two, and for the first time having a crowd by his practice court ('Let's face it,'

Murray said, 'the hype surrounding me has been over the top, as I haven't done anything – everybody's making out as if I'd pretty much won Wimbledon').

His other reward was to be promoted to a bigger stage, Court One, for a second-round match with Radek Stepanek, a Czech player who bore some facial resemblance to Homer Simpson, and who had something of a reputation for cartoon behaviour and gamesmanship. So Murray would have been prepared for Stepanek pulling funny faces at him, among other tricks. Stepanek, a top-20 player at the time, had not been helped by his coach Tony Pickard. Murray had been aggravated by what Pickard had said to his mother Judy about it looking as though he was training in Spain to run away from his British contemporaries. Plus, he had heard on the locker-room grapevine before this encounter that Pickard and Stepanek didn't rate him much. When Murray defeated Stepanek, Petchey walked over to shake Pickard's hand and to tell him, 'tough luck'. According to Petchey, Pickard responded: 'That was a terrible match. Both of them played badly. It was embarrassing. I can't believe that was on Court One.' When Murray heard about the post-match exchange, he was amused, but also regarded it as typical of the bitching in British tennis.

While Murray had been saying throughout that grass was not his favourite surface, there was no denying that playing his first match on Centre Court was a thrill. So far that summer, Murray had formally introduced himself to Britain's tennis public; his third-round match against David Nalbandian, a former Wimbledon runner-up, was the occasion that he launched himself at a wider audience. Sir Sean Connery, sitting in the Royal Box, was not the only person who got a little carried away as Murray took the first two sets. Murray was comfortable playing in the white heat of grand slam competition, before Bond and a television audience of millions. Unfortunately for Murray, who was playing only his seventh match on the main tour, fatigue and cramp began to take hold of his legs. Never before had Murray played a five-setter, and he was so exhausted after his defeat that he did not have the energy to stand up in the shower.

At least that happened behind the scenes; at the back end of summer, at the US Open, Murray's problems were all too public. New York also brought further signs that Murray was not going to mind his Ps and Qs with the tennis establishment. Both Murray and Petchey had expected that the teenager, the winner of the previous year's junior title, would be given a wild card into the main draw of the US Open. And the United States Tennis Association had indicated their willingness to do a trade with the All England Club, with one spot in the draw for the following summer's Wimbledon to be kept back for a young American. But the offer was rejected, and it was a moot point who was angrier, Murray or Petchey.

Murray, with a sore shoulder, and with a long American summer in his legs, would have to qualify. When he won his third and final match, he raised a finger to his lips, a gesture that was telling his critics, all those saying he was not fit enough, to be quiet. When Murray vomited on the court in his opening match in the main draw, against Romania's Andrei

Pavel, he blamed it on his electrolyte drink: 'I felt like I was going to burp and then I threw up. It was pretty funny.' Some of the sick went over Pavel's bag. Murray was not so much embarrassed as surprised, and once the court had been wiped down, he scored his first five-set victory. Still, after the burn of lactic and stomach acid that Murray had experienced against Pavel, it was not altogether surprising that he was not at his freshest for his next match, against Frenchman Arnaud Clement, which he lost with a 6-0 fifth set.

That long summer in America, which Murray felt was almost like a road movie, had allowed him and his coach to form a fast friendship. There are few jobs that involve a man in his thirties sharing twin hotel rooms with his teenage employer, even spending Christmas together, but this was one of them. Still, their relationship was not without its strange moments; when Murray would not stop honking the horn of their rental car as they drove through a rough part of the States, Petchey felt as though he had no option but to whack the boy on the arm. He didn't want to meet his end outside a trailer park. On their return, Murray became a lodger at Petchey's family home in Wimbledon.

A recurring theme was Murray's desire – after feeling maligned and misunderstood – to prove people wrong. When Murray had openly declared at the start of 2005 that he wanted to break into the top 100 that season, there were a few who had told him he would have been wiser to have kept those ambitions to himself. It was at a tournament in Bangkok that autumn, when he defeated Sweden's Robin Soderling to reach the quarter-finals, that he collected the points to give him a double-digit ranking, and he sent his mother this text message: 'I did it, Mum.' Murray also collected a bonus of £400, as a group of friends had all pledged to pay £100 each to whoever was first to make the top 100.

When Murray won a couple more rounds, putting him in his first ATP final, where he would play Roger Federer, Judy could not help herself in Dunblane – she danced about her house in her dressing gown and slipper socks. For Murray, playing Federer was like 'being a character in my own video game', but he showed plenty of composure. The only time he lacked clarity of thought was during the prize-giving ceremony when he could not be sure whether to kiss the beauty queen who presented him with a bouquet of flowers. There was some blushing of Scottish cheeks. 'She wasn't that great up close, Mum,' Murray later told his mother, to which she immediately replied: 'I'm sure she said the same thing about you.'

As much as tennis is an international sport – look at where tournaments are played around the world, and you will see that the sport has colonised more countries than the Romans or the British ever did – it can feel parochial at times. The rest of the sport did not much care that Murray had been drawn to play Tim Henman in the first round of the Swiss Indoors in Federer's home town, Basel. By then, Henman and Murray were friends, their friendship borne out of backgammon, and the 2004 US Open – while Murray had been winning the junior title, Henman had reached the semi-finals of the senior event for the first and only time.

Murray, who had first met Henman when he was 13, at a tennis clinic, had never understood why the British public were so hard on a man who had played in six grand slam semi-finals, including four at Wimbledon. Murray was grateful for the time that Henman had spent welcoming him to the tour. There are few occasions when someone will weep into a towel on making the second round of the indoor tournament in Basel, but this was one of them. Henman had a sore back and his post-match comments were cuter than the tennis that had come before it. 'Is is a torch? Is it a baton? Whatever it is, I've passed it on.'

Petchey would not have known it at the time, but his decision to miss the tournament in San Jose in California, which Murray played in February 2006, did not help him to stay in employment. In the opening month of the season, Murray had not had the Australian Open he would have wanted, playing some tame tennis to lose in the first round to Argentina's Juan Ignacio Chela, which had him calling out 'this isn't me' on the court and afterwards suggesting that the media were expecting too much from him (his future coach, Brad Gilbert, subsequently wrote a column for the *Melbourne Age* about how disappointed he was in Murray for his remarks). Petchey would have felt some extra responsibility for what had happened in Australia, as the decision to spend Christmas in South Africa – where Murray had only his coach to hit with – meant that he had been a little unprepared for the full weight of shot coming from his opponents as he began his first full year on the tour.

The tournament in San Jose fell during half-term, and

Petchey chose to stay at home with his wife and children, and to talk Murray through his matches on the telephone. Murray's companion for the week would be Kim Sears, who had a week off from studying for her A-levels. One of her first tasks, on landing, was to do something about Murray's hair, which had not been cut for a year. Murray didn't want to go to the barber's, but did allow Sears to attack his mop with a pair of nail-scissors.

No one could suggest that Murray's first title on the main circuit came at a 'soft' tournament. In the last couple of rounds, Murray beat two players who had previously been the world number one, Andy Roddick and then Lleyton Hewitt. To celebrate, Murray climbed into the crowd and kissed Sears. If the tournament had strengthened how Murray felt about Sears, it had done nothing for his relationship with Petchey.

The week after San Jose, Murray played in Memphis (Petchey was now with him once again) where he gathered the points which made him the British number one. However, there were signs, on both sides of America, that all was not well with Murray and Petchey. Reports in California had them arguing on a practice court at the Indian Wells Tennis Garden, and eating separately – when once they would have had all their meals together. In Florida, at the tournament in Miami, Murray complained publicly about the heavy schedule set by his coach. There were differences of opinion over strategies. Just before the start of the European clay-court season, and with Murray entered to play in Monaco, they sat down at a cafe in the French Riviera and he sacked Petchey.

Murray, who had had the best months of his tennis life with Petchey, was keen that the situation did not drag on any longer. He did not feel good about doing it. After all the time he had spent with Petchey's family, including living in their London home, and pulling Christmas crackers, this felt very personal. Indeed, Petchey's wife and children were in Monaco when this happened, as they had flown out for a family holiday. From Petchey's side, this was not unexpected and it did not permanently sour relations between the two men. This could be seen from the interviews they did together during the 2012 US Open, for Sky television, that the split had not stopped them from going back to being friends again.

There is no more spectacular place to play tennis than the Monte Carlo Country Club, with the Mediterranean on one side and the limestone cliffs on the other. It is a setting to lift the spirits. Yet for his first match without Petchey, Murray wore all black. Even his towel was black.

Brad Gilbert calls himself 'a neurotic, redneck Jew'. The actor Robin Williams, a friend of Gilbert's, thinks of 'BG' as 'a tennis sensei'. Andre Agassi had credited Gilbert for turning his tennis life around. Nothing would have prepared the American for the barracking he received from Andy Murray – a verbal assault on his dignity – during the most expensive coaching experiment in tennis history.

Whatever Gilbert was being paid by the Lawn Tennis Association – he was said to have been invoicing them somewhere between half and three-quarters of a million pounds a year – this gig would not have been easy on his ego. Money, sunglasses and a baseball cap didn't offer much protection. In Gilbert's bestselling book *Winning Ugly*, subtitled 'Tennis Warfare – Lessons From A Master', he advises the reader on how to relieve tension on court: try breathing like you have asthma, have 'happy feet', or sing a song ('I'll get a Tom Petty song going to myself').

What the manual doesn't recommend is Murray's foam-flecked approach, which was to whirl around to Gilbert and to gob a mouthful of invective his way. On at least one occasion, Murray was heard raging at Gilbert, the man who had guided Agassi back to world number one, 'You're giving me nothing out here.' There is a YouTube clip that shows Murray at a low moment in a grand slam; as he gives Gilbert a sarcastic thumbs-up, he also says something rude in Anglo-Saxon.

Gilbert is the most talkative person you will ever encounter (or have a largely one-sided conversation with) in tennis; it has been said that he is probably capable of talking underwater. Gilbert, an analyst for the American broadcasters ESPN, also has his own special way of 'calling' tennis, using colourful phrases as well as nicknames he has invented. It goes something like this: 'I smell a beatdown – Dr Ivo [Karlovic] is going to be taken to the woodshed.' Translating that from Brad-speak into plain English: it's bad news for Karlovic; Gilbert thinks he is going to lose heavily.

Francesca Schiavone, a former women's French Open champion, is 'Frankie Goes to Hollywood', while the Australian player Bernard Tomic is 'Weekend at Bernie's', and if you ever

hear Gilbert talking or tweeting about 'Gael Force' he is refer-
ring to the French player Gael Monfils. In Gilbert's universe of
beatdowns and woodsheds, Roger Federer is 'FedFan' and
Murray 'Muzza' or 'Muzzard'. As John McEnroe once said to
Gilbert, 'You do know that you are allowed to use the players'
real names?' So Gilbert likes to talk almost as much as
McEnroe does.

But, when Murray got angry and started to vent, and the
television director zoomed in for a close-up of Gilbert, he
would sit there in silence – neutered by a young man's anger.
What was the alternative? Scream back? Walk out? Other
tennis players register their frustrations by destroying rackets,
threatening to stuff tennis balls down line-judge's throats, or
snarling at the umpires. But surely few have ever abused their
coach like Murray mistreated Gilbert. Not once did Murray
remember to call Gilbert 'a tennis sensei'.

'Andy had the hunger. He also had the temper,' Gilbert once
said. 'McEnroe got furious at everything. Andy mainly got angry
at Andy for not doing it perfectly. Sometimes he took it out on
me. That's okay. I knew it was mostly frustration with himself.'

But Murray had never screamed at Mark Petchey. The way
that Murray was sometimes carrying on, Gilbert must have
been almost nostalgic for those gentle days when McEnroe
shouted at him over the net at New York City's Madison
Square Gardens: 'You don't deserve to be on the same court as
me.' That was a one-off, a match that sent a fried McEnroe
into temporary retirement. With Murray, Gilbert was being
verbally abused more regularly than that.

Maybe, in some ways, Gilbert had not been that different to Murray in his playing days; angry and with plenty to say. McEnroe once recalled: 'Eeyore had nothing on Brad; he had a black cloud over his head from the moment he went out there and never seemed satisfied until he got you pretty gloomy too. It almost seemed to be his game-plan. He'd look like he was going to commit hara-kari in the warm-up. Then he did a running commentary when he played, berating himself on every single point and justifying every mistake he had made.' The difference being, of course, that Gilbert's anger was not directed at a coach.

Initially, Murray had been attracted by Gilbert's past. Gilbert had coached Andy Roddick to the 2003 US Open title (the only grand slam title he would win) and to the world number one ranking, success which Gilbert partly attributed to talking Roddick into abandoning a sun-visor for a baseball cap. Murray was more interested in the work that Gilbert had done with his boyhood idol Agassi; in their eight years together, Agassi had harvested six of his eight grand slam titles.

The Las Vegan has often spoken of how much he owed to Gilbert. In 1997, Agassi had spiralled down the rankings to number 141 in the world, and he would later disclose in his memoirs how it reached such a low that he found himself snorting lines of crystal meth – a highly addictive stimulant more commonly associated with America's under-class than former Wimbledon champions – off the top of his coffee table. It was Gilbert who talked Agassi into dropping down to the Challenger circuit, the level below the main tour, so he could build up some confidence and momentum. Agassi took his advice, and rode the wave all the way to the top of the rankings.

Gilbert's Hollywood moment came during the 1999 French Open final, when Agassi, hoping to win the Musketeers' Cup for the first time to complete his set of grand slam titles, found himself two sets down against Ukraine's Andrei Medvedev. When the rain came, and stopped play, Gilbert gave the pep talk of his coaching life. Agassi has said that he would not have won that match if Gilbert had not found the right words. Murray knew all that. As a player, Gilbert had made the most of his limited talents – his highest ranking was fourth – but it was as a coach that he had made his mark on tennis.

Murray had found, after firing Mark Petchey, he missed having someone around to talk to, and felt down. As a temporary move for the 2006 French Open, he asked his boyhood coach Leon Smith to accompany him to Roland Garros. Smith's influence on Murray, when coaching the boy from 11 to 17, was such that Murray wanted peroxide hair too. 'Leon was a bit of a poser back then: tall, good-looking with bleached blond hair.' As with many of Murray's working relationships, he ended it because of the bickering. On this occasion, the root cause of the arguments was that Murray wanted more independence. But it was an amicable parting, and they remained friends, which was why Smith was pleased to help in Paris that spring. What Murray wanted, though, was a full-time coach.

One of the greybeards of men's tennis thinks that working

with a new coach is very much like having a new girlfriend. Hope springs eternal. You think to yourself, 'This is the girl/coach for me.' Murray linked up with Gilbert after that summer's Wimbledon, where he had beaten Roddick to reach the fourth round, only to play a pancake-flat match against Greek Cypriot Marcos Baghdatis.

In the early days, such as when Murray achieved his first victory over Roger Federer, at a tournament in Cincinnati, Murray and Gilbert patted compliments back and forth at each other, the American talking fondly of 'The Kid'. Some wondered what the LTA was doing paying for a millionaire's coach. But Gilbert had a theory that the LTA's decision to fund the arrangement had improved the usual player-coach dynamic. The relationship between a player and a coach is an odd and often fraught one; though the coach is the employee, he is the one giving instruction. Gilbert's thinking was that, because Murray was not paying his wages, there would not be as much of the usual conflict and tension. That was the theory, anyway.

'With Andy and Brad's personalities,' Tim Henman said, 'it was never a bed of roses.' How Ivan Dodig would have loved to have had someone of Gilbert's calibre to have screamed at, but that was how the other half lived. Gilbert was going to put some muscle on those Scottish arms. He was also going to give him the tactical guidance he needed.

Murray and Gilbert were spending an unhealthy amount of time together. They were together for breakfast, lunch and dinner, for practice sessions, matches, flights, car rides and while killing time in the player-lounges and locker-rooms of the world tour. When Murray yelled at Gilbert, it looked like a release after all those hours spent listening to Gilbert. Only in matches could Murray take the conversational lead.

Murray appeared to grow tired of listening to Gilbert. Gilbert was a morning person; Murray often didn't function properly until after lunch. Gilbert loved Cadillacs; Murray didn't even have a driving licence then. Gilbert was also somewhat neurotic, and had such a phobia for germs that he always carried a small bottle of anti-bacterial handwash with him. Making bets about British football – they had a £500 wager on the number of goals that the footballer Peter Crouch would score in a season – was not going to bridge this divide. 'Andy doesn't live an outlandish life and he has got to be the only Scottish guy ever who doesn't drink,' Gilbert recalled in an interview with the *Guardian*. 'His idea of a good time is studying his opponent's play on DVD. And then he plays video games seven hours a day. So if he is not playing video games or playing tennis, he is with his girlfriend. He lives a quiet relaxed life, focused on being a tennis player. But he is obsessed with video games. I don't play video games.'

From what Gilbert was saying to Murray, it was almost as if the coach thought it a problem that his player did not have any vices. So Gilbert suggested to Murray that he ought to consider blowing off some steam by sky-diving, bungee-jumping or stripping in public. How different this was to what Gilbert had been used to with Agassi. 'I knew Agassi years before I coached him. We were contemporaries. We were mates before we started. The day I started with Andy I didn't know him at all. It was the first time I had coached a non-American. Andy is very argumentative if he feels strongly about something. A lot of people in his team gave into him. I didn't so we would argue.' Even after they stopped travelling together, Gilbert and Agassi had stayed friends. But Murray would have been aware that Gilbert's relationship with Roddick had ended badly.

Even when Murray was playing well at the beginning of the 2007 season – he reached the fourth round of the Australian Open, where he took Rafa Nadal to five sets – he was not enjoying his tennis. Wasn't this supposed to be fun? He was tetchy and angry when he should have been happy that he was making decent progress in the profession he had chosen. It was almost as if he had forgotten the pleasure he could take from tennis, though it has to be said that any dissatisfaction in Murray's head stopped a long way short of how Agassi had felt about the sport. Murray never hated tennis.

The greatest pain that Murray has ever experienced on a tennis court came when, playing on his 20th birthday on the clay of Hamburg, he hit what he had imagined was an ordinary forehand. The wrist injury, sustained in a match against Italy's Filippo Volandri, would wreck Murray's summer, and leave Gilbert wondering whether the Briton was depressed and psychologically damaged. Murray and Gilbert were in agreement that the French Open was a write-off; there was no chance of Murray being in Paris.

Wimbledon was a different matter. Murray thought he was

not ready to play, but Gilbert believed that the Scot's wrist tendons were strong enough for him to have competed. Not for the first time, Murray thought Gilbert was not listening to him, and they were not communicating properly. Murray didn't like how, after he had lost at a tournament, Gilbert would occasionally get up early, put a note under Murray's hotel door, and fly home. So alarmed was Murray by Gilbert's suggestion he was depressed and might need help that he sought reassurance from his friends about his mental health, and even went to see a psychologist, who confirmed that he was not.

Murray wrote in an autobiography published when he was 21: 'Brad even wondered about the cause of my anger on court, whether it was just related to something in the past rather than just my frustrated perfectionism as a player. I know he meant all these things as a form of motivation and he has the best of intentions.' What Gilbert saw in Murray was 'one of the most negative people' he'd met, but that was not how Murray saw himself, and he found it difficult to relate to someone who saw him in that way.

In the circumstances, making the third round of the 2007 US Open, when he lost to Chinese Taipei's Hyung-Taik Lee, was a decent little run. Eventually, Murray tired of all things Brad. When Murray fired Gilbert in the autumn of 2007, he did so through an intermediary at the LTA. Maybe Murray should have fired Gilbert himself, but they weren't really talking then, and Murray couldn't ask his agent to do it for him, since Gilbert wouldn't have taken the call as the two of them weren't on speaking terms.

If Gilbert was no longer Murray's coach, he was still on the LTA's payroll; for several months he found himself trying and failing to coax more from Alex Bogdanovic, a British player who has the unfortunate career record of having turned eight Wimbledon wild-card entries into eight opening-round defeats (for some 'Boggo' had come to symbolise everything that was wrong with British tennis's culture of welfare dependency, with his first-round defeats at Wimbledon becoming as much a part of the summer season as Henley and Royal Ascot).

'I could have done more with Andy, but that's the thing in coaching – it's one-on-one, and if they're not feeling it, you don't want to stand in their way,' Gilbert has said. Murray would later confess that his treatment of Gilbert had been immature and silly. So he had learnt from his mistakes. The image that lingers, though, is of Gilbert sitting in the stands, feeling what it's like to be on the wrong end of a monologue.

Call them Andy Murray's Cross-Dressing Years. They were also the Miles Maclagan Years. Maclagan had Scottish blood and a floppy sun-hat, but much more importantly than that, in a post-Gilbert world, was that he had an easy-going nature. Coaches don't come much lower maintenance than Maclagan, who until he was hired had been best known for having held, but not converted, three match points against Boris Becker at the German's last tournament, the 1999 Wimbledon Championships. Unlike Brad Gilbert, Maclagan wouldn't talk at all, at least not in public, with Murray preferring his new coach not to give interviews. Murray, though sensitive to the charge that he wanted to surround himself with yes-men, was plainly in much greater control than he had ever been with Gilbert.

After ditching Gilbert, Murray had resolved to put together a gang of good people around him. Maclagan was the coach and he worked alongside physiotherapist Andy Ireland, fitness trainers Jez Green and Matt Little and the occasional consultant, such as Alex Corretja, a former French Open finalist and world number two. They became known as Team Murray, a term which the player himself was not keen on. When Murray was playing a grand slam, and all his backroom staff were there, mischief could be had during a change of ends by counting the number of people in his guest box, and then suggesting that this Scottish tennis player had an entourage that would not shame a Saudi prince. This was often unfair; while it was reasonable to count agents and media advisers and anyone who worked for his management company, it was going too far to throw his girlfriend and brother into the mix just to reach double figures and get a cheap laugh.

This Team Murray made their own entertainment. To keep their training and off-court life interesting, there were forfeits riding on their games of football tennis, played with two people on either side of the net, and used as a warm-up. That was why you might have seen Murray, or one of his staff, going out to dinner at a restaurant wearing women's clothing or a chest wig, dressing in a pink velour tracksuit or choosing a Hannah Montana film as his in-flight movie. Other forfeits included kissing the winners' toes, taking an ice bath without shorts on, clearing the plates away at lunch and wearing a cricket helmet to practice. There was a strict rule: if anyone from outside Murray's circle enquired as to what you were doing, you weren't allowed to say it was for a forfeit; you had to tell whoever was asking that you simply liked going to restaurants with your clothes on inside out. It may or may not have been a coincidence that, around that time, Murray was watching a lot of *Entourage*, the American television series about a Hollywood actor and his posse.

Twice during Murray's time with Maclagan – they were together for two and a half years, from the end of the 2007 season until after the 2010 Wimbledon Championships, during which time his ranking peaked at number two – he came within three sets of winning a grand slam. At the 2008 US Open, Murray became the first British grand slam finalist since Greg Rusedski had been the runner-up to Australia's Pat Rafter in 1997, also in New York.

For Murray, wearing a grey shirt, and with what someone called a geography teacher's facial fuzz, the final went by in a blur, and he did not win a set against Roger Federer. That was not entirely unexpected. Murray was not used to the emotions and the choreography of a grand slam final, while the other guy was arguably the greatest player of all time. 'This was a good effort at my age,' said Murray, who was 21 at the time, but he wanted more: 'I don't want to be remembered for losing in the final of the US Open.' Even then, Murray was saying that the only goal he had left in tennis was becoming a grand slam champion.

The second occasion that Murray went close was at the 2010 Australian Open, and again he had the misfortune to play Federer. Had Murray won the third set – he had been 5-2 up in games and had five set points in the tiebreak – the match could have got very interesting. But he didn't. Once again, Murray lost in straight sets to Federer and it all got too much for him when he was making his thank-you speech. The previous year's final had had Federer, after a defeat by Rafa Nadal, weeping during the speeches: 'God, it's killing me.' And now it was Murray's turn to lose control of his bottom lip, though almost immediately afterwards he thought of a genuinely funny line and returned to the microphone: 'I can cry like Roger, it's just a shame I can't play like him.'

The way Maclagan tells it, the end came when he realised there were three people in this tennis marriage. For a couple of months, Maclagan had been uncomfortable with the role played within Team Murray by Corretja. Though the Spaniard had initially been hired to help with Murray's clay-court game, as time went on his influence spread to other surfaces too. Murray had reached the semi-finals of that summer's Wimbledon Championships, losing to Nadal, and as Maclagan flew across the Atlantic to join his player at a training camp in Miami, he felt that it was the right time to speak openly about his concerns. He was aware that starting such a conversation could result in his unemployment.

'The issue was about Alex,' Maclagan recalled in an interview with the *Daily Telegraph*. 'Alex was a great player and he's a good coach and he had his ideas. And, with most of our ideas, there was some agreement between us. But there were a couple of things that we didn't agree on. The three of us sat down for a civilised chat and Andy and I decided to move on rather than coming to a compromise.' Maclagan was pleased that the trio did not try to throttle each other, and they parted amicably. 'I'm proud of the fact that we didn't have a big fight, that we didn't try to throw each other off the balcony. We ended things and shook hands. The next morning, I had breakfast with Andy and then flew home.'

For the second time, the first having been Brad Gilbert, one of Andre Agassi's former coaches played a role in Andy Murray's development. Darren Cahill was part of the adidas team of coaches who were made available to anyone sponsored by the German sportswear company. Murray often turned to the Australian for advice, and for a while it looked as though he wanted Cahill just for himself. The loose arrangement had its drawbacks. During grand slams, Cahill had his television commitments with ESPN and so was not always around when he was needed. Plus, there was the adidas versus adidas rule – if Murray found himself playing an opponent also dressed with three stripes on his kit, Cahill was not allowed to offer any tactical guidance. Where Cahill really helped, though, was encouraging Murray to consider appointing Ivan Lendl as a full-time coach.

The possibility that Murray and Lendl could work together was first raised in the spring of 2011 when the Scot, clearly still thrown by having lost to Novak Djokovic in the final of the Australian Open, was beaten by Alex Bogomolov Junior at the hard-court tournament in Miami. Lendl was the one who made the first move, not Murray, and there was initially some suspicion that Lendl was happy to have the idea floated in the media as a way of publicising his tennis academy. Without Cahill, though, Murray might never have entertained the possibility.

Cahill has recalled: 'I really encouraged Andy to consider. It's not easy, when players look at these former champions, to get their heads around the fact that they are going to fully commit to the coaching job because, to be quite frank, a lot of these guys can go off and in two or three days make the type of money that they can make from a full year of coaching. So it is unusual that a Lendl, a Connors or a McEnroe or any of these legends of the game would actually commit to somebody else's career. We felt that Ivan ticked a lot of boxes in what Andy was looking for.'

Ever since Murray had stopped working with Miles Maclagan, he had been urged to appoint someone with standing and gravitas as his coach. For a while, Murray's best friend, Dani Vallverdu, had been the closest to being the Scot's full-time coach. Murray and Vallverdu had first met when they were juniors training in Barcelona, and the Venezuelan had been an occasional hitting-partner and even more occasional doubles partner, but he had started to travel to most tournaments.

Could a big-hitter have helped change the outcome of the

2011 Australian Open final, with Murray's straight-sets defeat to Djokovic giving rise to the unfortunate statistic that the Briton had not won any of the nine sets he had played in slam finals? What Murray was looking for, when you boiled it down, was someone who had been there and done it. Vallverdu's ranking had peaked, in 2005, at 727; Lendl had won every major apart from Wimbledon. So Murray was curious. But Lendl was not going to come to him. If Murray wanted to talk this over, he was the one who would have to travel. Some observers, including American former professional Justin Gimelstob, interpreted Lendl's demand as a way of showing that he was not beholden to Murray; that he did not need the job.

So Murray went to have lunch with Lendl, and there was no avoiding the symmetries. At that stage, Murray had played and lost in three grand slam finals, while Lendl's first four major finals had brought four defeats. Along the way, a clever sub-editor at the *New York Post* had him as 'Choke-Oslovakian'. Murray was, of course, encouraged by how Lendl had then gone on to win grand slam finals (though it should be noted that Lendl had some good fortune in his fifth major final when he found himself trailing John McEnroe by two sets to love at the 1984 French Open, only for the noise leaking from a cameraman's headset to drive the New Yorker wild).

Would Murray have been so interested in Lendl, and vice versa, had Lendl won his first grand slam final? Probably not. But a rough run in slam finals was not all they had in common. All Murray wanted to do in tennis was to win a grand slam; everything he did on the match court, the practice court, in the gym or on the track was to further that aim. And Lendl knew all about obsession. Such was Lendl's desire to win Wimbledon – to add to the three US Opens, the three French Opens and the two Australian Opens – he twice skipped Roland Garros to give himself more time to prepare for the grass. That didn't work either.

A couple of Stakhanovites, they also had self-discipline in common. Maybe there are tennis professionals on the tour today who are more committed to hard work and self-improvement than Murray, but they have kept themselves very well hidden; and Lendl had been the first tennis player to take diet, fitness and training seriously. Boris Becker regards Lendl as the first modern tennis professional. Lendl would make a schedule and stick to it. A friend once said of Lendl that 'if the Pope was in Ivan's living room at bedtime, he'd say, "it was nice meeting you," give you that blank smile of his and disappear into his bedroom'. Lendl's attention to detail was such that he would ask the man who laid the courts at the US Open to also lay the practice court at his home so that he would be practising on the exact same surface. For the first time in his life, Murray had met someone as obsessive about tennis as he was. And both had been coached by their mothers.

In other ways, they were very different men. When Lendl was playing, he had displayed what some saw as paranoid behaviour. If he heard clicking on his telephone, he imagined that the Czech secret services had him under surveillance again, and he would spend the next few weeks on the lookout for eaves-droppers in restaurants. But when you have grown up under a communist dictatorship, perhaps that is less surprising. When Lendl returned to his house, with its high stone walls, expensive alarm systems and German Shepherds for guard dogs, people thought him a recluse. For all Murray's unease with fame, he has never hidden himself away, or wondered whether the couple on the next table were spies. Murray is more popular with his peer group than Lendl ever was with his, though that needs qualifying: Murray is living in a more corporate and civilised age. The current generation don't spit insults like 'communist son of a bitch' at each other like the old boys did.

More than anything, what Lendl brought was authority. Miles Maclagan would later suggest that Lendl was probably telling Murray many of the same things that he had been, including to be more aggressive and assertive from the off, but that Lendl would have been doing so with a back-catalogue of achievement. Only Lendl, out of all Murray's coaches, was in the position to tell him what it was really like to win a grand slam. Murray was hoping that Lendl could assist with the mental side of playing slams, and how to deal with pressure and expectation. During that first meeting, Lendl had impressed Murray with his knowledge of the modern game, telling him how he would go about beating Roger Federer, Rafa Nadal and Djokovic. While Lendl had not been on the tour, he had clearly been watching enough matches on television, and talking to enough people, to have kept his tennis brain active.

Andy Murray could have beaten Ivan Dodig 6-0, 6-0, 6-0, having performed cartwheels and backflips during every change of ends, and still he would not have elicited a smile from his coach. Ivan Lendl never smiled when he was watching Murray play. It was something he had copied from his parents; they had never shown any emotion as spectators. 'Smiling is over-rated,' he said. Maybe Lendl did not have the choice, perhaps he was no longer even physically capable of smiling while tennis was being played. This much was clear: Lendl's unmoving, unsmiling face had been having a calming effect on Murray over the course of the season. When Lendl was around, Murray was much better at controlling his emotions than when his coach had stayed at home to play golf. What would have happened, you wondered, if Murray had ever dared to scream at Lendl in the same way he used to tear into Brad Gilbert? 'I really wouldn't recommend that he ever does that,' Boris Becker said.

So no one expected Lendl to smile, or to clap, to move or to do very much at all when Murray played Dodig for a place in the last 32. Dani Vallverdu was so excitable – up out of his seat the whole time – that Lendl wondered whether the South American might one day fall out of a guest box. Lendl, meanwhile, liked to hold the same position for as long as he could; with his chin resting on the upturned palm of his hand.

Still, there is plenty a coach can communicate to a player by doing nothing, as Chris Evert, once the ice queen of the women's game, and a winner of 18 grand slam singles titles, had noticed. 'When I first heard that Andy and Ivan were going to work together, I thought, "Oh yes, this looks interesting." Ivan is so poker-faced, so stoic and he never claps.

Ivan's intense but in a low-key way. Andy used to get so down on himself, and that was having an impact on his tennis. Ivan has stopped that. Ivan keeps Andy mentally balanced,' Evert said. 'If Andy plays a good shot and looks over at Ivan at the side of the court, Ivan looks back in a way that says, "Okay, but keep going." If Andy is down, Ivan is saying to him, "You can get out of this." Ivan's message to Andy is, "Don't get so heated or emotional – just chill."'

Murray's new calmness in a crisis was the biggest change since Lendl's arrival. Lendl knew that to have made any great technical changes to Murray's game – to have broken his game down and then put it back together – would have been 'suicidal'. What Lendl could change was Murray's strategy, and his willingness to take risks, to play some shots, to be bold. 'When somebody tells you to go for your shots, it's one thing,' Martina Navratilova has said. 'When Ivan Lendl tells you to go for your shots, you listen.'

By the time the US Open came around, they had had three slams together. While Murray had led Novak Djokovic in the semi-finals of the Australian Open, only to lose, he had lost in the right way, playing aggressive tennis. Murray, who was beaten in the quarter-finals of the French Open by Spain's David Ferrer, then played in both Wimbledon finals. Murray had recovered from the disappointment of losing to Roger Federer in the final of the Wimbledon Championships to beat the same opponent on the same court – Centre – to win the gold-medal match at the Olympics.

The Murray–Lendl collaboration had done everything apart

from win a slam, and Lendl had said from the start that it could take nine months to see the benefits in Murray's game. John McEnroe was having to begrudgingly admit that Lendl was doing a decent job. If Murray ever did win a grand slam, Lendl would achieve as a coach what he had never come close to as a player: popularity in Britain and across tennis.

There were not many dissenting or sceptical voices, but one of them was Jim Courier's. The American, a former world number one, had his theory about why Lendl had returned to tennis, and he shared it with a local television network during the Australian Open: 'There is a reason and it is a little bit mercenary. He hasn't been allowed to make any money from tennis for the past fifteen years because he had cashed in disability insurance. That's the reason Ivan is back.' Lendl responded that Courier was being ridiculous: 'Jim shouldn't be saying stuff like that. First of all, it's wrong, and he doesn't have the proper information. End of story.'

Behind the scenes, and on the practice courts, Lendl was tweaking, chatting and encouraging. Lendl had told Murray to take it easy with some of the service drills, asking him: 'Do you want your arm to fall off?' The idea was that the arm would stay fresher and he would serve better when it mattered, in matches.

On a number of occasions during the US Open, Annabel Croft saw Lendl and Murray at the practice courts having what looked like 'deep' conversations. 'Andy asks a lot of questions,' Lendl disclosed in New York. 'Sometimes he surprises me with his questions, because they come out of nowhere, so obviously he has been thinking about it. The more questions he asks, the happier I am. He shows he wants to learn. I don't like to push things on him unless I have to – as I do at times. He can pluck what he wants from this closet, that closet or that closet. I really don't know at times which is the best one for him – or whether any of them are right. Only he knows what he is struggling with inside.'

Earlier in the year, Lendl had told the *New York Times* magazine, for a feature about 'tennis's new odd couple': 'I want Andy to tell me things that will help me work with him, and some of them are very private and go very, very deep.' Even after Murray has retired, he will not share what was said between them, believing that a tennis coach should be following the same strict rules of confidentiality as a lawyer, a doctor or a priest. But Lendl, once that conversation or practice session was over, often left to play golf. Lendl was not being unfriendly or a total golf tragic; he had noted how some of Murray's previous arrangements had been spoilt by spending too much time together and wanted to avoid that happening this time round.

At first glance it seemed that, under the Lendl regime, all fun and fripperies had been been cancelled. Since Lendl had joined Murray's staff, no one had seen them playing games of tennis-football on the practice court, or carrying out any forfeits. The thinking went something like this: you weren't going to catch Lendl wearing a pink velour tracksuit or watching a Hannah Montana film, just because he had a lost a game of tennis-football, or whatever else, with his twenty-something employer. But let us not forget about the filthy jokes. Or how Lendl, covered in sweat after a training session, would cast around for someone 'dry' to bear-hug.

You knew that Murray had formed some sort of bond with Lendl when you heard about the potential forfeit riding on some doubles. Murray and Lendl were planning a challenge match with the British doubles pairing of Ross Hutchins and Colin Fleming, and if they lost, Lendl was going to have to rollerblade into the All England Club while dressed in white Spandex. Lendl was also trying to make New York laugh with music. All who compete on the Arthur Ashe Stadium are invited to select three songs for the stadium's DJ to play during the changeovers. Serena Williams tended to ask for rockers Green Day, Laura Robson was open about her liking for boy-bands, but Murray did not want to choose in case listening out for the tracks would be a distraction. The offer was passed on to Lendl, who requested Wham! and Culture Club.

The fun should never interfere with the tennis, though. One of Lendl's recommendations to Murray before the US Open was that he should move to a quieter hotel. When Lendl was competing for US Open titles, he would spend as little time as possible in New York City. Rather than staying in a hotel, he would commute from his Connecticut estate, and he would try to practise at his house rather than at the tournament; about the only time he went to the venue was to play matches.

As much as Murray has always enjoyed the noise and the chaos of Manhattan, he took his coach's advice over the hotel.

What Murray had not counted on, as he sought peace and quiet in New York, was Prince Harry playing a game of strip pool in a Las Vegas suite. And maybe Murray's new status as an Olympic champion had brought extra attention, too. On stepping out of his hotel lobby one morning, Murray was intercepted by a group of cameramen. 'They asked me whether I had seen the pictures of Prince Harry. I said, "No comment." And then they asked me what I thought of the crown jewels. I didn't comment on that either. I ran away.'

Murray had also resolved not to hang around the courts as much as he had in previous years. And it was not as if he dragged out his match with Dodig. Though this would be Murray's first match with Dodig, he has always been an anorak about other players on the tour, and he had buffed up beforehand by looking at video clips. So he knew all about Dodig's past ('not everyone has a rich federation to help them'), how he had beaten Rafa Nadal on a hard court the year before, and how the Eastern European likes to come to the net, making him a rarity in modern tennis. When Dodig tried that, Murray would be waiting.

There was a poise and a purpose to Murray's game which had been missing from his opening match, which would have something to do with the time of day for his encounter with Dodig; Murray's best tennis on the Arthur Ashe Stadium has often come after dark. Murray was on court for less than two hours and his 6-2, 6-1, 6-3 victory meant he had reached the third round for a total loss of just 13 games.

Still, it was not even the most notable British performance

of the day on that stage; that had come earlier in the day when teenager Laura Robson had shot the Belgian Bambi, beating Kim Clijsters to end her career. Murray was not the only British tennis player to have crossed the Atlantic with an Olympic after-glow, to have experienced an emotional high while representing Great Britain (let's not use that dead phrase, Team GB). Robson and Murray had won the silver medal in the mixed doubles competition, and now she was having what Americans would call 'a breakout party'. After beating Clijsters, she would go on to defeat China's Li Na, a former French Open champion, before troubling Sam Stosur, the US Open title-holder, in the fourth round. Greats of the women's game were starting to predict good things for Robson, talking up where she would be in two, three, five years.

For Murray, it was all about this fortnight. Next it was Feliciano Lopez, a Spaniard who had flirted with his mother on Twitter.

3

A Body like a Machine

Over Labor Day weekend, the rich flee Manhattan for the Hamptons, while all other New Yorkers make for Central Park, but in the blue-collar borough of Queens, tennis players are at risk of being fried at Flushing Meadows. (Those who haven't been shouldn't be fooled by the name into imagining it to be a green and pleasant place where you can stroll among the long grass, bluebells and butterflies; the reality is a lot of steel and painted concrete, every surface reflecting and magnifying the sun's heat). Spectators at the US Open can entertain themselves between games with one of tennis's changeover debates. Which of the grand slams provides the greatest physical test? Where is a tennis player's body most likely to plead with him to drop his racket in the middle of the rally, put his head under a towel and retreat to the locker-room?

Well, it's not Wimbledon, unless you're John Isner and Nicolas Mahut, and your first-round match has just gone into a twelfth hour. Many a tennis pro has been bushwhacked by the weather at the Australian Open, where temperatures can reach 40°C and higher, and the line-judges can find themselves peeling dead moths and summer-blasted players off the courts. There are days in Melbourne when the heat melts tramlines, and confuses players, their bodies starting to malfunction, into thinking they are cold. On those days, you find yourself wondering whether, with global warming and holes in the ozone layer, it is such a good idea to be playing a grand slam in the middle of the Australian summer. Some players dread the French Open, where the looping bounce means having to 'win' rallies two or three times; play against Rafa Nadal at Roland Garros, or against one of the 'dirt-rats' or specialist clay-courters, and your legs and lungs will know about it.

There is, though, a strong argument to be made for the US Open as the place where a tennis player's willpower will want to curl up in the shade. Melbourne is probably hotter than New York City. But in New York the field must contend with the high humidity, which can be nastier than Australia's dry heat. The biggest difference is that players are fresh when they turn up at the Australian Open, after an off-season, however short, of rest and training. By the time the US Open rolls around, the season is eight months long, and players' minds and bodies are tired.

When Andy Murray and Feliciano Lopez walked on to the Louis Armstrong Stadium for their third-round match at the

A Body like a Machine

2012 US Open, it was Saturday lunchtime, it was 32°C (and promising to get warmer), and on another court a couple of juniors would have to stop because of heat exhaustion. It was just as well that Murray was no longer one of the skinniest, gawkiest kids on the tennis block. He had turned himself into a gym-hardened modern professional, and earlier that summer had appeared in a video feature for a British newspaper, in which, stripped to the waist, he looked into the camera and said: 'My body feels like a machine.'

Tennis has never been more violent, or more explosive. There has, of course, been an arms race in frames and strings; the polyester strings have forced the greatest change in recent years by allowing players to stay in control even when swinging with maximum power. Forehands can be hit without compromise. The manufacturers often aren't subtle; there is a range of strings on the market called 'Big Banger'. But the tennis that is being played today – real matches and tennis video games have become almost indistinguishable – would not be possible if Generation Murray did not take their physical conditioning so seriously. Maybe once it was possible to win a grand slam without knowing what cardiovascular meant, or how you would go about fixing yourself a protein shake, but not now. Buy a ticket to a grand slam and you will be watching some of the world's greatest athletes.

In the 1970s and 1980s, tennis players would have thought 'kinetic energy' was something that came served in a cocktail glass. It is a different sport now. Watch footage of matches from those years and you find yourself marvelling at how slow it was. Almost absurdly slow. So slow it can be frustrating to sit through. Back then, a first serve struck at 125mph was considered 'big'; now a delivery at that speed would not be worthy of comment. Television companies use the Hawk-Eye cameras and computer, based on missile-tracking technology, to measure the speed of forehand winners, many of which are travelling at 100mph-plus. Tennis's Studio 54 days, when a player could roll out of the nightclub and on to a practice court, have gone the same way as the haircuts. Every modern tennis player has to work as hard on his strength and fitness as he does on correcting any technical faults. If not harder. What would be the point of having grooved groundstrokes if, when a match goes into the fifth hour, your body fails you? If Murray was to have any chance of winning a grand slam, he had to compete physically.

His rivals were dedicating themselves to improving their bodies. Rafa Nadal is no longer the same player who, as a teenager, bounded on the tour in three-quarter-length trousers and muscle-vests. In recent times, he has been having platelet-rich therapy to combat his knee pain, with the injections bringing tears to his eyes.

Nadal regards Roger Federer as a 'freak of nature' for never picking up the serious injuries that others do. There is no doubt that Federer's smooth style and movement have been a great advantage over the years, but a great deal of effort has gone into making it look easy ('When Federer is in full flight, he looks like he's gliding, almost like he's floating above the court,' said Jim Courier, a former world number one). Federer's longest-serving member of staff, who has been with him before he started winning grand slams, is his fitness trainer Pierre Paganini.

Federer knows that without excellent fitness, genius can't flow from his racket. Excellent fitness means excellent footwork, and that means he can glide or float to wherever he wants to be on a tennis court. Over the course of every season, Federer will have a couple of training blocks, maybe more, when he will work on his footwork and speed around the court rather than on his strokes. The drills are designed to replicate movement during a match. Andre Agassi's hill-running around Las Vegas, as impressive as it undoubtedly was, now looks a little unscientific.

Tennis has witnessed some weird science and some bogus science. There was once a Swiss player on the women's tour, Patty Schnyder, whose coach (who believed he had found the cure for AIDS and cancer) convinced her that she ought to be drinking two litres of fresh orange juice every day. But there is no reason to snigger at anything that any of the leading men have done.

Anyone still using that mocking line 'anyone for tennis?' without irony, needs to sit down in front of a television showing replays of Novak Djokovic's last two matches at the 2012 Australian Open – all 11 hours of them. Djokovic was on court for almost five hours in beating Murray in the semi-finals, and then for close to six hours in defeating Nadal in the final. Djokovic's tennis was astonishing, with the Serbian reaching balls that he should not have even been getting close to, and then really cuffing his shots. Strange to think that Djokovic was once derided for being soft, for always whining about his physical ailments, for hating the heat, and for being too eager to retire from matches. A joke from Andy Roddick at the US Open one year – the American said Djokovic was dealing with 'cramp, bird flu, anthrax, SARS, and a common cold and cough' – would have stung. He knew he had to change.

It was a very different Djokovic who won three grand slam titles in 2011, putting together one of the greatest seasons in tennis history. Djokovic's parents used to run a pizzeria halfway up a Serbian mountain, so you could say he was brought up on margheritas, but a doctor persuaded him to cut the carbs and the gluten from his plate. The same physician also told him not to eat in front of the television, but to sit at the table where he could be 'present with his food'. Djokovic has also occasionally sat in an egg-shaped, pressurised chamber that gave him some of the benefits of being at altitude. Djokovic's fitness trainer, Gebhard Phil-Gritsch, has been quoted as saying that the player's body ran with the power and precision of a Formula One car. He also said that he is forever looking for that one per cent change to Djokovic's conditioning that could 'make a big jump'. 'The better you get the more you have to go into details, to optimise every little angle of the game.'

Like Djokovic, Murray has transformed his body since joining the tour. Back when he was being called 'a scruffy Hugh

Grant', it was not necessarily a compliment, but a comment on his need to bulk up.

In those early days, after reaching the third round of the 2005 Wimbledon Championships, where he lost a five-setter to Argentina's David Nalbandian because of cramp and fatigue, Murray was sensitive to the criticism that he was more familiar with the Starbucks drinks menu than the weights-room. Murray felt as though there should have been more attention paid to his achievement of going that far in the tournament, and less on any physical deficiencies he might have shown against a former finalist. Certainly, no one should have expected an 18-year-old, who just weeks earlier had still been playing junior tennis, to have been at the peak of his physical powers.

More recently, however, looking back at that summer, Murray has appreciated that some of the observations were fair comment (in 2012, he recognised that his upper body had been too small when he first played on the full circuit, but said he never had too much of a problem with his legs as he had inherited strong calves from his mother). He will surely also see that, at the time, he was not doing everything in his power to prepare his body for tennis. For all the hours he was doing on the court and in the gym at Barcelona's Sanchez-Casal Academy, he wasn't eating properly and on one occasion fainted in the loo. At the 2005 junior French Open, he had been running on baguettes and chocolate spread, and during his first senior Wimbledon he would send his mother Judy out for Starbucks frappuccinos. And while he hardened up over that long American summer in 2005, and did well to qualify for the US Open, he faded in the second round of the main draw to France's Arnaud Clement.

Seven years on, at the 2012 US Open, Murray was a very different animal, thanks to years of dedication and a sophisticated training programme. You don't get to challenge for grand slams simply by upping your broccoli intake and doing more chin-ups.

One of Brad Gilbert's ambitions as Murray's coach had been to have his player wearing a Nadal-style muscle-vest at Wimbledon, with his biceps on show for the Royal Box. We will never know for sure whether Murray would have considered that even for a moment, as Gilbert and Murray's time together included only one Wimbledon and Murray did not play because of injury. What we do know is that, when Murray sustained that wrist injury, one of his concerns was whether there would be further debate about his physical fitness (or lack thereof); he felt considerable relief when he saw that it had been accepted as a freak accident, and that he would not come under further attack for supposedly being a slacker.

Indeed, Murray has not been at fault for other freak injuries over the course of his career, such as when he was involved in a minor car crash in New York that left him lying on the floor of a yellow taxi cab with a bump on his head and mild whiplash. Or the prang during the indoor tournament in Paris one autumn when he stepped out of the crumpled vehicle with a stiff back. Or the time at the French Open when he broke his tooth by biting into a baguette.

A Body like a Machine

Early on in their relationship, or 'right off the bat' as Gilbert said, he told Murray that he wanted a couple of things for him: an extra four kilos in weight and eight more miles per hour on his service speed, and that 'the second won't happen without the first'. Gilbert introduced Murray to an old buddy and neighbour, who also happened to be a former Olympic sprint gold medallist: the American Michael Johnson. The day that Murray and Johnson spent on a track in California was, in Johnson's words, a great shock to Murray's body, as it was the first time that the Scot had done anything like it. They parted with Johnson giving Murray some exercise routines and warm words of encouragement. Murray spent more time with another of Gilbert's friends, Mark Grabow, a fitness coach for the Golden State Warriors, an American basketball team. You could not fault Gilbert's contacts. Despite all of this, Murray was still some way short of some of his main rivals; there was always more that he could have done to improve his fitness.

Soon after sacking Gilbert, and at a pre-season boot camp in Miami in the final weeks of 2007, Murray committed to whatever his new team – fitness trainers Jez Green and Matt Little, and physiotherapist Andy Ireland – demanded of him. Murray told them: 'Look, I've spent the last two years not pushing myself as hard as I should. If I don't do a session properly I want you to tell me straight out. Tell me: "Your attitude's wrong." Don't let me get away with anything.' Green has since spoken admiringly of Murray's 'total dedication': 'He came to me when he realised this was an area he needed to work on and from the very first day he was prepared to do anything I asked.' Even if that included Bikram yoga, which involved holding positions in a studio heated to an 'insanely hot' 42°C, while trying not to faint. Or the pain and nausea of the track. There was no torture, Murray kept on saying, that he wouldn't consider, which was brave, as Green used to be a kick-boxer. And because, just before the camp, Murray had been on a drip in hospital for two days because of an extreme case of food poisoning.

Other players require their fitness staff to sign confidentiality agreements, so fearful are they of any secrets leaking to the locker-room, and taking away any competitive advantage, but Murray and his team appear to have been very open about the work they have been doing. Mostly, because being secretive is not in Murray's nature. And also, you suspect, because he does not mind people knowing how hard he has been working. Murray once collaborated with *Men's Health*, a fitness magazine for office workers obsessing about turning soft guts into hard abs, to take readers through his regime. Such as how he does chin-ups with weights wrapped about his waist, or tied around his neck. About the only legal thing Murray would refuse to do is to borrow one of Djokovic's books on New Age spiritualism, which Djokovic reads on his doctor's recommendation.

Murray was happy to share a video on his website from that training camp which showed him lying down on his back in the crucifixion pose after doing twenty 100-metre sprints around the track. When Murray got up, he had left an exact imprint of his body, in sweat, on the grass. Though Murray had spent that day with Johnson, this was the first time he had done a full programme of track work, and he became all too familiar with the pain of doing sprints with only short intervals in between. The 400-metre repeats tended to be the worst. There were longer runs, too, up and down the sands of Miami's South Beach.

'Andy has never thrown up – that's not the aim,' Green has said. 'But Andy will tell you that he's been in pretty dodgy shape at the end of sessions, he really pushes himself to the limit.' Only once or twice has Murray failed to finish a set of sprints. One of those occasions was when he could manage only seven of the ten 200-metre runs he was supposed to be doing. Green gave Murray a ten-minute break, and then made him go back to the track to do the rest. The other time was when Murray went out too fast when asked to do five 400-metre runs, and after three found himself lying on the ground and crying out for oxygen. And, at the end of every session, Murray had the horror of the ice-bath, when he would sit in water chilled to 10°C. Not for masochism's sake, but to flush the lactic acid from his muscles.

It was at the 2008 Wimbledon Championships that Murray first seemed proud of the shape he was in; after coming from two sets down to beat France's Richard Gasquet, a victory that had taken him to his first quarter-final at the All England Club, he rolled up his shirt sleeve and flexed his bicep as Popeye might when trying to impress girlfriend Olive Oyl. Murray hadn't suddenly become the Narcissus of men's tennis, and he also wasn't trying to tell tennis that he had the biggest biceps in the draw; that would have been extremely foolish when he was to play Rafa Nadal in the next round (a match Murray lost). The gesture, which was copied by teenage girls standing behind the wire fence at the practice courts the next day, was about Murray thanking his team, and also showing them all that time at the track had been worthwhile. The hard work has continued ever since. That celebration reappeared in New York at that summer's US Open, and people took notice. Murray was playing a match on the Arthur Ashe Stadium when he looked up at the video screen and saw that the actor Will Ferrell was kissing his bicep.

Men's tennis has its secret smokers; there are others who like a glass of wine with their pasta. It's to Andy Murray's advantage that he has never smoked and he hasn't drunk alcohol in any quantity since his mid-teens. The night that put Murray off booze was when, at the age of 16 and living in Barcelona, he 'got completely hammered on vodka, wine and champagne', vomited outside a nightclub and 'tried to catch it in my hands – it went down my arms and legs and splashed on my shoes. Unbelievably, the nightclub let me in, but I can only imagine that I wasn't a popular clubber that night.' The headache in the morning was horrendous, and so was the self-loathing; he was embarrassed at how he had behaved. About the only time since that alcohol has passed his lips was when he won the title in Miami one year and, while having dinner with his girlfriend, he had a small sip of her strawberry daiquiri. One sip was enough (he prefers the taste of lemonade to alcohol), and he went back to his soda.

A Body like a Machine

Someone once looked at the number of calories Murray was putting away when he was training in Miami – 6,000 a day – and thought it sounded as though he was on an 'Elvis Presley suicide diet'. At his boot camps, he has consumed almost 4,000 calories a day more than the average man. Breakfast alone was a slog, almost as much of a physical endurance test as running around a track. He started with protein shakes and bagels with peanut butter; the peanut butter would stick to the roof of his mouth. Yoghurt and fruit would follow.

Almost every professional tennis player seems to have a thing for sushi, but Murray is the king of the California rolls; his record for one sitting is getting on for 50 pieces. Murray has also tried cutting gluten and dairy from his diet – Novak Djokovic's 2011 season had started a gluten-free craze in tennis – and has even stuck to it when he had the torture of sitting in restaurants, waiting for his food to arrive and watching everyone else at the table eating bread smeared with butter. One thing you will never find Murray eating is the humble tennis banana, as he regards it as 'a pathetic fruit' (he even hates the fact they're not straight). During tournaments, Murray shows great self-discipline. One Wimbledon, an opportunistic British supermarket sent a crate of their own-brand jelly sweets to Murray's house, after reading how much he liked them, but they remained untouched for the fortnight, only to be opened when he had played his last match.

About the only time he eats junk is when he is at home between tournaments; he has shown that he is more than capable of putting away three or four Feast ice-creams in a day.

'When I'm home and away from tournaments I don't eat particularly well for a week or so. I'm not really into chips that much, and sweets hurt my teeth now – I had too many of them when I was younger. Ice cream is the only thing I'll eat a lot of when I'm back around the house, and I can have it from midday until I go to bed.'

Greg Rusedski's story has scared many tennis players, Murray included, from using supplements. Rusedski, who tested positive for nandrolone, was exonerated after a tribunal accepted that the banned substance had entered his system when he had taken a contaminated supplement. So Murray will not bulk up using supplements, believing that it would be difficult to recover from a positive test, even if that 'positive' had come about because of a mistake made by a pharmaceutical company.

As much as Murray understands the need for having a rigorous testing programme in tennis, and he would hate to think that anyone on the tour is taking any chemical short-cuts, he has often spoken of his annoyance at having his privacy invaded. Murray, like everyone else in the tennis elite, must tell drugs-testers exactly where he will be during a one-hour slot on every day of the year. For 365 days of the year, Murray's time is never quite his own. Players can choose any hour between 6am and 11pm, and most go for the earliest possible slot as that means they will be in bed and so won't forget where they are meant to be and miss a test. However, when the drugs-testers do come visiting that means being woken up at what Murray would consider to be an ungodly hour.

A Body like a Machine

After one early-morning visit to his home in Surrey, Murray, who had been in bed with his girlfriend, took to Twitter: 'Nice little 6am drug test to start the day off. Must be a weird job being a drug-tester – waking people up, staring at their privates and leaving. Surely there is a law against that.' The testers don't always come at that allotted hour, as Murray discovered one summer, three days before the start of the Wimbledon fortnight: 'They said it was an out-of-hours test. So you fill in the forms but they come when they want. It's pointless.'

There have been frustrations at tournaments, too. Within a couple of minutes of one defeat at Wimbledon, he noticed he had a new shadow: a tester, and Murray politely said to him, 'Can you give me some space? I'd like to be on my own for five minutes.' Murray did a urine test after his semi-final defeat to Novak Djokovic at the 2012 Australian Open; but then was told he could not leave Melbourne Park as he had to stay seated for half an hour before doing a blood test. If Murray is ever inconvenienced by a tester, you tend to know about it. Only Rafa Nadal has been more outspoken about the intrusion of the testers. 'I just want to enjoy a normal life,' Murray has said, 'without people bashing on my door [in the middle of the night].'

Andy Murray has never punched anyone in the face. But, for almost as long as he can remember, he has been fascinated by boxing. At his first Wimbledon, he watched videos of Ricky Hatton's fights between matches. And he probably knows as much about obscure boxers as he does about obscure tennis players, which is a hell of a lot. Nothing gives him an adrenalin rush like boxing; watching a world heavyweight title fight once, he became so alarmed at how much he was getting into it that he switched the television off.

There is a theory that tennis players are drawn to the sport because they like having the physical barrier of a net between them and their opponent, that they want competition but abhor contact. If that's true, then that fear of physical contact would make tennis players very different from boxers. But Murray has always thought there are plenty of similarities between tennis and boxing: 'agility, speed, aggression, co-ordination and tactics' play a key part in both sports. Murray has also taken inspiration from the way fighters prime their bodies and minds for competition.

On a visit to David Haye's gym in Miami, Murray was taken by how basic it was; whereas tennis can be very neat and nice, this was sport at its purest. Boxers, Murray has realised, train hard to fortify their minds. Murray has started to think the same; if he has worked hard, he knows that he can last five sets. 'Staying more controlled mentally stemmed from taking my fitness more seriously. When you're doing track work, sprints and so on, it's pretty painful, but that does make you feel better prepared and therefore mentally stronger when you're going into a match,' Murray said in an interview with *Men's Health*. 'You know, without a doubt, that you are strong enough to last.' In the life of a tennis player, some of the biggest mental and physical challenges don't come on court at the grand slams, and on live television, but away from the crowds and cameras, and in training. So when Murray walks on court, he knows that whatever happens, it's not going to be any worse than what he has already been through.

Murray's comparisons between boxing and tennis were shared by Brad Gilbert (so there was something they agreed on). 'Andy is a fighter. The great thing about tennis is that it's like boxing in the sense that you go into the ring and it's just you against the other person. One guy tries to pound the other guy out of the ring,' he wrote in the *Guardian*. 'It's beautiful because it's basic.' (One thing Murray has not copied from boxing is the pre-match trash-talking. Haye would never send Murray a 'good luck' text message before an important tennis match, as boxers don't believe in luck. Instead, he will urge Murray to 'smash in' his opponent.)

The 2008 Beijing Olympics taught Murray a lesson about what happens when you are 'unprofessional'. When Murray arrived in China, he was already dehydrated from the plane, and had skipped some meals during the journey. Going to the Opening Ceremony, sweating for hours in the Bird's Nest Stadium, didn't help either. By the time Murray played his first-round match, he had dropped four and a half kilos; after his defeat, he was concerned people would think that he had been cavalier about the Olympics, that it looked as though he didn't gave a damn about the five rings and a possible medal. The disappointment in the singles tournament, plus losing in the second round of the doubles event when partnering his brother, left him with a new determination always to prepare properly for tournaments and always to travel on planes with his protein drinks. And always to stand on some scales on arriving at a tournament so he can then maintain that weight.

Murray has never understood why other tennis players don't work hard. He can't stand the indolence of some other British players, of how he has turned up at the National Tennis Centre in Roehampton, south-west London, at the weekend looking for someone to practise with, but has found the place to be like 'a ghost-town'. There was the occasion when he called James Ward, who has been the British number two, to ask where everyone was. Ward was on the train home; he had already been at the centre but, also finding no one to 'hit' with, had left. Murray was grateful that Ward returned to Roehampton, as otherwise he would have gone without practice. Murray has undoubtedly benefited from the Lawn Tennis Association's wealth – as we have seen, Brad Gilbert came for free – but has wondered out loud whether the annual Wimbledon surplus has harmed players as much as it has helped them.

During Murray's time, some young British players had their funding cut after posting pictures of themselves on a social-networking site which showed them eating junk food and partying, including, in the case of one girl, with her leg draped around a condom machine in a nightclub toilet. Another player had his money stopped when he was spotted in a bar during the Wimbledon Championships. No one could ever accuse Murray of pissing the LTA's millions up against the wall.

It was a long time ago that someone called Andy Murray soft or a tennis weakling. Instead, in the spring and summer of

A Body like a Machine

2012, a number of talking heads created another controversy about Murray's physical conditioning. Murray kept on hearing how he was making the most of any pain or strain, how he was trying to create the impression he was in a medical crisis, when he wasn't. While they did not allege that Murray had 'cheated', the implication was that he had been unsporting. Murray's irritation with Virginia Wade, with the former world number two Tommy Haas, and with John McEnroe, was revealing. Was Murray still as sensitive to criticism as he had been as a body-conscious teenager?

Wade won Wimbledon so long ago that the celebrations included the Centre Court crowd singing 'For she's a jolly good fellow' in her honour as she put her cardigan back on, and privately Murray probably considers that she has never experienced anything as physical as his matches. Wade, whose victory at the 1977 Wimbledon Championships is still the last time that a British woman won a grand slam title, was in the Eurosport studio during the 2012 French Open, discussing Murray's second-round match against Finland's Jarkko Nieminen, when she called him 'a drama queen'.

Murray felt as though his injury had been very real; his back had gone into spasm, he had been unable to put all his weight on one leg, and he was serving at 60mph, which is about the speed of delivery you expect from a veterans' competition at Dunblane Sports Club. Murray, after having treatment on the court, came from a set down to win in four sets, undoubtedly helped by his opponent's loss of concentration. When Murray was told what Wade had said, he was furious; one eye-witness reported him to have been 'red-lining just this side of apoplexy'. Suddenly, thanks to Wade, everyone was being invited to have their say, and just before Wimbledon Haas shared his views with a German television station (this debate had gone international): 'Sometimes he looks like he can barely move, then comes the trainer and then he moves like a cat.' McEnroe's opinion was that Murray's injury was possibly more mental or psychological than physical.

When that comment reached Murray, he responded by asking whether McEnroe and others (Boris Becker had also had his say) would care to have a look at his medical records? Or to consider why, if this had been an imaginary injury, he had gone to the bother – the extremely painful bother – of having eight-inch needles stuck in his back? Still, Murray's reaction did not stop his first-round opponent at Wimbledon, a Russian called Nikolay Davydenko who is one of the tour's eccentrics, from saying that other players occasionally 'laugh' at his behaviour. 'Sometimes he walks on court, he looks tired, like he doesn't want to run any more, and then he runs like an animal. He has done it all his career. Maybe it is a special Scottish thing.'

It is a rare event when a modern tennis player walks on court free of all pain, with absolutely nothing to trouble the masseurs. It is about degrees of pain. Taking pain-killing pills or, if it comes to it, pain-killing injections, is one of the realities of playing professional tennis. Take Murray's bipartite patella, or split knee-cap, which has been causing him pain since his teens. Murray can only 'manage' the knee, which, every now and then, feels as though it's on fire. While no one talks about Murray's knee problems in the same apocalyptic way that they discuss Rafa Nadal's chronically cranky knees – the Spaniard has had to take lengthy breaks from competition to rest his body – he often finds himself in great discomfort. The pain is often worse when he is playing clay-court tournaments.

Many players, Nadal included, feel that soft clay is much more forgiving on their bodies than playing on hard courts, but that is the surface which makes Murray screw up his face. Sliding around the clay, Murray has to work much harder at keeping his balance, and that puts more stress through the knee. It is a problem that Murray has had throughout his time on the tour, and it is not one that is suddenly going to disappear like a puff of clay-court dust.

Murray has done what he can to avoid aggravating the knee, but that has led to the odd storm in a Pimm's cup in British tennis, such as when he skipped Britain's Davis Cup tie against Argentina in 2008. Murray didn't think that flying to Buenos Aires to play on clay, when he had just played the hard-court Australian Open and when he had indoor hard-court tournaments to come in Europe, was going to do his knee any good. He knew that his withdrawal would start another round of bitching, but he always remembered what Jean-Pierre Bruyere, a French chiropractor, had told him when they worked together: 'Don't let anyone mess with you. Take care of yourself. I don't want anyone to stop you by pushing you too hard when you're young. It's your body and your life. If you're hurt, regardless of what anyone says, don't play.'

As Nadal has observed, playing sport is good for most people's bodies, but not for professional athletes, because of what they have to endure to compete. You only have to look at a tennis player's bare feet, gnarled and beaten-up, to see it is not the effete sport that many people used to think it was.

Ever since that first Miami boot-camp in 2007, Murray has continued to put great emphasis on his physical fitness. He goes there every winter to work on his fitness. He has also got into the habit of having a mid-season training camp, after Wimbledon and before his first tournament of the North American hard-court swing, though that was not possible in 2012 because of the Olympics.

There are a few players on tour who are more flexible than Murray; he has often been astonished at some of the things that Gael Monfils is capable of on a tennis court, and how Novak Djokovic can almost do the splits on court. Murray isn't as quick around the court as Nadal, and he knows he doesn't move as 'effortlessly' as Roger Federer does. He is never going to be as good in the air as Jo-Wilfried Tsonga. And perhaps there are a few characters in the locker-room that Murray wouldn't challenge to an arm-wrestle. But Murray is a fine all-rounder. He has become increasingly flexible. Over a short distance – and most of the time in tennis you want to travel only a short distance to reach the ball – he is one of the quickest. 'In tennis you don't have to be incredibly fast or incredibly strong, you just have to be very good at many different aspects. I'm an all-round athlete.'

Jez Green, writing in the *Daily Mail*, suggested that Murray had 'the stamina of a middle-distance runner, 800-1,500 metres, and the speed of a sprinter – his speed over twenty metres is exceptional. He is able to take incredibly quick steps.' In the gym, Green said, the 'prodigiously strong' Murray had 'the capability of a rugby player, even though he is a tennis player and cannot be that bulky. He is a ridiculously natural athlete and when you combine that with the work ethic he has, you come up with something very special. I suppose as an athlete you could call him the complete package.'

There is no doubt that men's tennis is getting taller. There are some, such as Ivo Karlovic (six foot ten inches), John Isner (six foot nine inches) and Juan Martin del Potro (six foot six inches) who have to duck under doors before walking out on court. And yet the leading four players from the past few years are not exceptionally tall. Murray, at six foot three inches, is the tallest of the quartet, with Djokovic an inch shorter, and Federer and Nadal each an inch shorter still. Murray is tall enough to get some extra pace and bounce on his serve, but not so tall that he struggles with his movement, or low pick-ups. Six foot three inches is a good height for someone aspiring to win the US Open. And it matters not one bit that Murray's body is not totally in balance; he has a weak left shoulder, because it never gets to work as hard as the right, and his left leg is a little stronger than his right. But that's just the way it is, with tennis being 'such a diagonal sport'.

By the time Murray walked out into the New York haze to play Feliciano Lopez, he and Ivan Lendl were eight months into their relationship. Inevitably, when Murray played, Lendl got more 'air-time' than anyone else in his staff. The coach was getting all the close-ups. But Murray would never have become the force he was if it had not been for his fitness trainers and for a physiotherapist who, according to Murray, believes in aliens, and who, when they started working together, had known next to nothing about tennis. They had been together for years.

There are few things more mortifying for a tennis player than when your mother has a crush on your opponent. At least, when Andy Murray played Feliciano Lopez for a place in the fourth round of the 2012 US Open, he already had some previous experience of playing through the embarrassment of his mother's affection for a Spaniard she had nicknamed 'Deliciano'.

It had become very clear at the 2011 Wimbledon Championships, where Murray and Lopez had played at a grand slam for the first time, exactly how Murray felt about his mother flirting on Twitter with one of his rivals. Murray and Lopez had been practising together before the tournament – before the draw had been made and so before they knew they could end up playing each other in the quarter-finals – when he noticed that his mother was standing by the side of the court, and he called over the net to his friend: 'Feli, if we sit down for a drink, could you pose for a picture with my mum, because she thinks you're beautiful?'

Judy went the same colour as the strawberries, and cried, 'I'm not doing it. I'm not doing it.' Before their match, there was so much interest in Judy's admiration for Lopez that

Murray said in his press conference, 'It's about time to stop with that nonsense – it makes me want to throw up. It's disgusting, yeah, disgusting.' British bookmakers were even offering odds on whether Mrs Murray would wolf-whistle at the Iberian as he walked out on to Centre Court (she didn't). Still, that can hardly have been much of a distraction for Murray as he defeated Lopez in straight sets, and then, when they met again at the US Open later that summer, this time in the third round, the Scot once again did not drop a set.

Now, a year on, here was 'Deliciano' once again. 'It's good to meet Andy,' Lopez said, 'so we can have this story another time. I know everyone has been joking about Judy and me but we are good friends and I admire her personality and charisma.'

In truth, Murray should not have been that displeased that he was playing Lopez. After all, he had beaten him six times on their first six meetings, conceding just the one set. Lopez's game suited Murray's. Lopez liked to get to the net to play a volley, but probably not as much as Murray liked having an opponent rush forward, giving him a target to aim for. Plus Lopez, for all his other talents, did not exactly have a reputation for mental fortitude; perhaps he would disagree with the heat.

Jez Green has disclosed the attention to detail that goes into preparing Murray on the day of the match, including how the players' team is immediately informed when the Scot has got out of bed (perhaps, as the US Secret Service does for the President, they also have a code word for him for all radio communications). Murray isn't allowed to choose his match-day breakfast on a whim. 'The nutrition routine is set,' Green said. 'He has to get a certain amount of calories in, all monitored.' Next, Andy Ireland 'wakes up' Murray's body with stretches, before the player pedals on the exercise-bike in the gym to raise his pulse, and then does what Green called 'some dynamic flexibility work'. After a light hit on a practice court, he 'refuels'. Twenty minutes before he is due on court, he returns to the gym for an 'explosive work-out, sprinting and everything quick and fast, he gets a sweat on and he goes directly from the gym to the court'. Green, who was talking to the *New York Times* magazine, also disclosed that throughout match days Murray has an osmorality check to ensure that he is properly hydrated, with the right percentages of water and minerals in his urine. Before Murray played Lopez, as before every match, nothing would have been left to chance.

Lopez's performance took many by surprise. He had decided to be bold. He was teeing off on shots, and more often than not the ball was landing in the court. He was also 'going' for his second serve, and that meant that Murray could not get the depth he wanted with his returns. Over the course of the four sets, Lopez would win more points than Murray, 162 to 154. Murray, after taking the first couple of sets with tiebreaks, twice led by a break of serve in the third set but somehow contrived to lose it 6-4.

Murray would have to stay out in the New York sun for a while longer; during each change of ends, he and Lopez had the option of wrapping themselves in ice-towels, but within

seconds of getting up, they could feel the burn again. Murray
took the fourth set and the match with the third tiebreak of
the afternoon (it was just as well that the Spaniard had made
a hash of all three of them), and then the Briton would talk
about the contest as if it had been a good way of toughening
him up for the rest of the tournament. Tennis players like to
put a gloss on most situations; had he zipped through the
match in three easy sets, he doubtless would have spoken
about how important it was to have conserved energy for the
second week. On this occasion, after a 7-6, 7-6, 4-6, 7-6
victory, he was saying it was no bad thing that he had had
to suffer.

The first stages of post-match recovery included an ice-bath,
stretches, protein shakes and making a reservation at a sushi
restaurant. Some players are so superstitious that they can go
whole grand slam fortnights sitting at the same table in the
same restaurant, ordering the same food – Goran Ivanisevic's
victory at the 2001 Wimbledon Championships was fuelled
by eating fish soup, lamb and chips and then ice cream with
chocolate sauce every night. Murray, though, likes to vary his
diet, and at the US Open he was eating fish, chicken and steak
in rotation. After the exertions of four sets with Lopez – and
still burning through calories for some time afterwards –
Murray knew he would have to 'eat a lot'. 'I'll try to get about
one hundred and fifty grams of protein in me today, tomorrow,' he said, as it had been one of those matches when he
could easily have lost two or three kilos. His muscles were
hungry for that protein.

The nature of a tennis tournament is that you don't have long to sit back in your ice-bath and enjoy your victories, and thoughts quickly turned to his next opponent. To a young Canadian called Milos Raonic who likes to eat red meat before matches and whose serve had a top speed of 155mph, not far off the record. Since he had started to play at the biggest tournaments, Raonic's pre-match steaks – always medium-rare, so still a little bloody – had come from gradually more expensive cuts of meat. He was also increasingly spoken of as the man of the future, as the young gun who was going to start going deep into grand slams and roughing up the elite. You don't get many vegans near the top of the men's game.

4

The Joke that Went Wrong

Andy Murray has never felt unloved at the US Open. At Flushing Meadows, he has never overheard a woman hissing into her mobile phone, 'there goes that Scottish w———', as he walked past. Or had letters sent to his locker telling him, 'I hope you lose every match for the rest of your life.' Or, when he has been on court, been reminded of the crowd's affection for a retired player, and how he compared (not so well). All that happened on the other side of the Atlantic, at the All England Club's summer garden party, otherwise known as Wimbledon, a place of ivy-covered walls, hanging baskets and mutual unease.

There is nothing complicated about Murray's relationship with the New York tennis set. If he likes playing in front of them during daylight hours, he loves it at night, so he would have been thrilled that his fourth-round match with Milos Raonic at the 2012 US Open was to be under the floodlights on the Arthur Ashe Stadium, as that experience never gets old. And, in return, they like watching him.

The first time Murray saw a night-session match at the US Open, which was in 2004 when he was in the city for the junior tournament, he sat near the back row of the upper section; up there, spectators have a better view of the Manhattan skyline than they do of the tennis, so far are they from the court. But Murray was not as interested in following the ball as he was in the energy and the noise, in the music being played over the sound system between games, and how the spectators grew ever more vocal, fuelled by the beer and the atmosphere. The first time that Murray played a night match, as a senior, only reinforced how he felt about the city and the grand slam. Winning the junior title clearly also helped, and Murray has always appreciated what he regards as the upbeat, positive nature of the average American tennis fan.

If only Murray's dealings with the British tennis public could have been similarly straightforward. In any young athlete's media training classes, there must be a module about Murray's joke that went wrong, the one about supporting 'anyone but England' at the 2006 football World Cup. Somewhere out there, there is a parallel universe in which Murray chose not to say anything when asked which team he wanted to win the tournament (since Scotland wouldn't be there). But Murray couldn't resist.

Throughout the joint interview, Tim Henman had been

teasing Murray about Scotland's failure to qualify, and so he laughed at his friend's gag. It was not the funniest joke anyone has ever told, of the kind you could tell at the Edinburgh Festival and launch yourself into the stratosphere in stand-up comedy, but it was still a joke and anyone with an IQ above 17 should have been able to tell that Murray wasn't being serious. In Henman's words, that joke became 'a pain in the arse' for Murray. Among many other things, it would inspire the creation of the Facebook group 'Andy Murray hates the English, so we hate Andy Murray'.

'Not nice,' Murray has said of the abuse he suffered for daring to make a joke about English football, and that's putting it mildly. Not nice is walking through drizzle from Southfields Tube station to the All England Club; this was having his character ripped apart on the air, in print, in the blogosphere or in his ear. And Mark Petchey, his former coach, has always said that Murray is a much more sensitive soul than people realise when they are listening to him cuss his way through an appearance on Wimbledon's Centre Court or New York's Arthur Ashe Stadium.

It would take six years, and Murray's big fat grass-court summer of tears and Olympic medals, for the player and the British (or, more precisely, English) public to start showing some genuine affection for each other.

Middle England has been a little confused as to what they want from their tennis players (apart from the obvious, a grand slam title). Tim Henman was too straight, they said.

The public applauded when John McEnroe urged Henman to show more emotion on Wimbledon's Centre Court, perhaps by effing and blinding beneath the Royal Box, or by putting more effort into those little fist-clenchers. They laughed when a comedian cruelly described Henman as 'the human form of beige', and they debated, often at dinner parties, whether a middle-class upbringing had held him back. And, as if that had not been enough, they gave him the worst possible nick-name: Tiger Tim. Some thought him to be a loser, for having reached only fourth in the world rankings, and for having played in six grand slam semi-finals, including four at Wimbledon, but never in a final. When Andy Murray came on the scene, with that first Wimbledon in 2005, he was a tartan novelty and so he had a period of grace, 'with everyone saying to me, "You're a breath of fresh air." Whatever Tim Henman or Greg Rusedski were like, I was different.'

But it was not long – it began in 2006, during Murray's first full year on the tour – before Henman's supposed defects became virtues. Virtues to attack Murray with. Suddenly, Murray was having a tennis racket wrapped around his neck for not being Gentleman Tim (that was how the Judy Murray–Jane Henman comparisons got started). With Henman coming to the end of his career, maybe some realised they were going to miss him. Whatever the underlying rea-sons, Middle England said Murray should show some respect by shaving. He should get a hold of himself and his emotions. He should wash his potty mouth out.

McEnroe's advice – and, depending on your point of view,

this was either a man speaking from experience, or the most hypocritical remark in tennis history – was for Murray to stop 'spewing negative energy'. Murray should ask his barber for a short back and sides. The Centre Court crowds were making it quite clear to Murray that they hadn't quite let go of Henman; Murray and his team would make bets on how long it would be before someone in the crowd cried out: 'C'mon Tim,' and whoever had the first minute would win. Aorangi Terrace was still Henman Hill. After Henman's retirement, it felt as though Murray was competing for oxygen with someone whose appearances on Centre Court now came while wearing a suit and sitting behind a BBC microphone.

Why all the fuss and fury? One reason: tennis was not immune to the modern cult of personality, and nothing reveals personality like playing a tennis match.

Perhaps it was just tennis's chattering classes wanting to make conversation. That was one theory anyway, that Middle England had grown so tired of discussing why no British man had won Wimbledon since the 1930s that they now entertained themselves by picking at the players' characters. Britain needed some 'proper conversational balls to hit back and forth over the net', Paul Hayward wrote in the *Guardian*. 'The tear-inducing British exit from the grand slam tennis event exhausted itself as a breakfast-table subject long ago, so the middle classes make merry with character assassinations . . .'

It was quickly becoming apparent that Murray was Britain's greatest talent for 70-odd years, one who would soon surpass both Henman and Rusedski, but that didn't give him a free pass.

A good few newspaper columnists didn't want to get too technical or too tennis-y, because they didn't know enough about the sport, and also because they didn't think their readers would care about the mechanics of a backhand volley; far better to focus on Murray's behaviour or appearance. Henman was the warm-up act; no British tennis player has ever had his language and behaviour scrutinised as Murray has. 'McBrat' offered up plenty of material for armchair and laptop psychoanalysis, especially as the on-court microphones and television replays meant you never missed a 'f——', a 's——' or a mangled racket.

There had been the suspicion during John McEnroe's 'Superbrat' days that the British public had enjoyed being shocked by his language and behaviour, and maybe there was an element of that with Murray. When they said they were appalled, maybe they were actually thrilled by the naughtiness of it all. Was it the hypocrisy of a tennis crowd which likes to see a tennis player smash a racket, or fill the air with stars and asterisks, but then tuts when they do? Murray has his own theory, that tennis has a great fear of emotion, of letting it all out. 'It wouldn't make me feel good to bottle up my emotions. Saying nothing and standing there makes me feel emotional and flat. There is a fear of emotion in tennis,' he once told the *Daily Mail.* 'If someone boos, everyone looks at them as if to ask, "What the hell are you doing?" Yet in other sports it happens all the time.'

Some of the outrage was real, some of it artificial, after Murray told an umpire at a Davis Cup tie that he was 'f——— useless'. There was the business of Murray cursing at Brad Gilbert. But, mostly, the swearing was directed at himself, as part of the longest running show in tennis, The Murray Monologues. If a match wasn't going well, or even if it generally was but he had just played a couple of duff games, Murray would mutter and chunter, using cuss-words as verbs, nouns and punctuation. Effing this, and effing that. So consumed was Murray by the moment, he would forget about the microphones, or that he should have been using the sound of the crowd for cover. More often than they would have wanted, television commentators found themselves apologising for Murray's language.

Murray, not accepting the charge that he was the anti-Christ in tennis shorts, was taken aback by this obsession with his swearing. There were plenty of other athletes, he said, who cursed every week without launching a thousand phone-ins and newspaper editorials. 'There are things I say on the court that I probably shouldn't say, but off the court I'm not stumbling out of nightclubs or throwing up in front of the paparazzi. I don't mean to upset people.'

When Murray was cross, words often weren't enough. He went through a period of self-harm, when he would bloody his knuckles by punching the strings of his racket. Sometimes he slapped the palm of his hand against his face, or smashed rackets by swinging them hard against his shoe. Or he grabbed at his clothes. Every sub-clause, comma and semi-colon of Murray's body-language – the times when he moped, or when his chin appeared to be staple-gunned to his chest – was debated. Murray could hardly walk on court without someone quoting P.G. Wodehouse's remark, 'It is never difficult to distinguish between a ray of sunshine and a Scotsman with a grievance.'

That was when he was venting, how about when he was happy? A few disliked Murray's celebrations – all those clenched fists and stentorian cries – about as much as they disliked his anger. The satirical magazine *Private Eye* printed a photograph of a howling Murray alongside one of a werewolf for their lookalikes feature. The public and media scrutiny included detailed studies of his appearance. Was this really allowed, a British player walking out on to Centre Court with what one critic had called 'a bum-fluff tache'? It would have been a big event in the shires the first time Murray played at Wimbledon with a sensible haircut and a smooth chin, and without a baseball cap. In short, Middle England thought Murray was a moody, scruffy young man, and didn't find it easy to like him. Even before Murray made a joke about the English football team, there were grievances. 'Wimbledon,' said one Centre Court regular, in reference to the spectators rather than the committee men, 'used to be so snotty about Murray.'

Despite appearances – an American once looked at Centre Court and all he could see were Paul Smith stripes and Oxbridge educations – Wimbledon can be a tough crowd. Murray and Henman weren't the first British players to have felt the disapproval of the tennis public and establishment. And you can't simply put that down to Britain's post-imperial tennis angst, with the nation kept waiting since the last days of empire for another male grand slam singles champion.

Spool all the way back to Fred Perry, who called himself 'a

rebel the wrong side of the tennis tramlines', and you will see that he was cold-shouldered too, perhaps more than anyone. In the 1930s, Perry, a son of a Labour MP, was no friend of the public school-educated members of the All England Club. After winning the first of his three Wimbledon titles, he was lying in a hot bath in the locker room when he heard a member say to his opponent, Australia's Jack Crawford, 'This was one day when the best man didn't win.'

As the champion, Perry was due a club tie, but it was presented without a smile and a handshake; instead, he got out of the bath and found it lying on a bench. Perry's disenchantment with British tennis, even after winning three consecutive titles from 1934-36, would persuade him to turn professional and move to America, and that hardly improved his standing at home. Bunny Austin, the beaten finalist in 1938, was also not always made to feel welcome; for many years, he was blackballed by the All England Club for being a conscientious objector during the Second World War. Some haven't helped themselves, such as Buster Mottram with his politics; to quote the *Observer*, he once had 'a dalliance' with the National Front, and more recently he tried, when he considered himself to be working in the interests of the United Kingdom Independence Party, to broker an electoral pact with the far-right British National Party. Some had a decent ride – John Lloyd and Roger Taylor – but many others didn't.

Jeremy Bates never went deep enough into Wimbledon – the fourth round was his limit – for the public to have made any great emotional investment in him. The Canadian-born

Greg Rusedski tried hard, probably too hard, turning up to his first Wimbledon in a Union flag bandana, but there was always a distance between him and the crowd. Though he played in a grand slam final, and Henman didn't, Rusedski's achievement of finishing as the runner-up to Pat Rafter at the 1997 US Open never received the attention it should have done, even if he won the BBC Sports Personality of the Year award. That wasn't his fault; the match had taken place on the same weekend as Princess Diana's funeral. Wimbledon has had its summer flings, its one-match stands, with the lowly ranked players who had beaten, or threatened to beat, a seed. But most were quickly forgotten.

Wimbledon is not unique as a grand slam for being hard on its own players. It was only at the 2012 US Open that Venus Williams, a 32-year-old, two-time former champion and world number one, 'felt American for the first time' at Flushing Meadows. Until then, she had never thought she had had the full backing of the crowd. Australian tennis fans have never all warmed to Lleyton Hewitt, despite his success, winning two grand slams and reaching the top of the rankings, as many considered him to be too difficult a character, lacking charm and refinement. The best young Australian, Bernard Tomic, is on probation with Melbourne Park. The Roland Garros crowds are notoriously hard on French players, which explained why talented, but perhaps emotionally fragile players such as Amelie Mauresmo and Richard Gasquet usually played better tennis on the other side of the Channel, at Wimbledon, than in Paris.

Admittedly, a Wimbledon crowd would never boo or slow-

handclap Murray, as the Parisians have done with French players. They would always support the British player; it's just that
they've been holding back, not quite putting everything into
it. And the crowd inside the gates of the All England Club is
one thing; those outside, who take a more casual interest in the
sport, have been even trickier to please.

It's unclear whether Andy Murray should be allowed to make
jokes or not. For years he was teased for being the grumpiest
man in tennis. When Tim Henman called Murray 'a miserable
git', it was said with affection, but critics, seizing on the quote,
kept pinning it to his T-shirt. *Headcases*, the satirical puppet
show, a modern version of *Spitting Image*, did a sketch about
an Andy Murray Misery Chatline, with 'each call costing just
a little bit of your hopes and dreams'. And another which
introduced a Murray puppet with the observation, 'Andy
Murray's joyless moaning is the sound of summer,' before
having the doll sing in monotone, 'the sun has got his hat on.'

Turn on your television or radio halfway through an interview with Murray, and you can't immediately tell from his tone
of voice whether he has won or lost. Why, critics said, couldn't
Murray just sound happy? Pat Cash, a former Wimbledon
champion, thought he knew why: because Murray has the most
boring, monotone voice in the history of the planet (Murray,
when told about the Australian's comments, did agree that his
voice wasn't that interesting).

However, the caricature of Murray was just that, a caricature. It ignored the fact that Murray had a dry sense of

humour and laughter in his life. Perhaps that's why it threw people when he made jokes. Take the time when he played an April Fool's joke in 2011 by announcing on Twitter that he had hired his good friend Ross Hutchins as his new coach because he felt as though he needed 'another yes-man'. The background to the hoax was the constant speculation about who Murray was going to appoint as a replacement for Miles Maclagan, as well as the accusations that he was surrounding himself with an entourage of pals who would never challenge him for fear of being bumped from the inner-circle and the pay-roll. Hutchins, who was in on the joke, wrote on his Twitter page that 'having this opportunity to work with such a special player and such a close friend is one I have wished for all my life', and within minutes the story was breaking on the Press Association news-wire and in the Sky Sports television studio.

There was some embarrassment and irritation in those news-rooms when they had to retract their stories later that evening, and it was an episode that seemed to reinforce people's opinion of Murray. Those already sympathetic to Murray thought it cast him in a good light, showing that he did not take not take himself or his job too seriously. For others, it strengthened their dislike. They didn't stop to consider that they were trying to have it both ways: they were saying Murray was a misery, while also suggesting that he should take his responsibilities as a public figure more seriously.

Murray still remembers the time when a 'sexist' joke became a global news story. After Murray played a match at a tournament in New Zealand in 2006 that had featured a lot of service breaks, he told the crowd, during a jocular post-match interview, that he and his opponent had 'played like women'. Some of the ladies, and a few men, gently booed Murray, but they knew that he had not meant anything by it and that he had not just revealed himself as a male chauvinist pig. This was a long way from the opinions once offered by Richard Krajicek, a former Wimbledon champion, who had let it be known that he thought the majority of female tennis players were 'lazy, fat pigs'. Krajicek had meant what he said, though he did eventually apologise; Murray was joshing. Unfortunately for Murray, when the story was reported by a news agency, it was made to sound as though the crowd had taken great offence, as if he had been booed out of Auckland. Murray was woken up the next morning by a radio station wanting him to expand on his supposed sexism, and by columnists across the world harrumphing from several thousands miles away.

The different reactions to Murray's gags about English sporting teams was telling. When asked for his views on the Ashes cricket series, he replied: 'I'm Scottish. I wanted Australia to win.' That played well in Australia. And the joke didn't annoy the Barmy Army, or have people torching his effigy outside Lord's.

But if England's cricket fans could take a joke, some of England's football fans plainly couldn't. Perhaps they were too dim to realise that Murray wasn't being serious, or maybe they were fully aware that he hadn't meant it, but had gone along with the outrage anyway. The story very quickly got out of control, with Murray's comments discussed on BBC Radio Four's *Today* programme. The fun went toxic. Even now, there are those who believe that Murray bought a Paraguay football shirt to wear for when they played England.

The worst of the abuse was online. The general rule for the comments underneath newspaper articles is that by the time you get to the twentieth message, someone will have mentioned Hitler; with articles on the tennis page, that rule is you can't get to the tenth post without 'anyone but Murray' graffiti. Offline, it wasn't pleasant either. 'I was still a kid and people were sending notes to my locker saying that they hoped that I lost every tennis match for the rest of my life. That's at Wimbledon. Even people within the grounds were saying stuff to me,' Murray has recalled. 'It wasn't nice and I felt as though I hadn't done anything wrong.'

For someone who is supposedly anti-English, he has been leading a curious life. He has an English girlfriend, many of his friends are English, several members of his entourage are English, and he has chosen to live in Surrey. If he hated the English, he would hate his English grandmother. The reality, of course, is that he doesn't loathe the English, or carry a membership card for the Scottish National Party in the back pocket of his shorts.

What Murray doesn't like – and he has been quite open about this – is when people think he's English. He is proud to be Scottish, and it annoys him when people get that wrong. Initially, as he made a life for himself on the circuit, and played international tournaments for the first time, he found some people thought 'British' and 'English' were one and the same. An American once asked Murray, then a teenager, to explain the difference between being Scottish and English. 'I was born in Scotland. If somebody says to me I'm English, I correct them because it's not true. And I don't mind when people call me British, but it really annoys me when I get called English. I'm not from there. It's like calling someone from France German.' At the 2011 French Open, he was not impressed when he was introduced to the crowd as 'l'Anglais'. But that's not the same as hating the English, not the same at all. As Murray has said, 'Being Scottish is just a fact, not a racist state of mind.'

Every time Murray has tried to explain himself, and reminded everyone about all the English people he has chosen to have in his life, it has not had the effect he would have wanted. The best example of this anti-Murray prejudice was a column in the *Daily Mirror* in 2008, written by Tony Parsons, an English author: 'If the English can survive the attentions of the Luftwaffe, the IRA and al-Qaeda, then I quite fancy our chances against Andy Murray. I don't really object to anyone despising the English – we can take it – but hypocritical back-tracking gets right up my Wembley Way and puts my Morris dancer out of joint. It's a bit rich for Murray to decide that he loves the English after all.'

The difficulty for Murray was that he was talking to two different audiences. The more he spoke of his fondness for the English, and how he was British as well as Scottish (there has never been any confusion in his mind over that), the greater the risk that he would upset a few Scottish opinion-formers. Take the column in the *Scottish Sun* in the summer of 2009, which was reacting to Murray's comment, another attempt at ending the cross-border sniping, that he had always got on well with the English. Under the headline 'He's one of us, not one of them', the columnist wrote: 'Andy Murray's new best mates? The English. Aye, but I bet he jumped for joy like the rest of us when Portugal knocked them out of the World Cup in 2006. I suppose Murray's climbdown from his anti-English comments before the World Cup three years ago is to appease relations with the notoriously snobby Home Counties set who hang out at SW19. Don't let them hijack you when you win by draping you in a Union flag.'

Murray's joke had been useful for something: revealing people's prejudices on either side of Hadrian's Wall. There was a clear attempt at hijacking by the English edition of the *Sun* in 2010, with the newspaper campaigning during that summer's Wimbledon to claim him for the Home Counties. They printed 'Come on Surrey' headlines, and a tenuous list of 25 reasons why Murray was 'more English than he lets on', including that he had played in front of the Queen at Wimbledon one year and he listened to music on an iPod, which had been designed by a Londoner. As the saying goes – and you hear this a lot from international tennis fans teasing the English – Murray is British when he wins and Scottish when he loses. When, during past Wimbledons, British papers have printed a daily swing-ometer for where Murray stands that morning – something like 'totally Tartan' at one end and 'Rule Britannia' at the other – it has been hard to know whether they were being snide or just showing the whole thing up for how ridiculous it is. But then, as everyone knows, you can say what you like about Murray.

Some critics don't like it that Andy Murray has never needed a crowd's love or approval to play his best tennis (as Tim Henman probably did), and that he has never cast himself as the saviour of British tennis. He has never chased popularity. He has politely declined, as one observer once put it, 'the role of darling to the middle classes and corporate lunch-munchers'.

When he resolved to tone down the on-court swearing and the gore (punching strings), it was not to endear himself to the Wimbledon queue, but because he thought that if he became more of an emotional flat-liner it would improve his tennis. Murray has made the odd concession to the mob, and for a while he took professional advice from Stuart Higgins, a former editor of the *Sun* turned public relations consultant who specialised in what his website called 'crisis management support' (his other clients had included supermodel Kate Moss after a newspaper had published photographs which they claimed showed her using cocaine).

Murray was willing to shave and to take his baseball cap off before playing at Wimbledon, but he wasn't going to manu-facture a new personality (and Higgins didn't ask him to either). 'You need to try to be yourself as much as possible, but at the same time if people don't like you it's not really your problem. You need to stay true to yourself and the people around you and hopefully things will turn around,' Murray has said. So while Murray would naturally always choose popularity over unpopularity, and was annoyed that people had taken his jokes the wrong way, he had accepted he would never be universally loved or liked. Since he wasn't playing tennis for the love of strangers, he was okay with that.

It is to Murray's credit that he has never claimed to be the shining knight in Wimbledon whites, the player to rescue British tennis from the dark forces of failure and mediocrity. He hasn't spent his life obsessing about Fred Perry and British tennis. About winning a grand slam, yes, but not directly about Fred. For the 2009 Wimbledon Championships, Murray's then clothing sponsor, the label which Perry had started, dressed the Scot up in retro kit which referenced what Perry used to wear. Had Perry still been alive, he would have been 100 years old that year, and Murray, thinking it was a bit of a fun, played along. Murray was relaxed about the stunt, and did not consider that it could possibly add to the expectation on him.

Murray has always been clear in his mind that tennis is an individual sport. Murray is British and Scottish but he plays primarily for himself; he wanted a grand slam title for his own personal satisfaction and sense of accomplishment; if that meant he would also end Britain's long wait for a male grand slam singles champion and would be the first since Fred, then that would be great, but that was not why he was enduring a lifetime of bikram yoga and ice-baths. The 70-odd years that had passed without a British champion, that wasn't his responsibility. 'I want to win a grand slam for the people I work with, and for my parents, who helped me when I was growing up,' Murray said in 2010. 'Then, doing it for British tennis and British sport would be excellent as well.'

People have kept missing the point that this is an individual sport. Murray is the only British man with a respectable singles ranking, so you often hear how terrible it must be for Murray to be out there on his own. But, in an individual sport, it's hardly possible to be anything else but 'out there on your own'. About the only other time you will see other British men playing singles is during the first week of the Wimbledon fortnight, thanks to the All England Club's gifts of wild cards, as their rankings aren't high enough for them to have gained automatic entry into the main draw. Then, most years, they go back to the chorus line until the next summer's Wimbledon wild cards are announced. The lack of other British men is often presented as a problem for Murray, as if it has somehow been a barrier to his chances of maximising his talent. Wouldn't Murray benefit from sharing the spotlight, from watching it burn through someone else's whites for an afternoon or two each summer?

'Not really,' Murray will say, just as Tim Henman used to say when he was the only Briton thought to have had a shot at winning a grand slam. In tennis, you play for yourself, apart from during those rare weeks when you are playing in the Davis Cup and, rarer still, in the Olympics. Who could blame Murray for not prioritising the Davis Cup when, without a decent second singles player, Britain had zero chance of winning a competition which was last in British hands in 1936? (One person was former British captain John Lloyd, who said: 'Call me old-fashioned, but when is it an inconvenience and a not a privilege to play for your country?')

It's difficult to see how, in recent years, having a second British man around would have made any difference whatsoever to Murray's performances. At the 2006 Australian Open, where he lost in the first round, he said the media had been expecting too much from him, but he was young then, and he wasn't on his own either, as Tim Henman and Greg Rusedski still had not passed into the tennis after-life. Look back at how Murray has played at Wimbledon over the years, and you will struggle to find a match that he lost because he was fretting about the British public.

'I've never felt stress and pressure from playing in front of a home crowd. I've never made it an excuse, and it's not going to go away so deal with it,' Murray said in an interview with the *Daily Mail.* 'I think we as a nation expect to win and when we don't we look for these big reasons. Why did Tim Henman not win Wimbledon? Why has Andy Murray not won Wimbledon? Well, sometimes you're not quite good enough. I can't say exactly why it hasn't happened for me there, but I'll tell you what isn't the reason: the pressure of the people and the pressure of the media.'

In a way, Murray finds playing Wimbledon one of the most relaxing tournaments of the year as he gets to sleep in his own bed. He has learnt to insulate himself. He tries not to read the

Giving his mother Judy a kiss after winning the title at Queen's Club in June 2009.

Murray found himself 'welling up big time' after winning a doubles title with his brother Jamie in Valencia in November 2010.

With his girlfriend Kim Sears during London Fashion Week.

Sacking Mark Petchey, a friend as well as his coach, was one of the hardest experiences of Murray's professional life.

Brad Gilbert wondered whether Murray was 'depressed'.

Murray reached two grand slam finals while being coached by Miles Maclagan.

The *New York Times* magazine called Murray and Ivan Lendl 'tennis's odd couple'.

Murray's fitness trainers, Jez Green and Matt Little, helped to transform the Scot into a gym- and track-hardened tennis player.

Murray flexes his bicep at the 2008 Wimbledon Championships.

Four key figures in Murray's life: his mother Judy, his manager Simon Fuller, his girlfriend Kim Sears and his physiotherapist Andy Ireland.

Playing doubles with Tim Henman, who has been one of the most influential figures in Murray's tennis life.

Punching his strings in anger leaves Murray's knuckles – and shorts – covered in blood.

For years, Murray didn't have the universal support of the British public, after a joke he made about the England football team.

Murray at an academy in Barcelona, where he could escape the bitchy world of British tennis.

Murray's victory in the boys' singles tournament at the 2004 US Open meant he would always love playing in New York City.

Murray's first title on the main tour came in San Jose, California, in February 2006.

Murray's first grand slam final came at the 2008 US Open, against Roger Federer.

Murray played his first Wimbledon semi-final at the 2009 Championships, when he lost to Andy Roddick.

(LEFT) In tears after losing to Roger Federer in the 2010 Australian Open final, Murray said: 'I can cry like Roger, it's just a pity I can't play like him.'

(RIGHT) Murray and Novak Djokovic meet at the net after the Serbian's victory in the final of the 2011 Australian Open.

Murray serves to Jo-Wilfried Tsonga during the semi-final of the 2012 Wimbledon Championships.

Murray's tears, after ultimately losing to Roger Federer in the final, helped him to 'reconnect' with the British public.

Murray speaks to Roger Federer at the net after beating the Swiss in the gold medal match at the London Olympics.

Murray poses with a post-box in Dunblane, painted gold by the Royal Mail.

Murray serves to Novak Djokovic during the final of the 2012 US Open final.

Murray is in shock after becoming the first British man to win a grand slam singles title for 76 years.

sports section of a newspaper. If he is watching television, and a story about himself appears on his screen, he zones out or turns over. Every year, when Murray is the last British player left in the tournament, it is said that he has been left 'carrying the flag'; it's an embarrassing phrase, and one which, in an individual sport, is almost devoid of any meaning. Between games, Murray doesn't sit there on his chair worrying about the state of British tennis, and feeling any great sense of responsibility for improving the sport (that is the Lawn Tennis Association's concern, as well as the concern of an all-party group of MPs and peers after Parliament got involved). And that's how it should be.

Had Tim Henman's dealings with the media been different, then Andy Murray's would have been, too. In addition to Stuart Higgins, Murray has taken professional advice from three different management companies during his career: Octagon, Ace Group and then 19 Entertainment, founded by Simon Fuller, who had managed the Spice Girls. And yet the figure who has arguably had more influence than anyone else on Murray's media relations has been an interested amateur, an Englishman who once went on the record to say that the British press is 'probably the worst in the world'.

'Unfortunately, that's part of the culture,' Tim Henman said in an interview with a Swiss newspaper. 'When you speak to tennis journalists, you notice how little they understand. I have asked them technical and tactical questions, and it was embarrassing. I was embarrassed for them. They knew nothing about the game. I've never been influenced by their opinions anyway, but now we are talking tennis and they didn't know anything.' Every Christmas during Henman's career, his parents would have a little treat for him; they would open up the box of newspaper cuttings they had collected from that year's coverage, and the family, looking back at what they regarded as that year's worst excesses from the broadsheets and tabloids, laughed all the way into Boxing Day. One of the cuttings they treasured was the front page of the *Daily Mirror* during one Wimbledon that declared: 'No Pressure, Timbo, But If You Choke Now, We Will Never Forgive You.'

The first time that Henman felt as though he had got burned by Fleet Street was after his disqualification from the 1995 Wimbledon Championships when, in a moment of anger, he had smacked a ball away and inadvertently struck a ball-girl. The next day, he bought her flowers and kissed her on both cheeks during an awkward photo-call, but that didn't stop what Henman saw as an over-reaction. His views were also shaped by the hysteria after his comments about equal prize-money and why there was a case for keeping a pay gap; the next day at the All England Club, he could not move for camera crews. The next time the subject came up, he decided to be 'boring' rather than 'sexist'. Henman had resolved to save himself the bother of being open; he never really lied, just deflected. Henman had enough to think about without inviting more drama and distraction into his life. 'If someone asked me a question, there might have been a truthful question and a correct answer. I would give the correct answer, then I wouldn't have to deal with all the extra attention. I felt I had to protect myself all the time.'

That, in turn, became Murray's coping mechanism. At first, dealing with the media was a fun game. The day after Murray lost to David Nalbandian in the third round of Wimbledon in 2005, he left with friends in a car for a day's go-karting, and immediately several paparazzi vans with darkened windows pulled out and followed them down the street. During that grace period, Murray knew he was saying things in interviews that he probably shouldn't have, such as the time he returned the kindness of a wild card into a tournament in Newport in America by being critical about the quality of their grass courts. He got away with that because of his age. But that did not last long, and soon enough, after the fuss over his jokes, he believed that the best approach was to be careful and guarded in interviews. Press conferences had once been 'fun'; now he was on alert for the 'traps'.

He could be confrontational. For a while, Murray imposed a period of radio silence with the BBC, refusing to speak to Auntie because he felt they had taken his remarks about suspected match-fixing in tennis out of context. Murray's quote that 'everyone knows that it's going on' was presented as if he was suggesting it was common knowledge in the locker-room that players were being offered bribes to throw matches. What he had meant by that was that it had been in the public domain that a few players had been approached.

Murray could not immediately forgive what he thought were underhand tactics by the BBC, especially as the radio broadcast led to a minor tiff with Rafa Nadal (they soon made up) and being called in to speak to executives at the men's tour about any new information he had (absolutely none). According to his account, the BBC had not told him they were researching a programme about alleged corruption in tennis, and had given him the impression they had wanted only a general interview. Plus Murray had other quarrels with the corporation, such as the article which had appeared on their website after he had been nominated for the shortlist for the 2007 BBC Sports Personality of the Year award. There was a 'did you know?' trivia-box for each of the nominees and Murray's was: 'Did you know that Murray was called "Lazy English" when he trained in Spain?' That was the first time Murray had heard that insult.

There was also a public falling-out with a couple of Sky's commentators, former world number four Greg Rusedski and Barry Cowan, best known for having once taken Pete Sampras to five sets at Wimbledon. Around the time of the 2009 year-end championships in London, Rusedski and Cowan were urging Murray to play with more adventure. Murray's response was that he didn't care for their opinion, or value it: 'Yeah, who are these experts? Barry Cowan? Greg Rusedski? I think I know more about tennis than Barry and Greg.'

Murray has laughed off some of the newspaper attacks on his character and his appearance, including the one that commented on the shape of his skull. But he couldn't laugh off all of them. Mark Petchey, who has seen how upset Murray had been by some of the criticism, once said to him: 'I don't envy you as a person. You're going to go through so much in your life that will be difficult. You're going to be incredibly success-ful and yet often you're going to read stuff that makes you sound like a failure.'

There had been two Henmans, Public Tim and Private Tim, and so there would be two Murrays, one of them more inter-esting, candid, funny and personable than the other. One consequence of Henman's pursuit of an easier life was that the public thought he was boring. They never really got to see the devil in Henman, or to appreciate his humour. Murray thought Henman had done a fine job in covering up his 'real personality'.

So Murray stopped making jokes, because of the trouble they could cause him, and became reluctant to give much away. This became tennis's biggest secret: that Murray had a gentler side, that he could mind his Ps and Qs, that he was perfectly capable of polite conversation. If Murray was really as grumpy as his popular image had suggested he was, he would have been living alone in Surrey, and he would never have had friends popping by.

People who have met Murray away from the tennis court have generally been struck by his manners. One lady who bumped into Murray on Wimbledon Common, where they were both walking their dogs, described how when she said hello, Murray immediately pulled down the hood of his track-suit top – he wasn't a snarky young 'hoodie' – before making entertaining small talk. While Murray is not a reader of books (something else he has in common with Henman), he has always been interested in the world around him and the people he has met, and made an informed decision about who he would vote for in the 2010 General Election (but he never let on which party secured his vote; his politics have stayed between him and the polling booth). To borrow a phrase from Richard Williams, father of Venus and Serena, Murray could see there was a whole world out there beyond the baseline.

For a sign of Murray's good nature, you have only to look at how he gets along with his rivals. Which is just fine, as friendly as it is possible to be when you're competing against one another. That is despite some people's best efforts to will a feud between Murray and Roger Federer into existence. Those who had been brought up on the bitching and bad-mouthing of tennis in the 1980s, when John McEnroe, Ivan Lendl, Boris Becker and Jimmy Connors went rat-a-tat-tat with the insults, were still hooked on the idea of animosity in the locker-room. They wanted players to hate each other.

The British author Martin Amis wrote an essay in the *New Yorker* in which he elegantly riffed about the cult of tennis personalities: 'I have a problem with – I am uncomfortable with – the word personality and its plural, as in "modern tennis lacks personalities" and "tennis needs a new star who is a genuine personality". But, if from now on, I can use "personality" between quotation marks and use it as an exact synonym of a seven-letter duosylabble starting with "a" and ending with "e" (and also featuring, in order of appearance, an "ss", an "h", an "o" and an "l"), why, then personality and I are going to get along just fine.'

Using the Amis definition, the top of modern tennis has

been free of 'personalities' for some time. Anyone who wants aggro in tennis will have been left feeling disappointed by the Federer era; the Swiss would much rather start a bromance than a feud.

Clearly, Murray was unhappy when Federer observed, after Murray had just beaten him at a tournament in Dubai in 2008, that the Scot needed to change his defensive playing style, and stop 'grinding' several feet behind the baseline, if he was ever going to win a grand slam. Murray didn't think that it was Federer's place to criticise his tennis when he had just lost. But that was as vicious as it ever got. Federer, who thought he was just being honest, apologised for his critique. For years, people kept looking for tension between the two. Innocent comments that Federer made about Murray were dressed up as being little digs at the Scot. While Murray and Federer have never been the best of friends, it would be going too far to imagine they loathed each other. Even to say they disliked each other would be a stretch.

Murray and Nadal have always got on well, apart from those few days when Nadal was unhappy at hearing what Murray was supposed to have said about corruption in tennis. Murray and Nadal have known each other since they were on the junior tennis circuit, and they remain friendly. Murray has disclosed that he loves watching Nadal play. And, before they played a Wimbledon semi-final, Nadal said Murray was 'one of the good guys' of tennis, 'not one of the bad people or arrogant people – Andy is a normal guy who hasn't changed after all his victories and that's important.'

But the clearest sign of the collegiate atmosphere in the men's game came at a tournament in Miami in the spring of 2011, when Murray chose to play doubles with Novak Djokovic. This was the same man who, just weeks earlier, had beaten him in straight sets in the final of the Australian Open, and put him in a funk. There were no hard feelings on Murray's side, and his doubles partner said: 'I like the guy.'

Andy Murray is the only one of the big four in men's tennis who has a home grand slam. There isn't a major in Spain, Switzerland or Serbia. Everything is on a smaller scale for Rafa Nadal at Madrid's Caja Magica, for Roger Federer at Basel's St Jakobshalle, or for Novak Djokovic at the tournament his family owns in Belgrade, than it is for Murray at Wimbledon. That should be to Murray's advantage, but nothing is ever that simple. When Murray first came on tour, he would openly declare that the US Open was his favourite grand slam ('Everyone says Wimbledon's the best tournament – it's not'). And all this was before his joke about English football went toxic. This wasn't Murray being a teenage contrarian, and hoping to upset his elders, as he meant what he said.

Clearly, his views of the US Open had been coloured by his victory in the junior competition. He made comparisons between how the US Open and Wimbledon treated their juniors. At the US Open, the boys and girls stayed in hotels in Manhattan and were free to be in the same changing-rooms and lounges as the seniors. At Wimbledon, the boys and girls were housed in student digs and got changed in the pavilion at the practice courts, not in the main locker-rooms. Murray was upset with the All England Club in 2005 when they declined a wild-card trade with the United States Tennis Association, which meant he would have to play in the qualifying tournament for that summer's US Open.

There were other reasons, too, why he liked the hard-court championships in New York more than the grass-court tournament in London, one of which was that he thought his game was better suited to concrete than to lawns. Another was that he didn't like the all-white clothing rule at Wimbledon; he wanted to be free to wear whatever colour he pleased (there were echoes, here, of Andre Agassi's complaints at not being able to dress in ripped denim on Centre Court). A third was that he liked what he regarded as the friendly and enthusiastic nature of the average American fan; those weren't characteristics that he would necessarily have attributed to a British spectator.

With time, though, Murray came to appreciate Wimbledon for what it was, down to the silence around Centre Court as he prepared to serve (there's never complete quiet at the US Open). His views softened; he no longer expressed a preference for one tournament over the other. He has not lost any of his adoration for New York, just gained plenty for Wimbledon.

What of the other two slams? When Murray has played at the Australian Open, he has been 'Muzza', and Melbourne Park has always been friendly. But it has sometimes seemed as though Australians can't shake off a fascination with how the

'English media' have been beastly to the Scot. Americans wanted to watch Murray play tennis; the Australians wanted to see whether the mother country was crushing him with their expectations. And while Murray has been booed at Roland Garros that doesn't make him special.

If Murray had to select one match when he first realised the power of having the Wimbledon crowd on his side, he would probably choose when he came from two sets down to beat Frenchman Richard Gasquet in a fourth-round encounter in 2008. That was also the same occasion when Murray, standing by the side of the court, with his eyes popping out of his head, and with engorged veins on his neck, looked for half a second as though he was about to do a stage dive.

During the high that followed, Murray and others thought he had formed an emotional bond with the Centre Court crowd. Murray lost heavily in the next round, a quarter-final with Rafa Nadal, but he went further at the next three Wimbledons, making the semi-finals each time. After three semi-final defeats, to Andy Roddick in 2009, and then to Nadal in 2010 and 2011, there were concerns that he was becoming what Tim Henman had been, a serial beaten semi-finalist. The defeat in 2011, when Murray appeared to be in control against Nadal, only to miss one forehand and then lose his way, was the hardest for the crowd to take. Still, away from London, he had been in three grand slam finals by then – one at the US Open in 2008, and two at the Australian Open in 2010 and 2011 – and the public seemed to accept and appreciate Murray for what he was: an exceptional talent who looked to have the rare ability to win a major, and who had his faults, just like everyone else.

Andy Murray's tears after the 2012 Wimbledon final shouldn't be thought of as the moment that British tennis lost its stiff upper lip. It is not as if anyone had ever thought Murray was emotionally buttoned-up, that he had been keeping his feelings hidden.

What was different this time, though, was that the British public were seeing a different, softer side to Murray. They had become accustomed to watching him growl and gurn, to seeing him bounce around the court and pump his fist, but now they were watching him weep. For many, that was suddenly the moment, as Murray wiped his face with his hands and shirt-sleeves, when they came to like the guy. How disappointing, a friend would later say, that it took Murray sobbing into a microphone for the public to realise 'he has a heart'. But, in an age when you cannot turn on the television or flick through a magazine without seeing the puffy eyes or smeared mascara of another 'celebrity breakdown', it was almost as if the public had forgotten that it was possible to engage with someone without first seeing them blub. The next morning, Roger Federer's achievement of winning a seventeenth grand slam title almost became a footnote in some of the British newspapers, with pages and pages dedicated to Murray's failure to stop the tears. And to the images of his girlfriend Kim Sears, who at first had bitten her lip and put a hand over her mouth, but had then needed a hug from Murray's physiotherapist, Andy Ireland.

Everything at Wimbledon is new; you learn that every summer. Something hasn't happened in tennis until it has happened at the All England Club. It was not the first time that Murray had sobbed on a tennis court. He had cried as a teenager after winning his first meeting with Tim Henman in 2005, and there had been tears after he lost the final of the 2010 Australian Open to Roger Federer (so the 2012 Wimbledon Championships was the second grand slam at which the Swiss had made the Brit cry). And when Murray had the rare opportunity in 2011 to play in front of a Scottish crowd, at Britain's Davis Cup tie in Glasgow against the Grand Duchy of Luxembourg, he was just in the middle of a post-match interview on the court, 'I don't get the chance to come back here very often so . . .' when his voice trailed off.

And those were just the tears in public. He had cried as a teenager when he had a pain in his knee and thought there was a chance he might never play again (he would also have a quiet cry when he was alone in a hotel room in Toronto, just days after the London Olympics, as he reflected on winning a gold medal). So, in tennis circles, Murray's softer side was well known. But, until 2012, he had never sobbed on court at Wimbledon. There was a British television audience of 17 million in the weepy aftermath of Murray's first Wimbledon final. For most of those armchairs viewers, this was Murray crying for the first time, and they realised that these weren't the tears of a spoilt child wanting pity and attention.

Even before the tears that fortnight, there had been indications that attitudes towards Murray were shifting; a writer for

the *Guardian* spotted what he regarded as 'perhaps the ulti-
mate sign that Middle England has clasped Murray to its
bosom', which was the sight of a couple holding up embroi-
dered cushions with the Scot's name on. By beating France's
Jo-Wilfried Tsonga, Murray became the first British man to
appear in a Wimbledon final since Bunny Austin in 1938; no
longer could you say, entirely truthfully, that the last player to
have lost to a Briton in a semi-final at the tournament had
died in the Battle of Stalingrad.

So Murray's Wimbledon career was moving in the right
direction, ever closer to the prize of that golden Challenge Cup.
And, while Murray had not lost all of his rage, he had become
a much calmer soul since working with Ivan Lendl; some of the
rough edges had been smoothed away. The Wimbledon crowd,
who had learned to love Jimmy Connors, John McEnroe,
Andre Agassi and other assorted tennis vulgarians, were coming
around. Perhaps it was always going to take time for the crowd
to get on with Murray. It had taken Tim Henman a few years
of tea-time thrillers before Wimbledon truly formed an attach-
ment.

But the great, almost total, transformation in public opinion would not have happened if Murray had not cried. If the
tears did not change everything, they changed a hell of a lot,
with John Lloyd arguing they showed that Murray was 'not a
grumpy geezer'. A column in the *Daily Mirror* by Tony
Parsons, who had previously been so scathing about Murray,
illustrated this change in mood: 'For those of us who had
never warmed to Murray, it felt like, for the very first time, we

were seeing the full man. It was a moving and humbling experience. The end of Wimbledon resembled the final reel of *Avatar* – where everyone says "I see you" and then breaks down ... Like the young McEnroe, Murray just made the leap from being widely disliked to being unanimously loved.'

In the Royal Box, British Prime Minister David Cameron shook hands with Scotland's First Minister Alex Salmond without anyone starting off another debate about where Murray stood on the British–Scottish spectrum. This was as it should have been from the beginning; Murray playing at Wimbledon and enjoying the crowd's affection, without any background nonsense.

Just a few days after showing the British public he could cry, he demonstrated another important truth: that he could take a joke. There can't be many other beaten grand slam finalists who would dry their eyes and head to the filming of a comedy panel show where there was every chance they would be 'picked on'. All those who had changed their minds about Murray probably liked him even more after he accepted an invitation to sit in the audience for the BBC's *Mock the Week*. 'Keep it light when discussing the Wimbledon final,' the host of the panel show had said after informing the comedians on either side of him that Murray was sitting in the audience.

And perhaps the teasing was more gentle than it would otherwise have been for Murray, who was given a standing ovation. 'The three most emotional things I've ever seen on television,' said one of the panel, 'are *Terms of Endearment*, *Philadelphia* and Andy Murray trying so hard in his speech not to call Roger Federer a bastard.' Between rounds, one of the regulars behind the desk put a towel over his head and peeled a banana. And there were a number of references to how Ivan Lendl had no emotional range during matches. 'This is Ivan Lendl happy,' said one comic, and keeping the same non-expression, 'and this is Ivan Lendl sad.' Throughout the programme, the director was able to cut to images of Murray and his girlfriend laughing.

Murray's rehabilitation continued at the Olympics. There were some extraordinary sights at the All England Club during the London Games. Serena Williams celebrating her gold medal in the women's singles by shaking her booty on Centre Court grass with a 'crip-walk' dance taken from the Los Angeles ganglands. There was the bright pinky-purple Olympic signage around the grounds, making it seem as though Wimbledon had been hijacked by the Teletubbies. And there was Murray – clear-eyed, no tears – looking as happy and as self-assured as anyone has ever seen him on a tennis court. For the first time, Murray was completely at ease, relaxed and assured, when playing against the world's best in front of a home crowd.

So Murray played some accomplished tennis to beat Novak Djokovic in the semi-finals and then gave Federer a horse-whipping in the gold-medal match (there was an hour-long period in which Federer, the greatest grass-court player of all time, did not win a game). It was undoubtedly true that the Olympic crowd was not quite the same as a regular Wimbledon crowd; during the Games, Centre Court was more international, perhaps a little younger, certainly quite a bit louder. But that should not be over-stated; this was still a tennis crowd, and not just people who had bought tickets to anything at the Olympics and who didn't much care whether it was archery, Greco-Roman wrestling or tennis.

Murray had felt as though his tears, and the reaction, had allowed him to 'reconnect' with the British tennis public. It mattered that Murray's first significant victory had come while he was wearing the red, white and blue of the British Olympic kit designed by Stella McCartney, and not just a regular outfit. Over the years, Murray's withdrawals from British Davis Cup ties had led some to imagine he was selfish and unpatriotic. But his reaction to the victory – climbing up to the guest box to hug his lover, entourage and family – demonstrated that he cared deeply about being part of a British team. And there was more: Murray won a second medal later that day, taking a silver in the mixed doubles with Laura Robson.

When Murray set off for North America, he was as popular as he had ever been.

Ever since a retractable roof has been added to Wimbledon's Centre Court in time for the 2009 tournament, it has been possible to play after dark at the All England Club. These had never been scheduled 'night sessions', just afternoon matches which had run out of daylight hours and carried over into the evening, and there was a curfew in place, an 11pm cut-off which had been agreed with the local council. So when Andy Murray played the Cypriot Marcos Baghdatis in the third round in 2012, he found himself in the peculiar, exhilarating situation that Saturday evening of trying to beat his opponent before they switched the lights off. At the US Open, night matches were night matches, a key part of the show, and when Murray and Milos Raonic both made it through to face each other in the fourth round, their match was never going to be scheduled at any other time of day.

The United States Tennis Association was never going to 'waste' Murray and Raonic's first grand slam meeting on a lunchtime crowd, or give the match a mid-afternoon start time. So keen were the USTA to get Murray and Raonic played on primetime television that when word reached them that a rainstorm was on its way later that night, they dumped the first match that had been scheduled for the Arthur Ashe Stadium, moving it to another court, and had Murray and Raonic opening the evening session at 7.30pm.

Over a number of years, no young player had emerged to consistently trouble the fab four of Roger Federer, Rafa Nadal, Novak Djokovic and Murray. Perhaps Juan Martin del Potro would have done so, after beating Federer in the 2009 US Open final, but a wrist injury stopped him from building on that success. A number of players had promised much, and delivered little. Latvia's Ernests Gulbis, such a great talent, had become a serial disappointment and once spent a night in a police cell during a tournament in Sweden after being arrested on suspicion of soliciting prostitutes, after what he said was a misunderstanding. Donald Young had had all the help and wild cards that American tennis could throw at him, but that got ugly when, in a fit of Twitter rage that showed his frustrations at how his career had been working out, he said: ''F—— the USTA.' During the 2012 season, Young lost 17 matches in a row. There were others who had been hyped, such as Bulgaria's Grigor Dimitrov and Australia's Bernard Tomic, but by the 2012 US Open none had shown that they were ready, or quite good enough, to join the A-list.

But perhaps Raonic had the loose arm and ambition to become a Hollywood name in men's tennis. As a boy, he had grown up idolising Pete Sampras and wanting to serve like Pistol Pete. With his murderously fast serve – going into the tournament, with a personal record of 155mph, he had the third quickest delivery in tennis history – the Canadian now had his own nickname, the Maple Leaf Missile. The wider tennis world had first taken notice of Raonic and his serve at the 2011 Australian Open when, after qualifying, he had made the fourth round. At the 2012 US Open, he was in the last 16 of a grand slam for the second time. Calling himself one of the most 'dangerous' men in tennis, Raonic didn't lack for confidence. It felt as though there was more riding on this than a place in the quarter-finals. If Murray could neutralise Raonic's serve, that would also help to kill off the idea that someone half a generation younger than him could win a slam before he did. John McEnroe's view was that Murray was going to have to tell this young buck, 'Hold on a second, you wait in line.'

The night before making his first appearance under the arc-lights of the Arthur Ashe Stadium, Raonic did what he always does to prepare himself for a tennis match, which was to binge on beef-steak. If Raonic came to the court with possibly the best serve on the tour, Murray had arguably the best return of serve; you could see that with your own eyes, or by looking at the statistics, as he was regularly either at or near the top of the leaderboard. Murray's reach is such that Andre Agassi has referred to him as 'Extendo-Arms', but the Scot's real gift is his ability to 'read' an opponent's serve, to take educated guesses about whether they are going to fire wide, down the 'T' of the service box or to the body. Murray had shown in the past, against Ivo Karlovic, John Isner and Sam Querrey, that he could cope with a big serve.

They had played only once before – Raonic winning a best-of-three-sets match at a clay-court tournament in Barcelona earlier in the season – so it took a few games for Murray to get a good feel for the Canadian's serve. Once he had done that, Murray was totally dominant. His performance was full of flair and variety – in his words, he played the kind of shots that aren't really appreciated these days – and he hardly missed a ball. Murray, clearly showing no ill-effects from his efforts in the heat against Feliciano Lopez, didn't face a breakpoint on his serve all night.

At the other end, the Donny Osmond lookalike was thinking to himself, 'Murray has taken me out of the match – he's doing things I have no answer for.' There was no point getting angry, or trying to smash the place up. Before the rains came, Murray won in straight sets, 6–4, 6–4, 6–2. When they met at the net to shake hands, the Briton apologised for a couple of lucky shots, only for Raonic to respond: 'Don't say sorry, it was simply amazing, keep it up.'

So, for the eighth grand slam in succession, Murray had reached the quarter-finals. His last-eight opponent this time was Marin Cilic, a Croatian who at that time was best known in British tennis circles for having unwittingly been at the centre of a grass-court controversy earlier that summer, one involving a moody Argentine and a line-judge with a punctured leg. Cilic had won the pre-Wimbledon title at Queen's after his opponent in the final, Argentina's David Nalbandian, had kicked an advertising hoarding and accidentally injured the official. It was not the first time that Nalbandian had railed against British tennis during his career, as he is about the only player to have ever criticised Tim Henman in public, once calling him, 'the worst kind of rubbish there is', and, while having a bad day at Wimbledon one year, he once swore at the crowd in Spanish. If you want some gristle with your forehands and backhands, Nalbandian is your man. Nalbandian is a much better pantomime villain than Murray, the teller of one soft joke about the England football team, will ever be.

5

Lover, Painter, Driver, Hairdresser

Modern art terrifies Kim Sears, in much the same way that graphite rackets once frightened tennis traditionalists. Specialising in 'quirky yet emotive' portraits of pets, she has called her business 'Brushes and Paws'. Someone had made the observation that she was a well-groomed young lady painting well-groomed cats and dogs – she knew she was on the other end of the spectrum to Damien Hirst's pickled sharks and cows sawn in half. Sears is no *enfant terrible* of the art world, the Tracey Emin of pet portraiture, yet she thought it was about time she visited New York's Museum of Modern Art. On Manhattan's Sixth Avenue, on her first visit to MoMA, Sears stood considering some lacquered paintbrushes, before moving on to Van Gogh's *Starry Night*, and Andy Warhol's

Gold Marilyn Monroe, which she thought was heartbreaking. She was also taken by Boccioni's *Dynamism of Soccer Player*, which she felt 'beautifully and effectively captures the intensity of sport in the present day'.

As Andy Murray's girlfriend, Sears has watched enough tennis over the years, and sat in enough guest boxes at grand slam tournaments, to know what the intensity of sport looks like from just a few feet away. On this occasion, Sears was at the US Open's Louis Armstrong Stadium, where Murray was playing against Croatia's Marin Cilic for a place in the semi-finals.

Had you wandered in during the first set and a half, you might have wondered whether Murray's tennis was anything near as intense enough. Murray, having lost the opening set, trailed 5-1 in the second. At that stage in proceedings – this was around the time that Ivan Lendl, usually so calm and still, removed his baseball cap, and when Pippa Middleton arrived on the scene – Sears would have been forgiven for thinking that her boyfriend was doing a half-decent impression of Edvard Munch's *The Scream*.

Fred Perry, a Hollywood swordsman as well as a grand slam champion, had four wives and lots of flings with actresses, including romancing Marlene Dietrich, whom he taught how to play tennis 'with great patience and lots of little passionate hugs, punctuated with rapid kissing between flying balls', so her daughter said. Ilie Nastase has claimed to have slept with 2,500 women. Boris Becker, who at one time felt he was being 'hunted' by female admirers, fathered an illegitimate child on the stairs of a Japanese restaurant in London (just not in a broom cupboard, as first thought; he has corrected that version of the Nobu conception). The first time that Bjorn Borg played at Wimbledon, so many teenage girls ran on to the court after his matches that the All England Club felt compelled to write to the headmistresses of the local schools to ask them to control their pupils. Their heels were ruining the grass. In years to come, Borg's coach would take the hotel room next to the Swede so that he could hear any midnight knocks on the player's door. And, somehow, people kept a straight face when talking of how Bjorn had sexed-up tennis with his 'Borgasm'.

Like so many other facets of tennis from yesteryear, the womaniser and playboy has disappeared from view. There cannot be many better adverts for monogamy than the fab four of the modern game; at the time of the 2012 US Open, Roger Federer, Novak Djokovic, Rafa Nadal and Andy Murray were all in long-term relationships, and each had credited their girlfriend or wife for giving them the calm and emotional support they needed to play their best tennis.

None of the four took Andy Roddick's route to love, which was to use his agent as a romantic go-between; after seeing the swimsuit model Brooklyn Decker while flicking through *Sports Illustrated* magazine, he instructed his agent to call her agent to set up a date. Or Ivan Lendl's approach during his early days on tour, which, according to that same publication, was to ask friends to talk to women for him: 'If a woman interested him, he sent someone he knew to risk the opening line. He didn't trust his English, his face or his crooked teeth.'

All four had found companions without calling Jerry Maguire or using their friends to make the first introductions. Federer's first kiss with his future wife Mirka Vavrinec happened in the athletes' village at the 2000 Sydney Olympics. Federer and Mirka, a former top-100 player, now travel the world with their twin daughters and nannies. Mirka is said to have stopped Federer from being such a tennis obsessive; he had been in the habit of spending his time off either playing tennis computer games, often selecting his own avatar, or re-living real matches to consider what he should have done differently. For a while, Mirka helped to organise Federer's interviews and media relations, and occasionally stepped in as a practice-partner.

Djokovic, who has been in a relationship with Jelena Ristic from around the time he broke into the top 100, has said that she has helped him to win grand slams: 'Our love and emotional stability has much to do with my success.' Before Wimbledon 2012, he took Ristic to Scotland for a couple of days to celebrate her birthday ('I sent Andy Murray a picture, and he replied, "What are you doing there?"'). Djokovic and Ristic, who has studied finance to masters level, live together in an apartment block in Monte Carlo; she doesn't go to every tournament he plays, though when she does you can see the angst on her expressive face.

Nadal's circle of friends in Majorca struggle to remember the time before he was in a relationship with Maria Perello, also from the same town of Manacor. Perello has rarely been seen on the tour; she has a full-time job and no desire to follow him everywhere. As Perello said in Nadal's autobiography, 'He needs his space when he is competing, and just the idea of me hanging around waiting on his needs all day wears me out. It would asphyxiate me. And then he would have to be worrying about me. No, if I followed him everywhere, I think there's a risk we might stop getting along.' She added that she didn't want to get caught up in the celebrity environment, a factor that she believed strengthened her relationship with Nadal. It was not until the 2010 Wimbledon Championships that she sat by the court to watch him play a grand slam final; before that, she had been happy to follow his matches on television.

Murray met Kim Sears at the 2005 US Open, and they got to know each other by spending some time together in South Africa that Christmas; he was there to train with his then coach, Mark Petchey, and she was on a family holiday. They have been together ever since, apart from a short break of a few months that left both of them utterly miserable. Like Federer, Nadal and Djokovic, Murray has found that he is happiest in a long-term relationship.

Perhaps because he doesn't drink alcohol, and has no interest in hanging around bars, he has never had any desire to spend his evenings chatting up girls (his fitness trainers wouldn't allow it either). And no one has ever accused Murray of being a sex symbol. But that doesn't mean that he has been without female admirers; at his first Wimbledon Championships 'there were girls shouting out that they wanted to go out with me, and that was fun'. Another year, there was the opportunistic female fan who slipped a piece of paper with her number on it into his racket bag. 'I put my racket bag down to sign some autographs and when I went to get some grips out of it later on, someone called Natalie had left a note with her phone number on it,' Murray wrote on his website. 'So, Natalie, I'd appreciate a photo before I consider making a phone call because you could be a complete stinker.'

Before he broke on to the main tour, Murray was briefly in a relationship with a German girl he had met when they were both tennis students in Barcelona. He recalled: 'I liked this one girl. Then a different girl came and I started spending time with her. Then the first one got jealous and decided to go out with me. It just sort of happened.' But, with their training and playing commitments, they hardly saw each other, so Murray does not regard that as having been a proper relationship. However, he was relieved when the interview she did for a Sunday newspaper, for a fee, was revelation-free; it was perhaps not the kiss-and-tell that the publication had been looking for when they handed over the money.

While it may be true that a Miss Scotland came to watch Murray play at Wimbledon one summer, the relationship was purely platonic – Katharine Brown was an old school friend from Dunblane. Sears is the only serious girlfriend Murray has had. He has said he is aware that some professional athletes want to go out 'with a thousand girls rather than one', but that doesn't interest him.

'It isn't that I have anything against people who want to go drinking and find as many girls as they can – I know that's what most guys of my age do . . . I don't know whether that's because I've got an older head on my shoulders or because I'm lucky enough to have Kim, but the last thing I'd want to do is go out looking for women,' Murray wrote when he was 21, in his 2008 autobiography.

Cups of tea, chocolate biscuits, Classic FM and Jilly Cooper are what excites Kim Sears, not the prospect of a photo-shoot in *Hello!* magazine. She would much rather spend her days painting cats and dogs, or reading, or listening to the radio, than pose in a photographer's studio or be strafed by flashbulbs outside a restaurant. Drawing attention to herself is not her style, so when she was sent some gold wellington boots – presumably to be accessorised with her boyfriend's gold medal – she decided they were too flash to be worn out of the house, writing in her blog: 'I'm sure they would look great on Lady Gaga at Glastonbury, but they will not be featuring on Wimbledon Common anytime soon.' Sears doesn't care for fame, or for following her boyfriend around the world to every tournament, and that's the way Andy Murray likes it. In this regard, Murray is no different to Rafa Nadal; it is unlikely he would have stayed with a girl who sees every match sat in a guest box as a promotional opportunity.

The highlight of the year, Sears has said, isn't one of the four grand slam tournaments, but Bonfire Night in Lewes – near her parents' house in Sussex – which she describes as 'a totally ridiculous, offensive, amazing tradition that links our whole community and I wouldn't miss it for the world'. Unlike her teetotal boyfriend, Sears drinks alcohol, and is said to make an excellent sloe gin from the berries picked by her mother, but she is not known for her partying.

Only very occasionally, such as when they are invited to sit on the front row for Burberry's collection at London Fashion Week, do they take up the perks of Murray's fame, and the next day it's back to the brushes. Of course, every time she watches him play a tennis match, her clothes, hair and make-up are closely scrutinised by the fashion pack; until one critic mentioned it, Sears was presumably unaware that she was part of the 'glossy posse – a group of girls whose long shiny hair, bright eyes, luminous complexions and dazzling smiles make men sigh and women gnash their unbleached teeth in envy'.

During Wimbledon 2012, one fashionista noted, with approval, that Sears had the Duchess of Cambridge's knack for successfully mixing High Street clothes and designer pieces. Hair salons reported during that same tournament that more women were asking for 'The Kim' than for 'The Kate'. But none of that is her doing; it just happens anyway when she takes her seat by the side of the court, a sort of unwanted fame by default.

She declines interviews, saying 'it's about Andy, not me', and about the only reference to Murray on her 'Brushes and Paws' website is a photograph of the bouquet he was given at the Olympics ('it was so beautiful I couldn't bring myself to throw it away, so I dried it in the airing cupboard and now have it hanging in the office'), but even then it's an indirect reference as she doesn't mention him by name.

Few tennis fans would even know what her voice sounds like. And only once could you say that Sears has upstaged her boyfriend at a tournament, and that was one autumn at the Paris Masters, an indoor event in the east of the city. Even then, she hardly engineered it. During the warm-up, her face suddenly appeared on the giant video screen, several thousand Frenchmen wolf-whistled, and she immediately started to blush. When a member of Murray's entourage jokingly fluffed up her hair with his hand, there were more whistles, and more blushing.

There have been no scandals or controversies, not unless you count how much she enjoys Jilly Cooper's bonkbusters – she bought a second copy of *Polo*, as she has read the first so many times that the pages were falling out. Another favourite is *The Man Who Made Husbands Jealous*, and when Sears was studying English literature at the University of Sussex, she would have liked to have done her dissertation on Cooper (the author said she was thrilled when she heard that).

She may like Cooper, but Sears is not a fan of *Fifty Shades of Grey*, the sado-masochistic bestseller by E.L.James. 'One book you can't judge by its cover – as it is impossible to prepare yourself for what lies inside – is *Fifty Shades of Grey*. Proof of that is that is my brother "stumbled" across it when down-loading books for his Kindle, according to Mum. Worse still is now knowing that my mother has read it too. Luckily Dad doesn't own a Kindle, or possess the adequate know-how to download anything,' she wrote on her website. 'I'm not here to masquerade as a literary critic, but I do want to say that I was left cold by the book.'

'Kim's good for Andy because she's not looking for fame,' Murray's father, Willie, has said. 'And she has a good sense of humour, which she has needed. I have a lot of time for her.' When Murray first introduced Sears to his father, he just said, 'This is Kim.' It was only a few months later that Willie realised that she was his son's girlfriend. 'Kim's a gorgeous, lovely girl and they get on so well. At the time, I thought she might be his agent or something like that. She's a very beautiful girl. To be honest, I wasn't sure if Andy entering into a relationship was a good thing for her because of the amount of time he is away. But Kim is the best thing that has ever happened to him,' Willie said in an interview with the *Mail on Sunday*. 'She has her own life, and she's not a hanger-on.'

During the grass-court season, Murray's mother Judy stays with Murray and Sears in their home in Surrey, and the two women have become friends, often sitting next to each other during his matches (Sears knows that Judy doesn't like a running commentary from those around her, so recognises not to discuss every shot and shift in momentum).

Like Nadal's girlfriend, Sears wants more from life than being a tennis player's consort, and has no desire to be defined only by her relationship with her boyfriend. Murray has said that having so much time apart has meant that they appreciate each other even more when they are together, and that there is always something to say to each other. It has kept the relationship fresh.

For a while Sears aspired to be an actress, and Murray – despite being as bewildered when reading Shakespeare's

Measure For Measure as when Roger Federer speaks Swiss German – would help her with her lines. She has also expressed ambitions to write a novel. But, as recently as the 2011 summer grass-court season, she was still casting around for a job, and she was helped in her search by Andrew Castle, a former British player turned GMTV presenter and tennis commentator, who asked on the air during one of Murray's matches at Queen's Club whether anyone watching would like to employ her.

'I've just been speaking to Kim's dad, and he said Kim is struggling right now to find a job,' Castle told BBC viewers. 'So if anyone out there is listening, there's a lovely young lady who wants a job. This could be the first time that someone gets a job via a TV commentary.' Castle never did report back on whether anyone contacted the BBC offering her employment.

Not long afterwards, Sears chose to make a career from her art. Sears, who as a teenager had created a Warhol-inspired print of three dairy cows on a five-foot piece of cardboard, had always found that her pencils and drawing had given her a release. Sears has been happy to paint cats and dogs, even though she has a slight aversion to cats, thanks to watching the Disney cartoon *Lady and the Tramp* as a child and being frightened by the Siamese cats: 'Even now, that song still gives me the heebie-jeebies.' Sears, who was so busy during the summer of 2012 that she stopped taking on new commissions, clearly enjoys her work, though in her quieter moments she does sometimes find herself wondering whether, in another life, she could have been a country singer as she loves their values and their hats.

As Sears has been there from the beginning, it's clear in Murray's head that she's not with him for the money or the profile. When they met, introduced by Murray's then coach, Mark Petchey, Murray was ranked outside the top 100 and had had to qualify for the US Open rather than going straight into the main draw. And Sears was still at school. The week that Murray and Sears 'went public' was the same week that Murray won his first title on the main tour, in San Jose in February 2006.

With Petchey staying at home with his wife and children, Sears used her half-term holiday to spend time with her new boyfriend. Murray hadn't had his hair cut for a year, and the *Sun* had started to compare him to Coco the Clown, so one of the first things she did on arrival in California was to give him a trim with a pair of nail-scissors.

To celebrate beating Lleyton Hewitt in the final, Murray walked into the crowd to kiss Sears on the lips, and the television commentator said, 'I'm not sure if he's going to come back on the court.' While she is believed to have later used a photograph of the kiss as the basis of a painting for her A-level art coursework, she was bewildered by the fuss over the embrace, saying it was 'nothing, and wasn't planned'. Wanting to carry on with the celebrations the day after winning that first title, Murray bought Sears a bag and a pair of sunglasses. Murray tries to be romantic. So if they are shopping and 'something catches her eye', he will try to pop back later to buy it for her; however, he has said that he has tended to ruin the moment by saying something stupid.

In a rare disclosure about the intimate aspects of their relationship, Murray once told the Spanish newspaper *El Mundo* that he is 'not one of those sportsmen who practises a strict policy of sexual abstinence before playing. Tennis is not like boxing. I remember a former world heavyweight whose trainer banned him from having sex for the six weeks before a fight. In tennis we play every week, so with a boxer's mentality we'd always be saying "no".'

Some six and a half years after that kiss in San Jose, there was another public display of affection, this time at the London Olympics. When Murray won the gold medal, he did what most do in the moment of triumph on Wimbledon's Centre Court, which was to climb up into the stands and find his guest box, where he kissed Sears (and hugged everyone else). 'At Wimbledon, everybody does it, especially the first time, as you want to share that moment with the people who have been with you all the time. Those are the guys who see what you are like after losing a Wimbledon final, and see how tough it is. It's nice to celebrate those special moments together.'

More than any other girlfriend or wife on the men's tour, Sears understands the sacrifices that go into being a tennis player, as she grew up around the sport. Or as Murray has said, 'She just gets it.' Her father, Nigel, has coached some of the world's leading female players, including the former world number one Ana Ivanovic, and former top-five players Daniela

Hantuchova and Amanda Coetzer. In a sign of how small a world British tennis is, when Judy Murray became the captain of Britain's Fed Cup she was taking on a position that had been vacated by Nigel Sears, who had also resigned from his job as head of the women's game for the Lawn Tennis Association.

Sears understands that Murray will be away for around two-thirds of the year, and when he is at home, he must concentrate on his training. A couple of days after Murray's tears at the 2012 Wimbledon Championships, Beverley Turner, the wife of Olympic rowing gold medallist James Cracknell, said she knew what life would be like for Sears. 'Living with an elite athlete can be a lonely, emotional and challenging business; the Murrays of this world tend to be intense individuals who bring their day-to-day vicissitudes home, where the partners have to soak up the disappointments and offer platitudes over a teetotal dinner of steamed vegetables and pasta,' Turner wrote in the *Daily Telegraph*. 'When they win, you can share the joy – even though it can feel strangely hollow as it is ultimately their own achievement – but if they lose, you'd better be tough … She must arrive at numerous birthday parties and weddings on her own and probably no longer questions the need to check Andy's diary with at least three other people.'

On a practical level, Sears has done much for Murray. Before he had a driving licence, she drove him everywhere (he bought her a Mercedes as a thank-you present). She has done his laundry (even when finding bags of dirty kit that have been sitting there for weeks), and she has been his hairdresser. And when Murray moved house the week before Wimbledon – there couldn't have been a worse time – Sears and Murray's mother organised everything so he wouldn't have to interrupt his preparations for the tournament.

On top of that, Sears has helped to soften and improve Murray's image, though that was not part of some master-plan to repackage her beau for public consumption; it just happened naturally over the course of their relationship. If Sears was so pleasant, people thought, can Murray really be the difficult customer he has been made out to be? Sears has also helped Murray from being consumed by tennis, of thinking and talking about nothing other than winning a grand slam. In the evening, Murray actually likes being able to talk to someone about a subject other than tennis. Sears, as the daughter of an experienced coach, and now a portrait painter, manages to stand both inside and outside tennis. However, they don't play each other at tennis, because, as he has said, 'She's not very good.' Sears is a much calmer soul than Murray. Willie Murray regards Sears as a 'stabilising influence' on his son.

Sometimes – and this has generally happened only around Wimbledon – the paparazzi have trailed Murray and Sears, but the images have never been more rock 'n' roll than the pair buying sushi in Kensington, strolling around Surrey with their dogs and takeaway coffees, or shopping for groceries at a local supermarket. There was one occasion when Sears loaded the trolley with fruit and vegetables, and Murray decided that he would buy Milky Way cake bars in such quantities that the lady at the checkout said to Sears: 'Do you think these are on special offer or something?' Sears replied: 'No, he just likes them a lot.'

Occasionally, Murray does wonder – or at least he says he does – what Sears is doing with him. While Murray is bright, he has recognised that she is considerably more intelligent than him. She is much better read than he is, but that is not too difficult, considering that he is known to have scanned only boxing magazines, a few passages from Harry Potter books, and part of a wrestler's autobiography. That must have been why Murray was so pleased with himself after beating her at Scrabble once that he announced the victory on Twitter (his winning move, 'hernias', was definitely a sportsman's word).

Central to Andy Murray's domestic life with Kim Sears are their dogs, a couple of Border Terriers called Maggie May and Rusty. Once, when asked by his brother Jamie what he would save first if his house was on fire, Murray jokingly replied: 'I would save my dogs, probably. Is that wrong that I said that over my girlfriend? I'd take my dogs, I'd take them for sure.'

One of the happiest days of Murray's life was when his girlfriend's parents gave her Maggie May as a present for her twenty-first birthday. Murray's affection for the dogs – Rusty came along later – has been such that he has forgiven them for chewing everything in the house, for working up huge vet's fees by swallowing pebbles, and for peeing on his shoes. Between tournaments, Murray can often be found walking the dogs and encouraging them to jump up to lick his face, and he further demonstrated his love for all things canine in the week after his defeat in the 2012 Wimbledon final when he and Sears went on a private visit to the Battersea Dogs Home. Occasionally the dogs have gone on tour, such as to Paris for the French Open, but most of the time they have stayed in England, running around the Epsom Downs, or the Devil's Punchbowl in Surrey, with Sears.

In a sign of the madness of modern life, Maggie May has more followers on Twitter than some of the players that Murray encounters on the tour. Maggie May has used the Twitter account – written by Sears – to flirt with Pierre Djokovic, Novak's pet poodle (naturally, he is also on Twitter), and also been open about her jealousy of other dogs: 'Kate Middleton's dog is stealing column inches. This has not gone unnoticed, and I'll step out without underwear tomorrow to compensate.'

Named after the Rod Stewart song, Maggie May has tweeted pictures of herself and Rusty wearing Murray's Olympic medals, one getting a gold and the other a silver, and has written a column for *The Tennis Space* website: 'Let's get this straight, I'm not your ordinary tennis player's dog. I don't even like tennis balls for a start. I'll chew them, sure, and rip them to pieces – but don't even think about asking me to fetch. Ivan Lendl came round for dinner the other night, which I was pretty excited about. I'm a soft touch when it comes to men, you see. I flirted my Border Terrier socks off and even allowed him on my sofa, but he didn't let me kiss his face, which I thought pretty harsh. Maybe it's a Czech thing ... We get to jump on Dad's face in the morning and there are plenty of socks and ankle braces to play with.'

A happy home life has always been hugely important to Murray; having, in his words, 'gone through' his parents' divorce, he had resolved to 'work hard at having a successful relationship'. When Murray moved out of London, from his penthouse flat with a roof garden in Wandsworth, it was to a Surrey village and a house that he would share with Sears. Leaving London would mean more space and more privacy, and it would also mean better sleep; in the flat he was often woken up early in the morning by the noise from the nearby skips.

As the estate agents around Oxshott like to say, it has gone from being a hamlet for pig farmers to one of the most expensive villages in Britain, if not the most expensive. They also say that Oxshott, sandwiched between the A3 and the M25, is part of the 'wealth corridor', with the village populated by footballers in their twenties and fund managers in their thirties. The other line, although not one used by the estate agents, is that the village is 'divorce central'.

The house that Murray bought, which had been on the market for around £5 million, is a mock-Regency property with an indoor swimming pool, sauna, jacuzzi, gym, library, cinema, games room, six bedrooms and a triple garage. It was also Murray's castle, which he thought needed defending one night when the alarm went off at 2.30am; while wearing just his boxer-shorts, and having picked up a tennis racket to use as a weapon, he ran downstairs to confront the intruder. He felt some relief on realising there wasn't a burglar, only that the alarm system was faulty.

Just a few months after they moved in, in the summer of 2009, Sears returned to live with her parents. When Murray and Sears broke up, his mood would not have been improved by the suggestions – entirely false – that he had ended the relationship because she was fed up with him spending so much time with his PlayStation. Murray's 'camp' strongly denied accusations that he would spend up to seven hours a day playing computer games.

It had been an amicable break-up and, as the publicists were saying, no one else was involved, but both were miserable apart. 'I work better in a relationship,' Murray has said. And he and Sears were not apart for long. By the 2010 Wimbledon Championships, the relationship was back on. Soon the press's attention would turn to whether Murray and Sears would marry. With the exception of Prince William, there cannot have been another British man under more media pressure to propose. Murray had seen how happy his brother was as a married man. Murray had been the best man when Jamie married his Colombian girlfriend, Alejandra, in Dunblane in 2010; even though he is teetotal, he had fulfilled his duties of organising a boozy stag night. Murray would joke how Sears was 'pushing for marriage'.

Pippa Middleton is about as well connected in tennis as she is in Boujis. Which is very. Just a day after being Roger Federer's guest at the 2012 US Open, and chatting backstage with Mrs Federer, Kate's younger sister sat with Andy Roddick's friends and family in the Arthur Ashe Stadium as the American made his last appearance before going into retirement. It was only after Roddick had lost to Juan Martin del Potro, and had given an articulate and emotional speech, that Middleton made her way to the Louis Armstrong Stadium to see whether Andy Murray could get his game firing against Marin Cilic.

Middleton was far from being the only one who arrived late for Murray's match; the attention on Roddick, while totally understandable, meant that the tournament's second largest stadium was not even half full in the early stages of the quarter-final. The challenge for Murray, and it was a challenge he was struggling with, was to create his own atmosphere on the court.

When Murray heard that his match, originally scheduled for centre stage at the US Open, had been moved to the Louis Armstrong Stadium because of rain, it is unlikely that he would have been whistling *What A Wonderful World* to himself. No two tennis courts are the same, but Murray, who has always loved playing on the Arthur Ashe Stadium, has often looked discombobulated in the Louis Armstrong Stadium. Claustrophobia could have been a reason, as the 'run-back' isn't as big in the Louis Armstrong Stadium, and there is less room at the sides of the court; and it also had the general effect of making Murray feel hemmed in. Or perhaps it was because the court surfaces play very differently, and the microphones picked up Murray telling himself that the cement there was 'ten times faster' than where Roddick had been playing Del Potro.

When a tennis player walks on court, it can be tempting to think back to past experiences there, good or bad, and Murray has had some rough days at the Louis Armstrong Stadium. It was there that Murray had played a long way below his best in losing to Nikolay Davydenko in the fourth round in 2006, where he had played a tame match for a third-round defeat to Switzerland's Stanislas Wawrinka in 2010, and where he had had to come from two sets down in the second round of the 2011 US Open to defeat the Netherlands' Robin Haase.

With Murray at risk of going two sets down against Cilic, thoughts also turned to the time that the Scot had, in one American critic's words, 'laid an egg on court' during a defeat to the same opponent in the fourth round of the 2009 tournament (that had been in the Arthur Ashe Stadium). Was this to be the sequel? This was certainly a very different Murray to the one who had dismantled Milos Raonic a round earlier – indeed, his form had been inconsistent throughout the tournament, flipping from average to excellent and then back again – and so concerned was Ivan Lendl that he took his baseball cap off; that may sound like a small act, but for a coach who usually doesn't like to move, some read that as a sign of great concern.

Lendl removing his headgear wouldn't have helped to improve Murray's game, but the arrival of Middleton and several thousand Americans undoubtedly did something for the Briton; the more spectators there were in the stadium, the more noise there was, the more it had the look and feel of a quarter-final of a grand slam championship. Sears, who of course had been there from the beginning, as she had been for all of his matches during the tournament, was doing a very good job of hiding her fried nerves. Lendl had momentarily lost his hat, if not his head; Sears remained as quietly reassuring and encouraging as ever.

There could be little doubt that Murray was better in a crisis under Lendl than he had been before. 'Sometimes in the past when I wasn't playing well I would get down on myself and not figure out exactly how to win all the time,' Murray had said, but he had found a way of staying focused, and 'using the time I had at the change of ends, and the time between points, better'.

In these situations, when one player is trying to turn a match around, it can often take two to tango – your opponent needs to be tripping over his own feet. Murray's tennis improved rapidly, also helped by the growing darkness which slowed the conditions down. But he would not have got back into the second set if Cilic had not faltered.

Malcolm Gladwell's book, *What the Dog Saw: and Other Adventures*, includes a brilliant essay, 'The Art of Failure', which is required reading for anyone who wants to understand how a tennis player thinks. 'Panic is the opposite of choking. Choking is about thinking too much. Panic is about thinking too little. Choking is about loss of instinct. Panic is reversion to instinct. They may look the same, but they are worlds apart. Why does this distinction matter? In some instances, it doesn't matter. If you lose a close tennis match, it's of little moment whether you choked or panicked: either way, you lost.' It looked like Cilic was choking, but Murray would have been happy with him panicking.

Having been 5-1 down in the second set, when Murray got back to 5-5, it was already looking as though whoever won the second set would reach the semi-finals. When Cilic took a 4-2 lead in the tiebreak, he appeared to have recovered his poise, and yet he then lost the next five points, and so the set, and the contest. Once Murray had that second set, he was not going to lose.

Cilic, who is six foot six inches, has a big serve and a seemingly brittle mind. Both Murray and Cilic would not have forgotten about their match in the semi-finals of the 2010 Australian Open, when the Briton had come from a set down for a four-set victory. Once again, Cilic's tennis was in desperate need of the Heimlich Manoeuvre. Murray ripped through the choking Cilic in the third and fourth sets, winning 12 of the 14 games, for a 3-6, 7-6, 6-2, 6-0 victory. As Murray said, 'This could easily have gone the other way.' What would have happened if Roddick and Del Potro's match had gone on for another half an hour, or if Roddick had given a longer speech, and those spectators had been delayed even further from taking their seats on Murray's court?

New York City had been hoping to see the concluding part of the Murray–Federer summer trilogy. As Roger Federer had beaten Murray in the Wimbledon final, only for Murray to have got the better of Federer in the Olympic final, there had been much speculation about who might do what to whom at the US Open in their projected semi-final. During Federer's quarter-final against Tomas Berdych of the Czech Republic, the Swiss kept on asking himself, 'Man, how is this happening to me?'

It was to be Federer's earliest defeat at the tournament since 2003, when Murray was a 16-year-old junior, and still another year away from winning the boys' singles title. It was a personal 'let-down' for Federer; it was also a let-down for the city. Most had imagined that the lights of the Arthur Ashe Stadium would see Federer through; after all, he had never previously lost at night in New York, a run which had started in 2000 and which had taken him to a 23-match winning streak for evening matches. But Berdych, while he was playing at night in New York for the first time, was not to be blinded by Federer's genius and star-power.

For the first time since the 2004 French Open, both Federer and Rafa Nadal would be missing from the semi-finals of a grand slam. For years, it had always seemed as though Murray would have to beat two out of Federer, Nadal and Novak Djokovic, to win a grand slam title. But now only one was left in the draw. 'What an opportunity this is for Andy Murray,' Boris Becker wrote in the *Daily Telegraph*. 'It is the first time for 33 grand slam tournaments that neither of the two biggest names in tennis – Roger Federer and Rafa Nadal – have reached the semi-finals. It is definitely too early to call it the changing of the guard. But this is the first one. There will be more. In the absence of the two senior guys, it almost feels as if Murray and Novak Djokovic are the new establishment.'

Had Murray played Federer in the semi-finals, there would have been no clear favourite. But most would now expect Murray to defeat Berdych to reach the final of the US Open for the second time. As Becker said: 'Who would you rather play? The greatest of all time, or somebody who has never won a slam?'

But this was not a free pass into the final. If, at that moment, you had compiled a list of the best players on tour not to have won a grand slam, Berdych would have been close to the top. Murray didn't need Lendl, who had good insight and intelligence on his fellow Czech, to tell him that no one on the circuit hits the ball harder than Berdych, the runner-up to Nadal at the 2010 Wimbledon Championships. When Berdych isn't in the mood, he can play some terrible tennis – witness his first-round defeats at the 2012 Wimbledon Championships and Olympics – but when he is in the mood, he can be a menace.

So, after Federer's defeat, New York would have to make do without the player whose face was on the side of the tournament vehicles. American television needed a new fixation, and during the Federer–Berdych match the camera had kept on cutting to Berdych's girlfriend, a model called Ester Satorova. For ten years, Berdych had been in a relationship with a female tennis player called Lucie Safarova, but since the glamorous Satorova had started accompanying him on the tour, he had been saying that it was easier to be with someone who also didn't hit tennis balls for a living.

'In the past, with Lucie, I was saying that it was probably for the best that we both played tennis. But then I didn't have any other experience. But now I can say that this one is way better because before it was too much tennis. Every day you have to play, practise, organise stuff, then winning, losing, handling that stuff, and it's quite tough to have it from one side. If you have to deal with the same thing from the other side, it's almost too much. So I'm really enjoying spending time with someone who has a different life.' This was how the *New York Post* reported Berdych's win over Federer: 'Now he is known for more than his killer girlfriend.'

It was Berdych's killer forehand that would have been on Murray's mind the night before their semi-final. Murray could not have imagined the match would be played in high winds which produced the worst conditions he has ever experienced on a tennis court, which is quite something, given that he grew up in Scotland. At the same time as trying to reach the final of the US Open, he would be keeping half an eye out for flying chairs, newspapers, hot-dog wrappers and other pieces of 'garbage'.

6

Fame and Fortune

And then, suddenly, a couple of knights, breathing Merlot and mayhem, gatecrashed Andy Murray's US Open. Whoever drew up Murray's carefully choreographed schedule of post-match print, radio and television interviews hadn't made room in the schedule for Sir Sean Connery and Sir Alex Ferguson dropping in on Murray's appearance in the main press conference room to pass on their congratulations. Sir Sean and Sir Alex could have waited until after the interview was finished, but then where would the fun have been in that?

With Murray into his fifth grand slam final, and his second at Flushing Meadows, this almost felt like a tartan takeover of the city; as the *New York Post* would later observe, here were the three most famous Scotsmen – 'with apologies to Ewan McGregor' – in one room. Watching all this, the American writer S.L.Price 'half expected Jackie Stewart, Fat Bastard and a blue-and-white faced Mel Gibson to come barrelling in next, flinging handfuls of haggis'.

Only Connery and Ferguson, New York's latest double act, could upstage a tornado. Murray and Tomas Berdych had started and finished their match in a gale, and the second semi-final between Novak Djokovic and David Ferrer had been suspended in the first set because the weather station's satellite pictures were flashing red with a tornado possibly heading towards the tennis.

'Excuse me for interrupting,' Connery said, and no one was going to stand in the way of James Bond's interlude. When Murray's mother, on the encouragement of Ferguson and doing her best Miss Moneypenny, moved forward to hug her youngest son, Murray told her, clearly enjoying this, 'Mum, you smell of wine.' Looking over at Ferguson, Judy said: 'He made me have wine. He's just been telling me that Scotland invented the world.' Ferguson responded: 'I explained how Scotland invented the world, and today we invented the wind.' And that was Connery's cue to say: 'Today we conquered the world.'

When Ferguson was finished, he turned to Murray and said: 'Continue your interview.' And if anyone couldn't quite believe that had really happened, a full transcript was soon available from the stenographers who record every word of every interview at the US Open. Or, alternatively, you could have gone almost immediately to YouTube to watch one of the strangest episodes ever seen at a grand slam tournament.

To say that the US Open likes the sprinkling of celebrity stardust across its concrete courts and walkways, and its media centre, would be to under-state what can look like a dependency; would the tournament have been quite the same if Eva Longoria had declined her invitation, or if Susan Sarandon and Alec Baldwin had not bothered, or any of the other regulars from *People* magazine had stayed at home? The 2012 US Open was like any other, with the celebrity spectators feted almost as much as the tennis players they were watching, sometimes more so. During every change of ends, the cameramen in the Arthur Ashe Stadium looked for famous faces to blow up on the big screen. While Wimbledon has gone more showbusiness over the past few summers, inviting more luvvies and television 'personalities', it still had nothing on the star-obsessed US Open.

Longoria, the *Desperate Housewives* actress, came to Flushing Meadows to watch her friend Serena Williams. Sarandon was photographed in a suite in the Arthur Ashe Stadium, having her shoulders massaged by her young lover as she watched the tennis. Jon Hamm, *Mad Men*'s Don Draper, was at the tennis, as was Red Foo, a singer best known for the 'Sexy And I Know It' track, who spent a lot of time at the tournament with Victoria Azarenka, the top seed in the women's singles, including sitting next to her at one of her press conferences. Nicole Kidman and her husband Keith Urban showed they were game; on noticing they were on the big screen, Urban leant across the lady next to him, the wife of the president of the United States Tennis Association, to kiss Kidman on the lips, and the crowd whooped. 'Over the last few years, tennis has become pretty attractive to celebrities,' Murray said. 'It's become a big sport and it gets a lot of attention now, so that obviously brings various famous people. You do get a lot of that in New York.'

Of all the players at the tournament, Murray was the one who was attracting the most attention from the world of celebrity. That had much to do with Murray's victory at the Olympics, but there were other factors, such as Rafa Nadal's absence, Roger Federer's relatively early exit, and that Novak Djokovic had made quiet, efficient, unremarkable progress through the draw until his semi-final on Super Saturday.

Kevin Spacey had made sure he was introduced to the Scot – and a few days later the actor had the thrill of a gentle hit with Murray on a practice court. James Corden, a British television presenter and actor who was finishing a run on Broadway, came to watch Murray play. Irvine Welsh, the author of *Trainspotting*, is a keen Murray-watcher, who had tweeted after the Olympic final, 'After winning hearts with his bubbling magnanimity at Wimbledon, I'd like to see Andy mix it up with a bitter, surly victory speech.' He was in New York to see his fellow Scot play. Murray's other supporters included *Star Trek*'s Sir Patrick Stewart and Andrew Garfield, the *Spiderman* actor and Murray lookalike.

But it was the two Scottish knights, Sir Sean and Sir Alex, who led Murray's celebrity fan club. While Murray had been in phone and email contact with Connery and Ferguson, it was the first time he had met James Bond and the manager of

Manchester United Football Club. This was quite a collection of famous friends for someone who considered himself almost an anti-celebrity, and who had once said that he wouldn't wish fame on anyone.

How was it possible for Andy Murray to maintain that he did not care for fame when he was represented by Simon Fuller, the creator of the *Pop Idol* television franchise, and the former manager of the Spice Girls? When Murray had the same management team as David and Victoria Beckham, Jennifer Lopez, Annie Lennox, Steven Tyler, Will Young and Lisa-Marie Presley? When his manager was the very same man who had spawned Simon Cowell? And hadn't Murray idolised Andre Agassi, who had willingly appeared in a campaign for a camera with the slogan, 'image is everything'?

Murray's decision to sign a contract with Fuller's XIX Entertainment had been intriguing, inviting speculation that he hoped to turn himself into a serious player in showbusiness as well as sport, that this was Tennis Spice making a move on Hollywood. As part of the deal – Murray and XIX started working together in the spring of 2009 – the Scot's interests in America would be looked after by the Los Angeles-based Creative Artists Agency, whose clients included a good portion of the film industry.

Up until that point, Murray had been represented by management companies who specialised in sport; first Octagon and then Ace Group, a more boutique company, and he had never intimated that he had any great desire to establish a

Brand Murray along the lines of Brand Federer or Brand Beckham. The major players in the sports industry, such as IMG or Lagardere Unlimited, would have been disappointed by Murray's news. Perhaps a little surprised, too.

Why had Fuller, who had built his business empire on pop music and reality television formats, and who in 2012 was said by the *Sunday Times* Rich List to have a personal fortune of £375 million, been interested in a 'mere' tennis player? Here was someone who had once been named by *Time* magazine as one of the 100 most influential people in the world. That was mostly off the back of his *Idol* creation, which was first seen in Britain as *Pop Idol*, became a huge ratings success in the United States as *American Idol*, and which was then sold in more than 100 other countries.

Fuller launched Cowell on the British and American public by employing his friend as a judge on both sides of the Atlantic. But there was a great, high-stakes falling out when Cowell launched a rival show *The X-Factor*; Fuller sued for a reported £100 million, dropping the law-suit only after a substantial out-of-court settlement. When you hear it called 'The Clash of the Simons' it sounds quite unremarkable, but theirs is an intense rivalry. A story has done the rounds in Los Angeles of how Fuller told Cowell he was on the waiting list for a sports car worth hundreds of thousands of pounds. So Cowell found one in Germany, had it shipped to Los Angeles and drove it to the set of a television network where he knew Fuller would be.

There is not another tennis player on the tour whose

manager is frenemies with Simon Cowell, or who has a star on the Hollywood Walk of Fame. Or who had discovered Amy Winehouse. The music promoter Harvey Goldsmith had picked Fuller as Britain's greatest entrepreneur. You could question Fuller's taste – he was also the Dr Frankenstein behind S Club 7 – but you could not knock his power or his influence. In short, Fuller was a big player, who the *Evening Standard* has described as 'The Man Who Wants To Rule The World' and 'the Mephistopheles of modern pop music'.

David Beckham wrote a piece for *Time* about how Fuller had helped to shape his career. 'We're both committed to being the very best at what we do – he's very hard-working and knows you rarely get an easy win in life,' Beckham wrote. 'He enjoys dealing with unexpected challenges. It's no surprise that he's as successful as he is because, despite being a nice guy and a modest character, he's also a real fighter for what he believes in. I admire him for that.' Beckham added that he had much to be grateful to Fuller for, not least that the entrepreneur had provided him with an introduction to Victoria Adams, who would become his wife.

Fuller was also instrumental in driving through Beckham's move to the Los Angeles Galaxy football team, in a deal which was reputed to be worth a quarter of a billion dollars. While Fuller didn't want any personal publicity – Goldsmith said that you won't see the Englishman 'hanging out with stars at parties, as his modus operandi is seeing opportunities, quietly grabbing them, staying under the radar, and delivering' – he has been brilliant at turning his clients into brands. When the

Spice Girls were at the height of their popularity, he was seen as the 'Svengali Spice' or 'the man behind girl power'; he was the one who drove all the marketing and merchandise deals, including the dolls and the deodorants, and the movie.

When Murray made the decision to sign with Fuller, the only other sportsman under XIX Entertainment's management was Beckham and it was a while since he had been 'just' a footballer (the racing driver Lewis Hamilton would follow Murray). Fuller had never worked with a tennis player before, so he did not have anything like the same knowledge of the tour as he did of the music industry. But Fuller was intrigued by Murray, believing that if this young Scottish player could ever win a grand slam title he could become – and he used the L-word here – 'a legend'. It had always been Fuller's intention to work with the 'hottest' designer, the 'hottest' singer and the 'hottest' footballer, and he believed that Murray had the potential to become the 'hottest' tennis player. To become iconic.

'I had seen a young man who was potentially a champion, someone who could make history. He had been so close, he was so young and I was projecting that if he were to win a grand slam tournament, I wanted to be part of it and I thought I could help. I was imagining a Brit winning a major and how massive that would be, and that's what appealed to me. My job is to complement sporting excellence with an understanding of what goes into being a superstar,' Fuller told *The Times*.

At the same time that Murray was moving through the draw at the 2012 US Open, one of Fuller's other clients, Victoria

Beckham, was launching New York Fashion Week by showing her 2013 spring/summer collection at the New York Public Library, and his country singer, Carrie Underwood, had an album at the top of the Billboard chart. There could be little doubt that Fuller was giving Murray advice and strategic thinking that no other tennis player was getting. As part of the deal, Murray's brother and mother would also be represented by XIX Entertainment, but the company would say that they had no plans to expand in tennis, that they were content to concentrate on this potential 'legend' of the future.

It was certainly never Fuller's intention that he would travel the world with Murray, accompanying him to every tournament; he was the celebrity overlord – or the Svengali of tabloid imagination – giving occasional, long-term guidance. Most of Murray's week-to-week media relations were handled by Matt Gentry of XIX Entertainment, while the company's Louise Irving helped to organise the player's travel and other media commitments, and Simon Oliveira, Beckham's spokesman, was also involved with the Murray account. Robert Dodds, the company's chief executive, was also in New York to support their client.

Sport had become a key part of the entertainment business, that's if it had not always been one; what exactly would be the point of tennis if it wasn't entertaining people? Tennis had certainly always had links with Hollywood. Take the man that Murray was hoping to emulate. Fred Perry had a very different take on fame than Murray; Perry embraced everything. Well, almost everything, as he turned down a film studio's two-picture deal for $100,000 because the Lawn Tennis Association talked him out of it. 'When Perry goes to Hollywood,' one American columnist noted, 'male film stars go to sulk in Nevada.'

Perry had actresses on his arm, he partied with Errol Flynn and David Niven, and, such was the strength of his own brand, he set up his own clothing label (as a pipe-smoker, he almost chose a pipe as his logo, before settling for a laurel wreath). Perry had never felt welcome in British tennis; he was much more at home in the world of showbusiness and entertainment, where they actually appreciated his looks, his success and his swagger.

Anyone who imagined that linking up with Fuller signified Murray's intention to take the Fred Perry approach or to air-kiss on the red carpets of film premieres had it all wrong. Certainly Murray would have been attracted to the idea of doing things a little differently to how the established sports management companies would have advised, but he was not interested in having parts of his life whipped up into celebrity froth.

Murray, for all his emoting and cussing on a tennis court, is naturally shy. And there was little chance – make that no chance – of Murray's girlfriend Kim Sears ever pushing for the couple to be sold as tennis's version of Posh and Becks. The only real equivalent to the Beckhams in tennis was Andy Roddick and Brooklyn Decker, who had had Elton John sing at their wedding, and she was arguably now the more famous of the pair, after a couple of films.

Murray had liked what he had heard from Fuller about how XIX Entertainment would help to position him, and how they would look after his image and business interests in the long term, rather than concentrating on the short-term and medium-term buck. During the getting-to-know-each-other stage of the business relationship, Fuller had visited Murray's home, and Murray had made it plain that he did not care for empty celebrity, that he didn't crave a bigger profile just for the sake of it. The last thing Murray wanted was for anyone to think he had become a 'fake', as buffed and polished, as rebranded and repackaged, as a Posh Spice doll. As Murray told Fuller during that meeting: 'For me, it's not about becoming a celebrity, it's about becoming the best tennis player I can be.'

One aspect of stardom that Murray has always been happy with is the personal interaction with the fans when they approach him at the practice courts, in a restaurant, in the street or at an airport departure lounge. He has signed every body-part he has been asked to, including foreheads. He has posed for pictures. He has never knowingly been rude.

Murray never had the option of becoming a celebrity refusenik. Publicity stunts are a regular part of an elite tennis player's life, with Murray and others called upon to promote tournaments beyond the tennis hardcore. In the course of his work, Murray has met the Miami Dolphins cheerleaders, he has stood on top of London's O2 Arena, he has tried Thai kick-boxing, he has played tennis with Venus Williams on Miami's South Beach, and he has stood on the helipad of the

Burj-al-Arab hotel in Dubai, hundreds of feet above the Persian Gulf. Murray hardly had much choice in any of the above, as the players are contractually obliged to do promotional activity for the sport.

But maybe he felt more comfortable about doing it because he wasn't selling himself, but the tour and the sport. Murray clearly cares about tennis, its image and its place in the world, and how the sport can possibly go about looking less elitist in Britain. When Murray has appeared on television talk shows, it has sometimes taken him a while to get warmed-up – he looked very nervous, for instance, when he sat down on Jonathan Ross's sofa – but then he has gone on to do a decent job of showing that he has a personality, a dry wit and a racket-bag of anecdotes to dip into.

If ever there was a television appearance which showed what Murray can be like in private, it was the interview he did with his former coach Mark Petchey in a corridor at the US Open one year. It was one of those rainy, dull days when no one has any idea when they are going to get on court, and Murray and a couple of his friends, the British doubles pair Colin Fleming and Ross Hutchins, had been killing time in the players' restaurant by laughing at each other's faults.

Their off-camera conversation continued on the air, when Petchey asked the three of them to do a live chat for Sky Television. Murray disclosed that he had been under attack from Hutchins for 'losing my hair quite early', but countered by mocking Hutchins' shoes. Telling Hutchins that his 'banter on Twitter' was poor, Murray then looked into the camera and advised viewers against 'following' the Englishman. Fire up YouTube for a five-minute clip which is, at once, entertaining, silly to the point of being puerile, and probably the best insight you will ever get into what Murray is 'really like' (that's not to say, in that trite phrase, that it's the real Murray, as the tennis player in business mode during his normal post-match media commitments is just as much the real Murray, too).

Murray's appearance on the BBC comedy series *Outnumbered*, for the Sport Relief charity fundraiser, showed that he could be a good sport. A little girl asked Murray what he did, and he replied: 'I play tennis.' So she said: 'But what do you do for a job?' A teenage boy, having already taken one photograph of himself standing next to Murray, then asked the tennis player to pose for another, 'because my friends are not going to believe it's you. Can we do another one when you're not smiling, where it's a bit more you?'

The first time that many of New York's fashion crowd would have been made aware of Murray – there is every chance they would have missed his appearance in the 2008 US Open final – was when he featured in American *Vogue* (anyone wondering what he was doing in the magazine should consider that the editor-in-chief, Anna Wintour, loves her tennis). The piece, which was published before the 2010 US Open, showed how Murray would look if he employed a stylist. The photographer Mario Testino, best known for his portraits of Kate Moss and the late Princess Diana, shot Murray in his Surrey home, in the garage, which also doubles as a weights room, as he wanted to capture him where he worked. It would have been the first time, though, that Murray has worked out while wearing a tuxedo and a bow tie, which Testino had to help him with.

When Testino looked at the images of Murray, he thought 'raw'. The writer of the piece noted Murray's 'green eyes, hot and fierce', and Christopher Bailey, the Burberry designer who had supplied the tuxedo, suggested that the Scot could become a 'global brand' and an iconic British sportsman. So this was Murray being love-bombed by fashion, with Bailey saying: 'He's so focused and driven in his craft. He's laser sharp: a wonderful person for the nation to celebrate.' Murray's appearance in American *Vogue* was certainly more successful than Laura Robson's in British *Vogue* when the teenager had been quoted as calling some female players 'sluts, who go with every guy and make such a bad name for themselves' (she would later apologise).

There is a line that Murray won't cross, or pirouette over. Greg Rusedski's appearance on *Dancing on Ice*, a reality show on British television, only confirmed in Murray's mind that he would never do anything similar; it also confirmed the same in Tim Henman's head, and whenever Rusedski was on, Henman and Murray sent each other text messages. 'Andy and I are pretty united in our certainty that we would never, ever appear in a programme like that,' said Henman.

Murray looked at Andy Roddick's cameo on *Sabrina the Teenage Witch*, and when the American hosted the comedy show *Saturday Night Live*, and thought: no way. Murray knows what he is capable of and what he isn't. Murray would not have been comfortable – and he almost certainly wouldn't have been asked either – to have played the love interest role that Rafa Nadal did in a music video for Shakira, a Colombian pop star. Murray's adventures in music have been restricted to an unfortunate rap on the album produced by doubles players and identical twins Bob and Mike Bryan ('During Wimbledon it really gets crazy. My hand cramps up and my mind gets hazy. I sign and I sign but the line doesn't end. Wake me up tomorrow and let's do it again. Autograph.') When Murray appeared on a TV show that embarrassed him by playing a recording of his rapping, he leant forward and buried his head in his hands.

Other players were happy for their images to be updated, but not Murray. Nadal's collaboration with Shakira and subsequent cross-over into MTV – the video saw him pouting like crazy, while a wind-machine blew his hair, and later misplacing his shirt – was part of The Sexing-Up Of Rafa. It was a process that he had presumably consented to. Nadal had once dressed as if he had just stepped off the beach in Majorca, with those cut-off piratas trousers, the vests and the bandanas, and he had the cartoonish enthusiasm and endeavour of Mowgli from *The Jungle Book*.

Nadal's image had arguably been too young and too cartoony for him to have appealed to middle-aged, middle-management tennis fans, so the ones that potential sponsors want to reach. Now Nadal wears conventional shorts, he has sleeves on his shirts and he does things that would make Mowgli blush. An advert for Armani had Nadal stripping in a car-park, while his campaign for an aftershave depicted him as a *demi-mondaine*. The sexualisation of Nadal appeared complete when *Sports Illustrated*'s 2012 swimsuit edition carried images of Nadal nuzzling with the Israeli supermodel Bar Rafaeli. Undoubtedly Nadal would have grown up anyway without the intervention of his advisers, but they pushed him along and they cannot be displeased with the result, an image which Bloomberg called a rare mixture of 'humility and virility', while others considered the Spaniard to be a 'safe rebel'.

Over time, Roger Federer had gradually become a citizen of the world. In the beginning, he didn't have Anna Wintour on speed-dial, and he didn't have perfect hair and the cool demeanour. As a teenager, he had been happy to slob around in jeans, he had experimented with hair-buns and peroxide, and he had had a reputation in Swiss junior tennis for being a hot-head throwing tantrums and rackets. No one is born a sophisticate, and Wintour and Federer's wife Mirka have had their parts to play. But that is not say that Federer has become a 'fake' or something he isn't; he has clearly changed, but he has never looked anything less than well-suited to the adulation, the private jets and the 'RF' monogram. Superstardom fits Federer as well as a white jacket with gold trim.

Since Djokovic started to make the most of his talent, and fully appreciated the connection between an appealing image and the size of his endorsement contracts, he has turned his personality down. The Djoker side of him hasn't quite disappeared, but certainly doesn't come out to play as often as it used to. There was a time when he couldn't resist any invitation to perform one of his impressions of tennis players – his Maria Sharapova is particularly good – but now there is a more serious, measured air to him (word would also have got back to him that Federer was displeased with the impersonations, saying that the Serbian was 'walking a tightrope').

Like the other three, Murray's appearance and image have clearly developed over the years, but any change had always seemed a bit more organic, and a bit less calculated. Anyone could see that he had been held back by that joke about the England football team, and as he lost trust in the media he became less inclined to be interesting. All that controversy happened before Fuller's time, so one can only speculate how he might have handled that situation differently. Fuller's challenge, after signing a contract with Murray, was to help turn the tennis player into a brand without his client freaking out that he had lost some of his integrity. And also to prepare Murray for what might happen if he ever won a grand slam title.

In Murray's mind – and it is impossible to refute this – there is nothing hypocritical about being shy and wanting to meet those he had seen on his television screen. Murray has always been interested in talking to actors, comedians and sportsmen, and the more successful he became, the more others asked to be introduced.

As a child, Murray had listened to cassettes of Billy Connolly's stand-up routines during long car journeys, so when he heard during the Australian Open one January that the comedian was in Melbourne for some live shows he gave him a guest-pass. Connolly, who enjoys his tennis, accepted the invitation and appeared to enjoy the experience, apart from when the host television broadcaster put a microphone under his nose and asked him for his thoughts. 'Leave me alone,' Connolly bellowed, though he even managed to make that funny, and there was laughter all around the Rod Laver Arena. 'He's a very, very funny guy. He's very normal, too. It's not like he really tries to be funny,' said Murray, who was invited to watch Connolly's show.

Murray is certainly no luvvie, but talking to Kevin Spacey in New York was fun. 'That was cool seeing him, because *The Usual Suspects* is one of my favourite films. I hadn't really met that many movie stars before. I had a little chat with him and asked him whether he played any tennis,' Murray said. Spacey's reply was that he had injured his hand on the set of his latest series, so had been unable to play recently. But when, just a few days later, Spacey had the opportunity to step on to the practice court with Murray and Ivan Lendl, suddenly the injury no longer seemed so bad.

Murray and James Corden's friendship began when they filmed a sketch for Sport Relief. When Murray was also invited on to Corden's *A League of Their Own*, the Scot was asked to perform the tennis version of the William Tell stunt by serving a ball to knock an object off the top of the host's head. Murray and Corden would go double-dating together, including to Murray's favourite restaurant, Nobu. So it was hardly surprising that Corden, who was in New York to finish the Broadway run of *One Man, Two Guvnors*, used a free afternoon to watch Murray play at the 2012 tournament. But the pair wouldn't be going out for dinner during the US Open, as Murray didn't want to change his routine or to be distracted from his goal of 'leaving everything out there on the court'.

One of the strangest encounters of Murray's life came when he was invited to No 10 Downing Street, and he ended up playing tennis with Prime Minister David Cameron in the State Dining Room. The room had been cleared of furniture before a reception for all the players who had qualified for the season-ending championships in London in 2010, and Cameron challenged Murray to a game; they came very close to hitting the chandeliers.

'I was scared as I didn't want to break anything. The Prime Minister was hitting the ball really hard at me,' Murray has recalled. 'I have no idea if everything in there is incredibly expensive but it looked very old-fashioned. There was a chandelier above where the dining table would normally have been. Some of the balls flew dangerously close to it. Mr Cameron definitely looked like he knew what he was doing. He spoke about tennis with a lot of knowledge and said that he tried to play a couple of times a month. He also explained how he'd had to change his grip as he had grown up using a wooden racket. These are strange experiences. When I played Wimbledon for the first time, it was a huge shock to me. But playing tennis at No 10 Downing Street? That's not something anyone would ever think they would do.'

Murray's meeting with the Queen, on the members' balcony at the All England Club after a second-round match at the 2010 Wimbledon Championships, was more controlled. In the days leading up to the Queen's visit – which was to be her first to the tournament since Virginia Wade won the ladies' singles in 1977 – there had been some speculation as to whether Murray would bow before her. You got the impression that it was the same people who had attacked Murray for his joke about the England football team who were now hoping that he was going to make a faux-pas, and then they could bash him for being a chippy, Scottish republican. Murray was understandably annoyed, and that probably made him more nervous, affecting his technique – when he watched the slow-motion replays, it confirmed his initial thoughts, which was that his bow had been far from perfect.

Murray has always taken the most pleasure from meeting other athletes, as he has appreciated the chance to talk about training and the demands of other sports. In addition to his friendships and acquaintances with boxers – Ricky Hatton has been his guest at a grand slam – he has also spent some time with Beckham. As early as 2005, Beckham was speaking about Murray's 'exciting talent'. And soon after Murray started his association with XIX Entertainment, he spent the day with the Beckhams as they promoted the Malaria No More initiative with an appearance at Wembley Stadium and by meeting Gordon Brown, the then Prime Minister, at Downing Street.

Murray's memories of the day were how normal Brown was, and also that Beckham gave him a pair of football boots, though the tennis player felt as though he had not impressed anyone with the quality of the free-kicks he had taken on the Wembley pitch. One thing is for sure, Murray did not come away from that day hoping to be even half as famous as Beckham. The footballer has since followed Murray closely. There have been times when Beckham has texted members of his management team for real-time updates on Murray's matches at Wimbledon and other grand slams, and when Murray played in his first Wimbledon final, Beckham was there to watch, sitting in the Royal Box with his wife.

Beckham is not the only leading sportsman to have dropped by at the All England Club. Rory McIlroy, the Northern Irish golfer, interrupted one of Murray's training sessions at Wimbledon one summer to say hello, and Lewis Hamilton has also been at Centre Court.

One of the first celebrities to have taken an interest in Murray was Sir Sean Connery, who had watched his fellow Scot play David Nalbandian in the third round of the 2005 Wimbledon Championships. The next day, Connery had phoned Murray. That was a great thrill for Murray, because as a boy he had spent his pocket-money collecting the James Bond films. 'Every December in our electronics store back home, they used to do a two-for-one offer on videos, and they had every single James Bond film. So when you lined them up, you could see the pictures of all the different Bonds,' Murray would tell the *New York Times* during the 2012 US Open. He said that *Goldfinger*, a Connery picture, had been one of his favourite Bond films. And, seven years after becoming a fan, Connery would break into a press conference to pass on his congratulations in person. Murray said afterwards: 'That was cool.'

*

Discussing money is never vulgar at the US Open. It's a tournament that always makes a point during the prize-giving ceremonies of announcing the number of noughts on the cheques, presumably encouraged by the applause from the crowd. It is also where the almost beyond-parody Donald Trump, the billionaire who wears his own range of cologne called Success, takes up residency for the fortnight in his private suite in the Arthur Ashe Stadium, and is treated like a rock star. The total prize-money pot in 2012 was $25.5 million, with the men's and women's champions to each receive a cheque for $1.9 million. Even for those who had performed well in the US Open Series, the events leading up to New York, there were bonuses.

So when *Forbes* magazine – the publication for the super-rich and the super-envious – produced a list during the tournament of the highest-earning tennis players of the past 12 months, it was bound to generate discussion, even if no one should have been at all surprised that Roger Federer was at the top, with an estimated annual income of $54.3 million. In the six years leading up to the 2012 US Open, *Forbes* calculated that Federer had earned close to a quarter of a billion dollars. (About the only way that Federer could possibly have made more money would have been if he had been born American, as that would have allowed him to have best exploited the American market, but that is debatable as being Swiss is also a commercial advantage; no one is ever offended when Federer says he's from neutral Switzerland.)

Next on the *Forbes* list was Rafa Nadal, on $32.4 million, followed by Maria Sharapova ($27.1 million), Novak Djokovic

($19.8 million), Li Na ($18.4 million), Serena Williams ($16.3 million) and Caroline Wozniacki ($13.7 million). Andy Murray was in eighth position, with *Forbes* calculating that, in the period between July 2011 and July 2012, he had made $12 million.

From reading those numbers you might consider it odd that one of the talking points of the 2012 season had been whether tennis players were grossly under-paid. But this was a debate which mostly centred around the sport's B-, C- and D-listers, who even talked about the possibility of boycotting one of the grand slams unless they were paid more for losing in the early rounds, arguing that they had been unable to make much profit because of the costs of touring. Boycotting one of the slams would have been a guaranteed public relations disaster for the locker room, as whatever the reality, the perception would have been of multi-millionaire tennis players striking over pay in the middle of a global recession. The A-list were doing fine, even if a few of the sport's most recognisable faces also wondered, with an eye on golf, and also on the high percentage of revenue which went to the athletes in American sports, whether everyone was due a pay-rise.

For the elite, prize-money was just the start. The breakdown of the headline figures in the *Forbes* list confirmed that most of their income was not from prize-money, but from endorsement contracts, appearance fees and playing exhibition matches. Tennis is an attractive sport for companies wanting to reach an affluent demographic, and especially an affluent female audience. Murray's figure was broken down into $5 million in prize-money and $7 million in other earnings. Around $6 million of that second number was estimated to have come from sponsors and $1 million from appearances and exhibitions. Going into the final grand slam of 2012, Murray had four major partners – with clothing manufacturers Adidas, the Royal Bank of Scotland, Swiss watch-makers Rado, and Head rackets.

According to the 2012 *Sunday Times* Rich List, which had appeared a few months before the US Open, Murray was, for want of a much better word, 'worth' £24 million, which was not bad for someone in their mid-twenties and only halfway through their career who was yet to win a slam. Tim Henman, by contrast, was said to have amassed 'only' £17 million. About the only people in their twenties on that money list who had earned comparable amounts to Murray either played football or had acted in the Harry Potter films.

A tennis player's most lucrative contract tends to be with his clothing and shoe sponsor, and Murray didn't appear to have broken that industry rule. In 2010, he began a five-year association with Adidas that was believed to pay him around £3 million a year. It was a good bit of business for Murray and 19 Entertainment as he had previously been operating at a much lower level – he had worn Fred Perry clothes, and had not even had a shoe sponsor, just wearing whatever trainers suited him and sometimes swapping from one brand to another when he changed surfaces. It was extremely unlikely that Nike, the American sportswear giant, would have signed Murray, as they already had Federer and Nadal as their male ambassadors, with

Sharapova and Serena Williams endorsing their women's lines; the Scot was not going to do better than Adidas.

As part of the deal, Murray would have access to the travelling team of coaches and consultants paid for by Adidas; it was a facility that he would make use of when he was between Miles Maclagan and Ivan Lendl. And while Federer and Nadal's contracts with Nike stipulated that they had to have 'clean' shirts, in other words with no other sponsors' logos anywhere, Murray was permitted by Adidas to have a couple of patches on his sleeves. That advertising space on Murray's arms was an important part of any negotiations with other companies. Murray played one Australian Open with nothing on his cotton billboard; his management company had unpicked the patches as they renegotiated the deals with sponsors other than Adidas. During the summer of 2012, one newspaper reported that Murray's agents were looking at the possibility of doing a deal 'with a film studio to advertise blockbuster releases on his shirt'.

There was considerable doubt among the tennis industry, though, whether it had been a smart move by Adidas executives to have ended their association with Djokovic so that they could start a new one with Murray. When the decision was made, Djokovic already had one grand slam title, which he had won at the 2008 Australian Open, and Murray was of course still without a major. At that stage, both Murray and Djokovic were trailing Federer and Nadal, and no one, certainly not any of the executives at Adidas, could have foreseen what would happen during the 2011 season when the Serbian won three of the four grand slams, with only the French Open eluding him.

For so long, he had been the third man of tennis, but no one had ever had such a brilliant season, not even Federer at his peak. Djokovic's success continued into 2012, when he won the Australian Open for his fifth grand slam title, and at that year's French Open he came within one match of becoming the first man since Rod Laver in 1969 to hold all four major titles simultaneously; only Nadal stood in the way. One respected industry figure was of the opinion that Adidas's decision to drop Djokovic and hire Murray was starting to look like 'a colossal mistake'. Djokovic was having so much success that Sergio Tacchini, the Italian company which had sponsored him after he was ditched by Adidas, had to wriggle out of the contract because they could no longer afford to pay all the win bonuses and other fees due to him (by the 2012 US Open, he was a few months into a new partnership with a Japanese company, Uniqlo).

While Murray had worn the three stripes, he had already lost three grand slam finals – at the 2010 and 2011 Australian Opens, and at the 2012 Wimbledon Championships – with the second of those coming against Djokovic, by the time he arrived at the 2012 US Open. Murray also lost to Djokovic in the semifinals of the 2012 Australian Open. There would have been some relief at Adidas, one has to imagine, when Murray became the Olympic champion. But, to make the partnership truly worthwhile, they wanted to see him win a grand slam.

Murray's relationship with the Royal Bank of Scotland, which had started when he was a teenager, was not without controversy. After the bank was bailed out by the taxpayer, there was a close examination of some of the sponsorship deals which had been signed off during the boom years, and Murray came under considerable pressure, from newspapers's City diaries and elsewhere, to volunteer for a significant reduction in his annual fee from RBS.

An important moment in Murray's commercial life was the announcement at the start of the 2012 grass-court season that he would be sponsored by Rado. Federer was a Rolex ambassador and Nadal wore a £250,000 Richard Mille watch which, at a time of Spanish financial crisis, seemed to some almost to border on the obscene; and now Murray had his own watch-deal.

Even so, there was no getting away from the fact that Murray was a long way from earning anything like the money which Federer and Nadal did from off-court deals. According to *Forbes*, Federer was paid an estimated $45 million and Nadal $25 million. Federer and Nadal each had around double Murray's number of sponsors.

When the US Open began, Murray was nothing like as attractive to sponsors as some of his colleagues were. While his nationality was worth a few million dollars or pounds a year to Murray, because of Wimbledon and the British tennis market, he did not have anything approaching the same international appeal as Federer, Nadal or female players such as Sharapova or Serena Williams. Murray certainly wasn't in the position to have even attempted what Sharapova did on the eve of the tournament in Manhattan, launching her own range of 'candy' that she was calling – don't laugh – Sugarpova.

Andy Murray: Champion

Those New Yorkers who didn't like Sharapova's sweets could instead buy some shoes she had designed, or eat a Federer-branded chocolate truffle or purchase some underwear from Wozniacki's range of lingerie. Some, such as Serena Williams, have been extremely proactive about using their brand to make money, with the Californian regularly making personal appearances on a home shopping network to push her own designs of clothes and jewellery. The week before the US Open, her older sister Venus had been in the Hamptons relaunching her clothing line, EleVen. Those sort of commercial opportunities – whether Murray wanted them or not – were not yet available to him.

There had been suggestions that perhaps Murray could have done better with his off-court business. That was no criticism of XIX Entertainment, and how they were handling his account, as the suspicion was that Murray himself was not as keen as others to chase every endorsement pound, dollar or euro as, with every deal he made with a sponsor, he would have to sign away a certain number of days per year and that would cut into his time for training, tournaments and recovery. It would be naive in the extreme to believe that Murray never had a thought in his head about hard cash, as almost every tennis player has a good sense of their own worth, but he has certainly never been greedy, or risked compromising his tennis with his commercial activities. When he set out in professional tennis, great wealth wasn't the lure, and he had never stood on a tennis court thinking about the money that was potentially going to flow from his strings. Murray is many things, but he never has been, or never will be, the Scottish Anna Kournikova.

Murray's reluctance to stray too far from tennis, and to push himself as a celebrity, also must have counted against him, with one analyst arguing that he needed 'more exposure outside tennis'. The counter argument, expressed by one marketing executive, was that Murray 'not seeking the limelight or acting up to the cameras would, in many ways, make him more bankable from a sponsorship perspective. He's all about credibility and raw emotion. Those two attributes are everything that almost every brand wants'. Murray's tears at Wimbledon had endeared him to American as well as British fans, but until he won the US Open he would not be a 'name' in the United States beyond the tennis hardcore.

Expectations of Murray's commercial success had been raised by the constant plucking of figures from the air during his career, usually accompanied by a 'Murray Minted' headline. Murray's former agent, Patricio Apey of Ace Group, did the player no great favours when they were working together by saying, 'Sixty million pounds, eighty million pounds, these figures could be dwarfed if things work out for the guy.'

Apey also once said of Murray, when the player was in his teens: 'He doesn't do commercial smiles. He's as genuine as you get. And that's what companies are attracted to.' Michael Henderson countered Apey's observations in the *Guardian*: 'Where does one start to rebuff this guff. First, "genuine". What is "genuine" about behaving in such a churlish, ill-mannered way that you put off people who, in normal circumstances, would be happy to see him prevail. A grumpy teenager is not, nor ever will be, a thing of beauty.' He went on to deconstruct the rest of Apey's comment before concluding with: 'Then, "that's what companies are attracted to". Some of them might be, now, in Britain, but the McBrat act will not play well in all the lands.'

If Murray had been reluctant to sell off parts of himself to corporations, he had never had any great problem with accepting large appearance fees, as taking the money wasn't going to do his tennis any harm. The rules of tennis allowed these fees to be paid at all tournaments apart from the grand slams, the Olympics, the Masters-level events and the season-ending championships. Turning up at Queen's Club, for some grass-court matches before Wimbledon, earned him a six-figure sum before he even started to think about prize-money. Of course, it suited Murray just fine playing Queen's before Wimbledon – and it is unlikely that the British public would have been particularly sympathetic if he had disappeared to Germany to play a tournament the same week because of a guarantee – but the tournament director agreed to pay a substantial fee, even if it's not something that anyone really wants to talk about in public. Queen's with Murray is a totally different tournament to Queen's without Murray (when there would be lower domestic television ratings, less interest from the public, and from sponsors and companies wanting corporate entertainment).

Murray's largest appearance fees are likely to have been paid by promoters in the Middle East, for his appearances at recognised tournaments in Dubai or Doha, or at the pre-season exhibition in Abu Dhabi. And when Murray has gone to the Far East, to tournaments such as the one in Tokyo, it has to be imagined that his guarantees have made the prize-money almost incidental to that week's financial rewards. But Murray was not in the same appearance-money league as Federer and Nadal. Whenever Federer or Nadal competed in the Middle East, each player's guarantee reputedly ran to seven figures. In the spring of 2012, at New York's Madison Square Garden, Federer played an evening of exhibition tennis in exchange for a reported one million dollars.

Simon Fuller and the rest of Murray's management team knew that, if Murray were to win a major, and so becoming Britain's first male grand slam champion of the professional era, he would have much more power in the marketplace (in addition to triggering any bonus clauses in his existing contracts). Depending on which industry figure you spoke to, Murray would double, triple or even quadruple his off-court pay by winning a slam.

'In individual sports, the financial spoils from product endorsements truly go to the largest winners,' *Forbes* magazine had noted. 'And the only way anyone else is going to get a large share of the endorsement pie is to knock off one of the greats – Federer, Nadal or Djokovic – in an epic slam final.' Still, as the same publication had noted, it would have been optimistic for anyone to think that Murray's first slam, however historic for British tennis, was going to propel him to the top of tennis's money list. Even with a first slam, Murray wouldn't have Federer or Nadal's history of success, and he still wouldn't have their polish. Don't think, *Forbes* had argued, that Murray could win his first major and start 'sniffing the Federer-Nadal stratosphere, as those two have simply been too good for too long and have achieved an iconic status in the sport'.

There was a debate to be had over whether winning a first grand slam title at Wimbledon or the US Open would have the greatest impact on Murray's market value. Winning Wimbledon would be the most romantic storyline. But winning the US Open would offer him an excellent introduction to those Americans who didn't follow the sport so closely.

In the beginning, money mattered a great deal to Murray. As a teenager, Murray had always been uncomfortable asking his parents for money. 'Mum and Dad always said, "Make sure you have enough money with you, make sure you take enough money out," but Jamie and I never really did like taking money. Then once I started to make money, I started to appreciate it even more. When you spend your first pay cheque and start being able to pay for things yourself, it's a very nice feeling.' When Murray went to North America in the summer of 2005, one of the motivations for playing so many tournaments appeared to be financial gain, because he no longer wanted to be reliant on his parents. Murray's first pay cheque – which he received at one of those Futures tournaments on the lowest level of professional tennis – was around £100. No one needed to tell him that he was now playing, at the 2012 US Open, for 'ridiculous' amounts of money.

*

Andy Murray's red Ferrari didn't last long. He didn't sell the car because of the cost of insurance, though that was high, but because he felt like a complete prat in it; he could no longer stand the embarrassment of sitting in the Ferrari at a red light or when parking the vehicle. It was a poseur's car, and he wasn't a poseur. People kept honking him at the lights. 'I'm quite a conservative driver, but when I was driving that I'd get beeped just for getting out of the car.' So Murray bought a more under-stated, elegant car, a gun-metal Aston Martin, and in 2012 he would be seen driving a Jaguar convertible.

But Murray doesn't spend all his time in fast cars. During Wimbledon 2012, for instance, he could have been driven in each day in an official tournament car, with a chauffeur and darkened windows; instead he preferred to travel from his Surrey village to the All England Club in the passenger seat of his friend's Volkswagen Golf. One spring at the French Open, he decided against taking a car on the way to a dinner in Paris, so he walked into the Metro and got lost beneath the city, an experience he almost appeared to enjoy.

A decent chunk of Murray's money has gone on properties. He knew he was fortunate when, at the age of 22, he was in a position to buy a house worth around £5 million. He has also bought a couple of apartments in Miami, and it has been said that they are big enough that when his whole entourage are in the city he can give them all a room each. Murray has other investments. His prize-money and endorsement cheques are passed to his accountant to manage.

Beyond the interest in fast cars, Murray has never been

particularly materialistic. When he set out on the tour, he didn't own much apart from his rackets, shoes, clothes, a bag and a PlayStation, and though he can now buy himself pretty much anything he desires, he doesn't feel the need to fill his house with shiny objects that he doesn't want or need: 'I haven't spent shocking amounts on myself because I don't need anything.' If Murray wasn't sponsored by Rado, you have to wonder whether he would ever wear a watch off court at tournaments. And while he had fun wearing a tuxedo for *Vogue*, clothes don't usually excite him. Spending money on others gives Murray more pleasure; though he once said that he would never buy underwear as a present.

Not all the money that Murray has earned should be seen as profit. Simon Fuller's XIX takes a percentage. And Murray must pay his staff; Ivan Lendl's contract would in all likelihood have entitled him to several hundred thousands pounds a year, plus bonuses. In addition, Murray has to pay for his entourage's travel expenses. Tennis players are extremely well-treated at tournaments. When Murray played at the season-ending tournament in Shanghai in 2008, for instance, the hotel had produced personalised bed linen and robes for him, so he had his name on his pillow and on the back of his dressing-gown. But living on the road is not cheap. So while Murray has not always bought first-class plane and Eurostar tickets, he has been extremely irritated if people have ever invoked the stereotype of the mean Scot.

If Murray was that desperate to hoard his money, he would have joined all number of other tennis players by moving to

Monaco (it has always seemed a little odd that Novak Djokovic, the great patriot who led Serbia to victory in the Davis Cup, avoids his country's taxes by retreating to a Monte Carlo apartment between tournaments). Murray doesn't see enough of his friends and family as it is. Moving to the Cote d'Azur, for more money and less time with those he cares about, is not something he has ever considered for a New York minute, for even an instant.

Mother Nature plainly isn't a tennis fan. Or at least she has no great love for the US Open. Sir Alex Ferguson may well suggest that 'Scotland had invented the wind', but Andy Murray had never experienced conditions like this at Dunblane Sports Club. In Scotland, you very rarely find yourself playing tennis in the high winds and high farce whipped up by an approaching tornado.

On so-called Super Saturday, with a gale blowing around the Arthur Ashe Stadium as Murray and Tomas Berdych attempted to play their semi-final, the look on the pair's faces alternated between exasperation and amusement. As if trying to follow the ball in a howling wind was not enough to contend with – the worst was when one of Murray's groundstrokes suddenly took a sharp right, and many other shots were stopping, moving and then stopping again – the semi-finalists also had to look out for objects flying through the air. Murray's chair took flight, and when it landed on to the concrete, it left a dark mark on the court surface, a bit like a tyre mark at a crash site. Murray felt fortunate that someone had got the furniture back under control; it would have been hugely unfortunate for his tournament to have been torpedoed by a collision with a chair. Paper napkins, pages of newspapers, ketchup-smeared hot-dog wrappers, ticket stubs, cellophane, paper cups, and all the other detritus of an American tennis crowd, was airborne. One ball-kid didn't have the strength to keep hold of the umbrella attached to Berdych's chair, so he called a friend over for help, and now the two of them were clinging on.

If, as a boy, Murray had ever experienced something similar in Stirlingshire – he didn't – he and his opponent would have walked off court as to continue would have been ridiculous. As a professional, Murray had once played two miserable sets of tennis in a desert sand-storm, in the final of the Indian Wells tournament in California, but there was no doubt in his mind that these were the worst conditions he had ever competed in, nothing less than 'brutal'.

Suspending this match was never an option presented to the players. Neither was closing the roof, as the Arthur Ashe Stadium didn't have one. While it was just about possible to understand why the stadium didn't have a roof – the United States Tennis Association had built it so big and open-plan in the 1990s that they were now struggling to find a way of covering the court – it was harder to appreciate why the tournament had never used covers and tarpaulins to prevent puddles and flooding (the reason given was something inexplicable relating to drainage). So the groundstaff had much drying and squeegeeing to do before the semi-final started late.

The wind generated a little controversy in the opening set when it blew Murray's baseball cap to the ground. As Murray's hat had dropped while a point had still been live, Berdych claimed the headgear had been distraction. The players came to the net, their pointed discussion moderated by the umpire, with Murray asking Berdych whether he was a hundred per cent sure that the cap had been a hindrance. The point was replayed, Murray's serve was broken, he threw his 'nonsense, nonsense, nonsense' hat aside and lost the set. It was just as well that Murray has a good tennis brain and plenty of resolve, as someone with a bit less intelligence and a bit less gumption could easily have fumed and grumbled their way to a straight-sets defeat.

Murray had always thought playing in the wind was a great skill. You couldn't always expect to play tennis in perfect conditions. Murray had noticed how Ivan Lendl would take extra interest in televised golf tournaments when the wind picked up, as he wanted to see how the players adjusted their technique and minds. The difference between tennis and golf is that golfers could talk to their caddies about strategy; Murray had to work out for himself the best way to adapt his game to the weather.

When playing into the gale, he kept the ball as slow as possible, flattening out his groundstrokes, and using slice whenever possible. Using topspin from that end would have been madness, as the wind would have got hold of the ball and slowed it up, and Berdych would then have controlled the rally. When Murray had the wind behind him, he used topspin as much as he could and attempted to dictate points.

As the match continued – they would be out there in the wind for the best part of four hours – it gradually became apparent that it was actually no bad thing for Murray to have played Berdych in what appeared to be the set of a disaster movie, *Tornado Tennis*, or somesuch. On a still day, Berdych's serve would have been a weapon, but the wind was causing so many problems with his high ball-toss that establishing any rhythm was impossible. Plus, on a calm day when Berdych could accurately predict the flight of the ball, and adjust his feet accordingly, he would have regularly been getting into position and unloading with his forehand.

Another factor was Murray's mental resilience. Berdych has the hardware to win grand slams – the build, the serve and the forehand – but there had always been doubts about whether he had the mental software to go with it. Murray won the second and third sets so easily that the watching Boris Becker would remark that Berdych had 'one of the most fragile minds in men's tennis', as well as suggesting that the Eastern European looked as though he was just 'going through the motions' in his first US Open semi-final.

Murray had found a way of coping mentally, and Berdych plainly hadn't. Murray was getting on with trying to win the semi, and Berdych was thinking that there should have been a rule in place to stop the match, as would happen when the rain was lashing it down. This is impossible, Berdych seemed to be saying to himself as he tried to get the ball into court. If a thought bubble had appeared over Murray's head, it would have said, 'This wind is doing me absolutely no harm at all.' While Berdych was much more competitive in the fourth set, Murray held firm for a 5-7, 6-2, 6-1, 7-6 victory, and so won the prize of a fifth appearance in a grand slam final, and the congratulations of a couple of boozy knights.

Some had been calling it the CBS Open, the implication being that this was an event run by and for television executives. For years, the tournament had persisted with the television-friendly Super Saturday, which meant that the two winning semi-finalists would be scheduled to play the final around 24 hours later (and they could only walk on court once the last of that Sunday afternoon's American football matches had finished). At all other slams, there was at least a day between the semi-finals and the final. So, even at the best of times, the schedule in New York could be controversial, as whoever won the second semi-final could be at a considerable disadvantage, with extremely limited recovery and preparation time.

Back-loading the schedule also ran another risk: that the weather could throw everything off, as there would be no days left to play with. It had taken time for the tournament to appreciate that change was required, and the 2012 US Open would see the last of the Super Saturdays, as, even before the chaos of the rain, wind and tornado warnings, the United States Tennis Association had agreed, under pressure from the players, to schedule a day off between the semis and the final from 2013 onwards. While the USTA said that Super

Saturday had been a strong platform, they recognised that 'the physicality of the game has changed', that it was no longer wise or kind to ask the players to compete over successive days.

A former head of CBS Sports made an interesting point in an interview with the *New York Times*, saying that killing off Super Saturday could have financial implications for the players, that the locker-room had lobbied for a move which could hurt their earning power. 'You could make an argument that the reason these guys make so much money is from that exposure. If they change it, they change the economics of it. Life's a trade off.'

After coming off court, Berdych argued that the semi-final should have been suspended: 'I think our sport deserves to have some rules if the conditions are like that. We are here in the States where they really love a show. Actually, this was not a show. This was just about someone trying to deal with the conditions and then trying to put the ball over the net.' Apart from rain, were there any other weather conditions that would persuade the US Open to suspend a match? We had the answer soon enough. David Ferrer was leading 5-2 – Novak Djokovic's head was all over the place, and he was telling the umpire that the conditions were unplayable – when the match was stopped because of a tornado warning, and the site was evacuated. The tornado would miss by a matter of miles, taking down power cables.

Not even the US Open would ask a player to complete a semi-final and contest a final on the same day. So, with Djokovic and Ferrer to resume their semi on Sunday, it meant that the men's final of the US Open would be played on a Monday for the fifth year in succession (there was also disruption to the women's tournament with the final, between Serena Williams and Victoria Azarenka, moved from Saturday evening to Sunday). The men's final would start around 4pm on Monday afternoon, which wasn't the scheduling to make a television executive cut the end off a Cuban cigar. 'The Monday finals the past four years were a sweet coda to the hectic two weeks,' the *New York Times* noted before the conclusion of the 2012 tournament, 'but murder on ratings.'

The US Open had been unlucky with the weather. But the tournament hadn't helped itself with the scheduling and the decision to build such an enormous stadium which meant that building a roof would be hugely complicated and expensive (the Australian Open and Wimbledon already had a retractable roof over their centre courts, while the French Open had announced plans to build a stadium which could be converted into an indoor arena).

The first of that run of five Monday New York finals, in 2008, had also been Murray's first grand slam final. On that occasion, the weather and the schedule had worked against him. Roger Federer, having finished his semi-final on the Saturday, had a full day off before the final. Murray's semi-final with Rafa Nadal had been incomplete on Saturday night and had to be finished on Sunday. That was another factor working against Murray in his first major final, the other being the great gap in experience.

This time, Murray would be the one who had a day of rest

before a Monday final, as Djokovic and Ferrer had a match to finish on Sunday. The tornado, or at least the threat of it, had helped to save Djokovic's tournament, as his head was a mess in the wind. Had they continued, he could have found himself in a much worse situation. As it was, they played only seven games on Saturday, and when they resumed the next day, on a calm afternoon, it was a totally different match. It was too late for Djokovic to do anything about the opening set – the first set he had lost all tournament – but he won the next three. If Murray was to win his first grand slam, he wouldn't have to beat Federer or Nadal in the final, but he would have to defeat arguably an even tougher opponent on this surface – Djokovic was on a 27-match winning run at hard-court grand slams.

All of Britain's Olympic medallists would parade through London on that Monday. A few hours later, on the other side of the Atlantic, Murray would have the opportunity to keep the summer rolling (as well as doing something which no living British man had ever achieved). It had already been quite a summer for Murray, what with playing in his first Wimbledon final and winning Olympic gold. And now, for the first time, he had reached two grand slam finals in one season. So, once again, Murray was one match victory away from achieving his lifetime ambition, and there was little chance of Sir Sean Connery and Sir Alex Ferguson missing the final.

Murray's boyhood idol wished him well, too. 'I don't know if I'm speaking from my heart or head, but if there's anybody who deserves a slam – because of the generation he's found himself in, and because he has still put himself out there and created some incredible memories for us – it's Andy,' Andre Agassi had said. 'I'd love to see him get over the finish line. I think he's going to win a tight epic.' As much as Murray wished for the same, there was also some fear mixed in; he was scared about how his life would change if he were to win a grand slam. Relax, Ivan Lendl told him, pretty much all that changes when you win a major is that you are offered the best tables in restaurants and free rounds of golf. Lendl was lying, of course.

7

The First Since Fred

Lady Luck hadn't just stomped on Andy Murray's toes; she had done so in her stilettos. In New York City, as everywhere else in tennis, Murray was trying to deal with two pieces of misfortune. The first was that he had been born into the 'Golden Era of Men's Tennis'.

Of course, for the one-eyed American sports fan in the bleachers – he was easy to spot as he came dressed in his tennis kit and the Stars and Stripes – this didn't look like much of a golden age; nothing like the days when John McEnroe and Jimmy Connors had brought low-brow bitching, high drama and glory, or when Pete Sampras and Andre Agassi had faced off. But Mr US of A was in the minority. Most who had bought a ticket to the 2012 US Open could appreciate and enjoy the international cast, recognising that a quartet of

Europeans – Roger Federer, Rafa Nadal, Novak Djokovic and Murray – were the most talented generation in the sport's history.

In many people's eyes, American or otherwise, Federer is the GOAT; to the uninitiated, that sounds like an insult, but is in fact the biggest compliment he can have about his tennis – that he's the Greatest Of All Time. By beating Murray at the 2012 Wimbledon Championships, Federer had extended his collection of grand slam titles to a record 17, and he had returned to the top of the rankings to move past Sampras' record of 286 weeks as the world number one. Others wondered whether, given time and a good run with pain-free knees, Nadal would go on to have a better career than Federer. Each was probably the best of all time on their preferred surfaces, the Swiss on grass and the Spaniard on clay.

Earlier in the tournament, Andy Roddick had retired from tennis because the 2003 US Open champion and former world number one didn't want to simply 'exist' on tour; existing was about all that was left for him given the dominance of those at the top. For John McEnroe and all other spectators, the golden age of tennis was a great treat, a great spectacle; for Roddick and for Murray, it was nothing less than the hardest era in which to try to win grand slam titles.

Murray kept running into all-time greats, on draw-sheets, on the court and in his head. Just consider that Federer and Nadal had achieved the near-mythical feat of the career grand slam, winning all the four majors at least once. Only seven men in the history of the sport had completed the full set, and two of them were Murray's contemporaries. And, at the 2012 French Open, Djokovic had come within a match of becoming the third man of this generation to achieve the career grand slam. Had he beaten Nadal in the Paris final, he also would have become the first man since Rod Laver in 1969 to hold all four slams simultaneously.

Tennis had never seen anything like this before: Federer, Nadal and Djokovic's domination of tennis was such that from the 2005 French Open until the 2012 US Open, a period spanning more than seven years, the trio had won every grand slam tournament apart from the 2009 US Open, when Juan Martin del Potro had finished as the champion. When the US Open began, Federer, Nadal and Djokovic had some 33 grand slams between them, with Nadal on 11 majors and Djokovic on five. Murray kept on going deep into grand slam fortnights, but without holding a silver or golden trophy above his head. Some wondered whether it was not a Big Four, but a Big Three And A Half.

Murray's second piece of misfortune followed the first. Federer, Nadal and Djokovic had, on each of their first appearances in slam finals, played and beaten opponents who were just as inexperienced with those occasions as they were. Indeed, they came up against players who, in truth, were not quite in the same class. Federer's first slam title came against Australia's Mark Philippoussis at Wimbledon 2003, while Nadal won his first major at the 2005 French Open by beating Argentina's Mariano Puerta, and Djokovic had defeated France's Jo-Wilfried Tsonga in the final of the 2008 Australian

Open. How Murray could have benefited from playing a grand slam final against someone who wasn't one of the greats of modern tennis. But it had never worked out like that for him. Three of Murray's first four grand slam finals had been against Federer – at the 2008 US Open, the 2010 Australian Open and the 2012 Wimbledon Championships – and the other, at the 2011 Australian Open, had been against Djokovic. He had played 13 sets, winning one and losing 12.

Now, at his fifth attempt to win a grand slam final, he would face Djokovic, the defending champion, and quite possibly the greatest mover on hard courts that the sport had ever seen. While Federer and Nadal had always looked more at home on the sport's natural, traditional surfaces – Federer on the turf and Nadal on the *terre battue* (beaten earth) – Djokovic had shown a preference for an 'artificial', man-made court: he was at his best on anything hard and unforgiving on the body.

And nothing's more hard and unforgiving than New York cement. No one has ever squeaked their shoes behind a Flushing Meadows baseline like Djokovic has, performing the sort of lunges and near-splits that you really shouldn't try at home (Boris Becker had watched one of Djokovic's matches earlier in the tournament and had worried about the Serbian's ankles: 'Most other people would have been in hospital now'). To avoid another defeat, all Murray had to do was beat someone who was on an undefeated run of 27 matches at the hard-court slams, a sequence which had included titles at the

2011 Australian and US Opens and the 2012 Australian Open. For Djokovic's last defeat at a hard-court major you had to spool back a couple of years, to the 2010 US Open final, when Nadal, playing his best ever tennis on the surface, had completed his career grand slam.

There had been some thin, less-than-golden periods in men's tennis, such as when Pete Sampras was winding down and before the full flowering of Federer's talent, and had Murray been around then you have to think he would have won a slam before he turned 25. Murray was certainly a greater talent than Roddick, who had experienced both a slam victory and a run at the top of the rankings.

But there wasn't much point in Murray thinking about how life would have been easier at any other time in tennis history, and he certainly never asked for anyone's pity. He was where he was, which was sitting in the locker-room before the 2012 US Open final, feeling more nervous than he had ever been before a big occasion. For all the self-confidence which Murray had gained from winning the London Olympics – a victory which had shown him that he had a place at the top of the sport, as well as showing others that tennis possibly had a Big Three and Three Quarters, if not a Big Four – he had never had butterflies like this before going out to play.

Murray was anxious because he knew that this was going to hurt, that a match against Djokovic would test him both physically and mentally. After all, their semi-final at that year's Australian Open had taken the best part of five hours. But mostly he was apprehensive because he didn't want to become the first man of the modern era to lose his first five appearances in slam finals. Agassi had been the runner-up in his first three, so had Goran Ivanisevic, and his coach Ivan Lendl had lost his first four. But Murray was in danger of breaking new ground. Whatever happened, Murray was going to make history: he was either going to become the first British male to win a grand slam since Fred Perry in 1936, or he was going to be confirmed as the unluckiest man in tennis.

Murray's disappointments during the 2012 grand slam year – coming so close against Djokovic in their Australian Open semi-final and against Federer in the Wimbledon final – had led him to doubt whether he ever would win a major. 'In some ways, I had been preparing myself mentally for it never to happen, to never win a slam,' Murray has disclosed. 'I would say I could live with it if I didn't, but in some ways that was me preparing for the worst.'

The night before, Murray had relaxed in his Manhattan hotel room by playing Scrabble and watching one of his favourite comedies, *The Wedding Crashers*, but now he was in Queens and he couldn't block out the negative thoughts. Lendl had told Murray to enjoy himself on court, as this was the moment that he had dedicated his life to. But that was precisely why Murray could take no pleasure from this match. Had Becker been right when he suggested that the expectation had started to 'eat into' Murray: 'You get to the point where, instead of enjoying reaching a major final, you become weighed down by nerves and expectations.'

It's never quieter in the locker-room than on the day of the final – everyone else has long departed the tournament – and in the last few minutes before Murray was called on to court he sat on a bench with his head full of self-doubt. 'What if I lose this? No one's ever lost his first five finals. I don't want to be that person. Can I do this?'

The conclusion of the 2012 US Open could have been an all-British match. Strange to think now, as Novak Djokovic travels the world on a Serbian diplomatic passport, draws tens of thousands of supporters to rallies in Belgrade's Parliament Square, or shaves his head to celebrate his country's Davis Cup victory, that he once had discussions with Britain's Lawn Tennis Association about the possibility of becoming a British citizen. Had he done so, he would have been playing for Great Britain's Davis Cup team instead.

Those conversations began around the time that Britain played Serbia in a Davis Cup tie in Glasgow in 2006; this was before Djokovic had become rich from the sport so it was understandable that he and his family, who had made so many financial sacrifices to get him that far, considered taking some of the LTA's money for what would have been a more comfortable existence. The discussions continued. Though the Djokovic family did not have any British ancestry, he could have qualified under the residency rules. The LTA's funding wasn't the only temptation: Djokovic also thought that the sponsorship opportunities would be better as a Briton than as a Serbian. It was a stressful, uncertain time for Djokovic, who was still a teenager and making his way in the sport, and he mulled over what to do. But then he had a moment of clarity saying to himself: 'Why the heck? I am Serbian, I am proud of being Serbian. If I play for Great Britain, deep inside, I'm never going to feel like I belong.'

If Djokovic had said yes to the switch, that would have had a huge impact on the course of Murray's tennis life. It is highly questionable whether the British public would have ever truly accepted Djokovic as a British tennis player. Greg Rusedski had qualified through his mother, who was born in Yorkshire, and there had been still those who had questioned what he was doing in a Union flag bandanna, and in a Davis Cup team with Tim Henman. The term of abuse for Djokovic would have been 'plastic Brit'; even after he won his first grand slam at the 2008 Australian Open (which, had he defected, would have been Britain's first in men's tennis for 72 years) he would have been called that.

Perhaps, in some ways, having Djokovic as a British tennis player, plastic or otherwise, would have helped Murray as there wouldn't then have been such scrutiny of his efforts to win his first major. But it also would have taken away much of the significance of any slam that Murray won; if it hadn't been so long since a British man last won a slam, there would not have been the same interest and emotional investment in the career of the player from Stirlingshire. In this counter-factual account of modern tennis history, it's also worth thinking whether Djokovic would have had the season he did in 2011 – winning three grand slams – if he had been British rather than Serbian. One of the factors that propelled Djokovic to such heights had been the pride and confidence he had taken from Serbia winning the Davis Cup for the first time at the end of 2010. Even if Djokovic and Murray had won the competition for Britain, would it have felt so special for someone who had learnt to play the sport halfway up a Serbian mountain?

Even without playing for the same country in the Davis Cup and the Olympics, there was plenty to link Murray and Djokovic. Both were born in May 1987, separated by just a week, with Murray the older. Pretty much ever since they had played as 11-year-olds in a junior tournament in the French town of Tarbes, near the Pyrenees, Murray had been compared and contrasted with Djokovic. While Roger Federer and Rafa Nadal have been the iconic players of this generation, Djokovic has arguably been a more central figure in Murray's competitive life. Nadal is just a year older than Murray and Djokovic, and Nadal had also been a rival in junior tennis, but, on the main tour, the Majorcan had always been ahead of the game on the senior tour, winning his first slam just after turning 19.

Murray won easily that day in Tarbes, at an event known as Les Petits As, beating Djokovic for the loss of just one game. But Murray would never again have such a lop-sided victory against Djokovic, and for long periods since those early days it has seemed as though he has been trying to catch up with the Eastern European. Djokovic was the first to make the top 100, and then he was the first to break into the top 10, and then he had been the first to win a grand slam. But for three years after that first slam, he could not win another, and he went back to being the third man of tennis, behind Federer and Nadal, with Murray following on as the world number four. During that time, there wasn't much between Djokovic and Murray, since the Scot was making grand slam finals.

But then, in 2011, Djokovic did so much more than winning another slam; he won three, he dominated, and he ended the Roger-and-Rafa duopoly. Djokovic now had a stronger mind, a stronger body and a stronger game. The quality of Federer and Nadal's tennis had forced Djokovic to become a better tennis player. In 2012, he had won a fifth slam, the Australian Open, and then almost a sixth at the French Open.

There was also no doubt that Murray had become a better tennis player because of the era he was playing in. Like Djokovic, he had had to push himself even harder if he was to have any chance of scoring a grand slam title. In another age, Murray could have been a worse tennis player and a multiple grand slam champion.

There weren't going to be any great tactical surprises in the Arthur Ashe Stadium. They had been playing against each other since the juniors – though there had been a two-year break during their senior careers when they had not played each other at all because, as third and fourth in the world, they were always on other sides of the draw, and so, with Federer and Nadal around, the chances of them playing a final together were always slim. The pair had also practised together on a regular basis, as well as occasionally playing doubles. And while they were not as close as they had been as teenagers – as Djokovic said, 'Common sense tells you we couldn't hang out' – they still sent each other text messages when the other had won a tournament. Or, in Djokovic's case, when he had been on a long weekend in Scotland, he sent a photograph to Murray to prove he hadn't been far from Dunblane. And on the Saturday of the final weekend, before their respective semi-finals, they had sat down together in front of a computer to watch Scotland and Serbia play a scoreless draw in a World Cup qualifying match. They watched the match in near-silence.

The US Open final would be their 15th match together as adults. Going into the final, Djokovic had won eight of their 14 matches, including their two previous encounters at the slams, the 2011 Australian Open final and the 2012 Australian Open semi-final, but Murray had come out on top in six of the last ten meetings. Murray knew what rubber-legged Djokovic was capable of on a hard court: ludicrous movement, ludicrous defence, ludicrous attack. To have a chance of beating Djokovic, Murray would have to turn in one of the best performances of his life. He knew he would have to give everything, although at the time he wouldn't have known that that would include a couple of toenails (they would turn black and drop off). For the first time during the tournament, he took painkillers before a match.

While the weather had calmed down since Super Saturday, the conditions were far from straightforward, and the match started in the swirl of another windy New York afternoon. That was no bad thing for Murray. He had shown, in beating Tomas Berdych in the semi-finals, that he could handle himself in the wind, while Djokovic had been befuddled in the opening stages of his match with David Ferrer. The *New York Times* noted, during the final, that Murray seemed to understand the wind: 'Murray, with his wind-blasted hair and his lean visage, looked like Bob Dylan in the post-Newport electric period: focused, intense, brilliant, but with a level of dishevelment that couldn't possibly be contrived, as he leaned and loafed at his ease, absorbing Djokovic's pace with the aplomb of a musician in a deep, timeless jam.'

During the early exchanges, as Murray and Djokovic found their range and rhythm, it became apparent that the crowd favoured the Briton. There were a couple of reasons for that. One was pro-Murray: those Wimbledon tears, which had shown the American tennis public just how badly Murray wanted to win one of these grand slam trophies. The other was anti-Djokovic: some of the US Open regulars had never quite forgiven him for his mini-feud with Andy Roddick, when he had reacted badly to the American's comments about the Serbian's fitness four years earlier. Ordinarily, Djokovic would have had the charm and the wit and the game – this was his fourth US Open final – for America to have grown very fond of him. But anyone who dares to speak ill of Roddick in New York is going to have to work hard to be the crowd's friend. Murray could tell Djokovic all about how a sentence or two out of place can stay on your record for years.

Despite the pre-match butterflies, the gusting wind and the unforced errors, Murray looked to be playing with purpose. Doubtless he had been encouraged and emboldened by his victory over Djokovic on an English grass court, in the semi-finals of the Olympics. Murray also should have taken something from his performance against the same opponent at that January's Australian Open; though he had lost, it had been mightily close.

The opening set in New York will be remembered for the 54-shot rally, which ended when Murray missed with his forehand. And for the tiebreak. Tennis fans of a certain vintage often talk about 'The Tiebreak', or 'The War of 18-16', which came in the 1980 Wimbledon final between John McEnroe and Bjorn Borg; 32 years later, Murray and Djokovic's shootout didn't contain quite so many points, but it was almost its equal for tension. The tape of Murray and Djokovic's 24-minute 'breaker' is going to get the television networks through a few rain-delays in years to come. Murray, having trailed 2-5, had set points at 6-5, 7-6, 8-7, 9-8 and 10-9, and you started to wonder how he would deal with the possible psychological trauma of losing the set. But, when Djokovic could not get his service return to land in the court, Murray converted his sixth set point, taking the tiebreak 12-10.

That first set, lasting almost an hour and a half, had all been too much for Sir Sean Connery, and he took a short break, leaving his seat in the presidential box (the New York equivalent of Wimbledon's Royal Box).

It was around the time that Murray took a 4-0 lead in the second set that Boris Becker, watching in the stadium, said of Djokovic, 'He's been stabbed in the heart and is starting to bleed' (the German, a former champion, was about the only person who could talk like that and not sound utterly ridiculous). But Djokovic wasn't about to give Murray the set. There was plenty more angst to come before Murray took a two-set lead. Djokovic got back into the set, breaking Murray when he served for the set at 5-4. Had this gone to another shoot-out – as it was, Djokovic was broken when he served at 5-6, after a game which included a big mistake by the Serbian with an overhead – you have to think that Connery would have needed another long break. This was a fraught night for everyone in the stadium. Sir Alex Ferguson was seat-surfing in the back row of Murray's guest box, and feeling helpless; he was accustomed to watching sport and having a degree of control over what was happening in front of him; but now there wasn't anything he could do but watch and wave his arms about.

The apologies were flowing on CBS, the host broadcaster. Sorry, they said, to all those viewers who had tuned in expecting *How I Met Your Mother* and *Two Broke Girls*, but we're going to be staying with the tennis into prime-time. And sorry, too, for Andy Murray's language when he was shooting his mouth off near the microphones: 'Take your time, you d—;' 'F—, man, f—;' 'My f——— legs feel like jelly now.' There was something unintentionally comic about that last cry, which led to the word jelly trending worldwide on Twitter. Not every burst of self-admonishment from Murray's lips needed to be immediately followed by an apology from the network. There was the moment when Murray – he has always been his hardest critic – railed at himself, 'The one shot you have to practise, the one thing, stupid.' It all added up to the sound of a tennis player who, having led by two sets to love, was now having to stop the night and his career imploding on him.

People shouldn't have been that surprised that the final was turning against Murray; for all those who wished him well, there had almost been an agony in watching the match going so well for a couple of sets, as they just knew that it wouldn't last. It just couldn't last. Murray had never had it easy in his tennis life, so who really imagined that this was going to pass off without too many complications, that he was going to win in straight sets? Especially as the man on the other side of the net was Novak Djokovic, who, over the past couple of years, had developed a reputation in New York for producing his best tennis when it looked as though he was close to defeat. In both 2010 and 2011, he had saved a couple of match points when playing Roger Federer in the semi-finals of the US Open before going on to victory.

Once again, Djokovic kept his very best for when he really needed it. Undoubtedly it helped that he had stopped falling over. For someone with a reputation for being such an athletic and confident mover around a hard court, it was curious how many times he had gone splat in the first couple of sets, and American television had started an on-screen count of the number of times he lost his footing. In the third and fourth sets Djokovic was a man transformed; he was staying on his feet – no doubt helped by a new pair of shoes – and he couldn't have put any more into his tennis or puffed out his chest any more. By then, he couldn't have cared less that he had 'skinned' both knees.

So the man with the rubber legs was now out-playing the man with the jelly legs. And perhaps Murray hadn't got his tactics quite right in the third and fourth sets, as the wind had lost some of the strength it had during the first couple of stanzas. When Murray later went through the match in his head, he would consider that, when the wind had died down a little, there should have been a change in strategies. But it's easy to think clearly when the match is done and you're off the court. Clarity of thought doesn't come easily in the white heat of a US Open final. Murray, still in high-winds mode, was perhaps guilty of guiding the ball and aiming for the centre of the court; and that allowed Djokovic, who had already decided that he was going to swing at everything worth swinging at, to control many of the points. Djokovic was, as Andy Roddick sometimes said, directing traffic.

Just as Murray had doubted himself before the match in the locker-room, so he was now questioning himself on court. He was thinking, 'What's gone on here the last couple of sets? What can I do to change it?' When Djokovic levelled the final, after taking the third and fourth sets 6-2 and 6-3, he had the momentum. He also had everyone looking through the history books; he was attempting to become the first man since Pancho Gonzales, the winner over Ted Schroeder in 1949, to recover from two sets down in a US Open final. It was time for the most important pee of Murray's life.

*

Sometimes Mats Wilander, who has seven grand slam titles and an excellent tennis brain, can go too far with his criticism of the modern generation. During Roger Federer's defeat by Rafa Nadal in the semi-final of the 2012 Australian Open, Wilander had likened the Swiss to Van Morrison's 'Village Idiot'. 'This means a lollipop to him,' Wilander said, on noting that Federer was – apparently – walking around the court with a smile on his face. That was not the first time that the Swede had been disparaging about Federer's mental approach, once saying that the GOAT 'lacked balls'.

While occasionally harsh, Wilander is usually right, and as he watched Andy Murray in the third and fourth sets, he was more than a little concerned. Wilander thought Murray was looking as though he wanted to leave the Arthur Ashe Stadium, as if he wanted the experience to be over with. And, if Murray went on to lose, Wilander predicted that the Scot would have 'a window of maybe another year of pleasure' and then would start to hate tennis. Just as Murray's idol, Andre Agassi, had come to hate the sport. Agassi had hated the sport because his father forced it on him; would Murray come to loathe it too because of the agonies and disappointments it kept inflicting on him? There was plenty riding on this fifth set. If Wilander was right, Murray wasn't just playing to win a first grand slam championship, he was playing to stay in love with the sport he had dedicated his life to.

Wilander wasn't the only one who believed that the night would forever define Murray's career. Even before anyone had opened a can of tennis balls, John McEnroe had been suggesting on American television that the final would be 'a crucial moment' in Murray's career. 'Either he turns the corner or it will be a really, really tough one to swallow. And if he wins he will become a whole now player, and he will feel different.'

When Novak Djokovic had taken the match into a decider, McEnroe would have been absolutely convinced that Murray's career was going to go one way or the other; there was now the very real possibility that the Scot could lose a grand slam final from two sets to love up. As the *New Yorker* magazine had noted earlier in the season, 'Tennis, more than most, is a sport dominated by psychological battles – or, at least, it is a sport whose observers fancy themselves experts in psychoanalysis.' That was never more true than when this match went to a fifth set. Among the armchair and studio psychologists the consensus seemed to be this: Murray was just a set away from possibly earning close to a million dollars – the runner-up would receive $950,000 – and having his world ripped apart.

It was common knowledge in tennis how Murray had reacted so badly to past defeats in grand slam defeats, feeling as though he had not only let himself down, but those around him too. After losing an Australian Open final, he had said to his mother backstage, 'I'm so sorry, Mum.' (Shocked, she responded by telling him that he had absolutely nothing to apologise for and that she had been proud of his efforts). And, after both defeats in his Melbourne finals, to Federer in 2010 and to Djokovic in 2011, he had been so badly affected that for months afterwards he had struggled for motivation. After losing grand slam finals, Murray has found himself in a 'why bother?' frame of mind, questioning whether all the effort – and all that time on the practice court, the gym and the track – was really worth it. It's a fallacy that defeat immediately inspires you to work hard; sometimes you find yourself examining whether you had become delusional about your chances.

The Olympics had saved him after the weepy end to the 2012 Wimbledon Championships; without the Games, Murray could have found himself hosting what Maria Sharapova likes to call 'a pity party'. Having to prepare for another tournament at the All England Club meant that he didn't have the time to sit around festering in his own disappointment. No doubt the public's reaction to the tears, and what Murray called 'reconnecting', also helped.

Back in the Arthur Ashe Stadium, this was the first time he had won two sets in a grand slam final. To falter from here would keep the stereotype of the British 'loser' going; of the Brit either not talented enough, or too inclined to choke. And while Fred Stolle, an Australian, had lost his first five slam finals, that had been back when tennis was an amateur and more gentle pursuit. Murray was a set away from the greatest moment of his life; he was also a set away from the greatest disappointment any modern tennis player had ever had. Ivan Lendl could speak from experience about how to come back from losing your first four slam finals. Five? Murray would be on his own. And Murray was supposed to enjoy this? This was where the work that Murray had done with Alexis Castorri, a psychologist, would hopefully come into play. 'When I looked at early films of Andy playing, he played with such happiness and excitement, so my initial thought was that he needed to bring back the zest, and I believe that you start that off the court,' said Castorri, who had been talking to Murray throughout the season, after Lendl made the introduction. 'Andy is a creative genius, a tactical and technical genius, so he needed to reconnect with his inner strengths.'

As the fifth set began, you couldn't help but downgrade the importance and the value of Murray's gold medal, with the five-setter in New York confirming that the four grand slams still stand above the Olympics. If Murray were to finish the year as the Olympic champion, but as a double runner-up at the grand slams, at Wimbledon and the US Open, would he look back on the season with something approaching satisfaction? Afraid not. Murray's primary ambition in life was to be a grand slam champion.

Lendl had told Murray that he would never be under as much pressure before a match as he had been before playing in the final of Wimbledon 2012. Watching Murray as he left the court after the fourth set, and then when he returned for the fifth – we weren't to know then about the pep-talk he had given himself – it was becoming more and more difficult to agree with Lendl on that. Was this really any easier to bear for Murray? If anything, this was the more stressful occasion. Murray had never been more nervous before a match. Now, many of Murray's fans in the stadium and across the world, while still hoping and keeping everything crossed, were also preparing themselves for his possible defeat. 'Expect the worst, prepare for the worst, witness the worst – this has been the British way in tennis for years,' noted the *Wall Street Journal.*

From where Lendl was sitting, mostly impassively, there had been indications in the fourth set that Murray was starting to raise his level; the coach thought it looked as though the Scot was coming back into the match. Perhaps, if one or two more of the big points had gone Murray's way, the match could have been over in four sets. But it wasn't. So Murray had taken a loo break that was never really about emptying his bladder, but about standing there in front of the bathroom mirror and telling himself to 'fight', about filling up his head with positive thoughts.

'We all know that it's a war out there. It's very unlikely that you're going to win a match like this in a blow-out, especially against a guy like Novak,' Lendl said later. 'At some point, it's going to come down to who wants it more or how badly do you want it. It's a question of how bad do you want to do this? What price are you going to pay and how can you execute under extreme pressure?'

That night, Lendl thought he would help his player by doing something extraordinary: clapping. There were moments during the final when Murray had glanced over at Lendl and thought that he almost looked bored. But that was just Lendl being Lendl: unmoved, with the same range of facial expressions as a net post. Lendl's decision to break with his own coaching protocol – this was an even bigger event than when he had taken off his baseball cap during Murray's quarter-final with Marin Cilic – was to tell the Scot to keep on doing what he was doing. 'Andy started hitting better forehands and I tried to show him, "That's the way,"' Lendl would later disclose. 'It's a war and he needs every bit of encouragement.' Lendl wasn't the only person in Murray's guest box who helped to give the player the mental fortitude he needed; it was no bad thing having Sir Alex Ferguson sitting with the rest of his entourage.

About the only person, either in the Arthur Ashe Stadium or in front of a television screen, who was in absolutely no doubt that Murray would win was Tim Henman. Even when, in Henman's words, it had 'gone pear-shaped' as Djokovic pulled back two sets, the Englishman still believed that the match would end with Murray as champion. 'I just thought, even during the third and fourth sets, that there was an air of inevitability about this,' said Henman. 'I still thought that Andy was going to do it. I thought to myself, "This is Andy's time." Mentally, Andy was incredibly resilient in that fifth set. He did well to stay in the present tense, and to not think back to past shots and past matches. In the context of what he'd been through, and all the baggage of having lost his first four slam finals, it was an incredible effort.'

Did the darkness help Murray? It was around 8pm when the fifth set began, and they were under floodlights, and into television primetime, which is where the match deserved to be. Daylight wouldn't have done this justice. In New York, the best matches are night matches, and Murray had always loved floodlit concrete. Now was Murray's moment to do what he had implored himself to do when he was in that bathroom: to give everything he had on the court. Every track and Bikram yoga session, and every ice-bath, even every post-training California roll, had contributed in some small way to this.

It was at moments like this, in a one-set shoot-out for a grand slam title, that Murray would have been extremely thankful for the work he had done on his physical conditioning. Throwing yourself around a cement court for almost five hours is not easy on the body; by the time Murray and Djokovic were finished, they would have been on court for four hours and 54 minutes, tying with Lendl and Wilander's match in 1988 for the longest ever final at the US Open. Nerves and fatigue had gripped Murray's legs in the third and fourth sets. But he was a different player in the fifth set. He wasn't physically spent. He had more to give.

Lendl had personal experience of the physical agonies of trying to win a first grand slam. Lendl put so much into beating John McEnroe in the 1984 French Open final – he came from two sets down to do it – that he was mentally and physically exhausted at the end. So much so that he later couldn't even recall talking to a friend in the locker-room. That match also gave Lendl an insight into how one match, or one set, can change a player's reputation. 'When I won my first grand slam, I went from being the guy who could never come up to being the guy who never gives up, but I knew I didn't deserve either of those descriptions.' Here was Murray's opportunity to transform people's perception of him.

On the resumption, the player suffering physically was Djokovic. The defending champion had put so much into squaring the match at two sets all that he was the one now hurting during the baseline exchanges. If Murray was going to lose this match, it was not going to be because he was left wanting, both mentally and physically; it would be because Djokovic had simply played better tennis in the closing stages to retain his title. Djokovic, because he could not move properly, resolved to smack almost everything.

The set could not have started any better for Murray, who broke straightaway after a game that had included a lucky net-cord. That helped to settle him down. He also had New York on his side. 'Having the crowd chant Andy's name, that was magical,' said Murray's manager, Simon Fuller.

There are all sorts of numbers and statistics that you can use to deconstruct and analyse a tennis match. By the time they were finished, Murray would have won just five more points, 160 to Djokovic's 155. Over the five sets, Murray hit fewer winners, 31 to 40. And also made fewer unforced errors, 56 to 65. But, to understand what happened in the shoot-out for the US Open title, the most instructive numbers were those relating to Murray and Djokovic's respective first serves.

During Murray's career, his first-serve percentage had been a periodic concern, because when it dipped too low, he struggled to impose himself on opponents. That is the case with most players, but that eternal tennis truth seemed to apply more to Murray than to anyone else. With Lendl in his corner, Murray had become more adventurous with his forehand, much more willing to hit out. And one of the other important pieces of advice that Lendl had given Murray was to stop hitting so many serves on the practice court, and, by easing off in training, the Scot had found that his shoulder was fresher at the business-end of a grand slam fortnight.

Now, more than any other time in his life, Murray needed to serve well, and his right shoulder and arm didn't let him down. Having landed only 45 per cent of his first serves in the fourth set, Murray would be successful with 70 per cent in the decider. And he would win 71 per cent of the points he started with a first serve, which was his best one-set number all match.

At the same time, Djokovic's serve was going the other way. The Serbian no longer had the strength in his legs to serve as he had done in the fourth set, when he had made 83 per cent of his first serves. In the fifth set, that percentage was slashed to 45. Marian Vajda, Djokovic's coach, was annoyed with how the scheduling and weather had worked against his player; a combination of television's Super Saturday demands and the risk of tornado-damage had left Djokovic competing over three successive days. Had Djokovic been British – and, as we have seen, he almost did end up representing Great Britain – then there would have been much complaining about how the tennis gods, otherwise known as the television rights-holders, had hampered him.

It was undeniably true that Djokovic's tennis in 2012 hadn't been of the quality of the year before, but it was never going to be. How could it be, when Djokovic had been so magnificent in 2011, not losing a match until the semi-finals of the French Open? But Djokovic hadn't fallen far in 2012. He had won a slam at the Australian Open, he had reached the final at Roland Garros, and he had been a semi-finalist at Wimbledon and the Olympics. And he certainly hadn't become a soft touch. Djokovic wasn't in a slump.

It wasn't going to be the greatest grand slam final in history, no one was claiming that, as it hadn't touched the heights of Nadal's victory over Federer at Wimbledon 2008. Or been the equal of Djokovic's victory over Nadal at the 2012 Australian Open, which had lasted for almost six hours, finished after 1am, and been a great show of skill, resilience and bloody-mindedness. But this match had provided plenty of entertainment. And wasn't it enough that the match could possibly end with Murray becoming the first living British man to win a grand slam title?

When Murray sat down on his chair with a 5-2 lead, leaving him just one service game away from the championship, Djokovic called the trainer on court for a medical time-out that took more than five minutes. It was a move which aggravated a few in the Arthur Ashe Stadium, but not Murray. After all the effort that Djokovic had put into the final, after all the long rallies that he and Murray had played, he didn't deserve to be booed by the crowd. That wasn't fair. But, unfortunately for Djokovic, it was another sign of how New York had never quite taken to him. Djokovic responded with a sarcastic thumbs-up. They would remember that.

The British monarchy had been going through an abdication crisis. The world's athletes were doing Nazi salutes at the

Berlin Olympics. The BBC began broadcasting on television. And the book *Gone With The Wind* had just been published. That all happened the year that a British man had last won a grand slam singles title.

When Fred Perry left New York in 1936 as the US Open champion, no one would have imagined that it would be another 76 years, and 287 grand slam tournaments, before another British man won a major; they wouldn't have even imagined that a couple of years would pass without British success. 'I don't suppose the Lawn Tennis Association thought that champions came along like buses, not being in the bus-riding classes, but no doubt they thought they could whistle up another champion as the club doorman whistles up a cab,' Simon Barnes wrote in *The Times*. 'Who needs Perry? Bloody man's turned professional . . . But that chap Bunny Austin has the makings of champion. But Bunny didn't. He was a triple losing finalist in grand slam tournaments. His last final was at Wimbledon in 1938, and he won four games.'

While Britain waited for another male grand slam champion, the Empire disappeared, the Berlin Wall went up, the Berlin Wall came down, man walked on the Moon, the world entered the digital age, and Tim Henman had been a tea-time tease. John Lloyd had reached the final of the 1977 Australian Open – during a time when some of the leading players didn't bother with the tournament as it was too far away – and Greg Rusedski played for the US Open title in 1997. But they still couldn't change the fact that Fred Perry was the last champion. To mods, skinheads, and the British band Blur, the name 'Fred

Perry' meant a brand of their favourite polo-shirts; to anyone in British tennis, and across the sport, his name was forever a reminder of all the years, the decades, that had passed without success.

Perry, who died in 1996 at the age of 85 after a fall in a hotel bathroom in Melbourne, probably would have quite enjoyed the idea of posthumously tormenting the British tennis establishment. When Murray prepared to serve for the US Open's silver trophy, the Scot gave a few seconds' thought to what he was possibly about to do for British tennis. For the first time in his career, Murray was thinking about Perry on court. This didn't change the fact that Murray was primarily playing for himself, not for queen and country, but it was almost inevitable that Perry would pop into his head; after all, he had been reminded of him almost every week of his professional life. Perry is up there smiling down on me, Murray thought. Maybe. More likely, given the nature of the match, and Djokovic's reputation for playing himself out of danger, Perry would have been on the edge of some celestial seat.

Here's what wasn't on Murray's mind: the money. Others might think that weird, given that he was playing for what would be the biggest one-off sum of his life, a cheque for $1.9 million (or at least an empty envelope which was said to contain a cheque for that amount, with the money paid later). But that was the way it had always been with Murray, and for most elite tennis players; on the court, you play for the glory and the place in history, and you leave any thoughts about cash for later.

It was a little after 9pm in New York, so just past 2am in Britain, when Murray first stood a championship point away from winning a first slam. While Murray's victory would have had a bigger television audience in Britain if it had happened at a more sociable hour, Sky Sports' live broadcast still attracted a peak of more than 1.5 million people. Most of Dunblane was still up in the small hours of the morning. Murray's father Willie, who had chosen not to fly to New York, watched every stroke on his television set. The Dunblane Hotel, which had been given a late licence until 1am, kept the locals going with popcorn, hotdogs and whisky.

Murray's maternal grandparents, Roy and Shirley Erskine, had tried to control their nerves earlier in the day by keeping busy; Shirley, having completed the housework by noon, took their dog for another walk, while Roy had gone to Stirling to play bowls. Now they were seated in front of their television in their house (given the dedication with which they followed their grandson's career, with several leather-bound volumes of newspapers cuttings, they were never going to miss this). Just a few hundred metres away, at the Dunblane Sports Club, they had champagne in the fridge, just in case. And the local butcher had been so optimistic about Murray's chances that he had been preparing some US Open specials to go on sale the next morning: Big Apple Bangers (pork and apple sausages with bacon and cinnamon) and Grand Slam Saltires (steak pie covered in streaky bacon). About the only person in Dunblane, you suspect, who had chosen to miss the match was Murray's paternal grandmother, Ellen Murray;

just as the final was starting, she had taken herself to bed with a cup of Horlicks. She would check the score in the morning.

Where were the tears? The dosey doe? The big embrace? The great emotional moment that the news channels could put on a loop? Truth be told, American fans were a little disappointed by Andy Murray's celebrations. They had watched him cry after losing a Wimbledon final, and they had seen him run into the stands to find his lover, staff and family after winning the Olympics, so surely he was going to do something spectacular after achieving his lifetime's ambition in the Arthur Ashe Stadium. 'The ending was poor television,' the *New Yorker* magazine noted. 'When it was over it seemed as if the sensational play on the court had sapped away whatever energy there might be around it. Djokovic did not seem all that dejected, and Murray did not seem all that excited.'

Murray didn't emote as many Americans had wanted him to. But, for a British audience, and for many around the world, this was a long way from being poor television. This was always about the achievement rather than the party.

There are few more tense moments for a tennis player than serving for a first grand slam. But Murray had rehearsed this so many times in his head over the years – and those rehearsals had given him butterflies – that when it happened for real, it was no longer so terrifying. Suddenly, Murray, at 40-0, had three championship points. Novak Djokovic saved the first one. At 40-15, Murray, having missed with his first serve, hit a decent second. At first, as Djokovic's return left his strings at some speed, Murray thought that it would be 'good'. Was Djokovic doing to Murray what he had done to Roger Federer in previous years when facing match points; which was to be both bold and brilliant? But Murray was wrong, wonderfully wrong. It was 9.04pm on 10 September 2012 in New York (or 2.04am the next day in Dunblane) when Djokovic's return bounced beyond the baseline, and Murray became the US Open champion and the first British man to win a major for 76 years. In the time it had taken a line-judge to call 'out', Murray's life had changed forever. As active as Murray's imagination had been, he was still totally unprepared. Murray crouched and covered his mouth with his hands; he was in shock. Djokovic walked over and gave Murray a hug.

So what next? New York waited. But there was to be no jig or scissor-kick or lap of the court high-fiving the front row, and he didn't collapse on to his back or start blubbing either. Fred Perry used to hurdle the net after winning matches, which was part showmanship and part telling the other guy that he had had much more to give. But 'celebrating in an opponent's face' has never been Murray's style. Murray probably thinks braggadocio is cold meat, and, anyway, he didn't have the energy.

Earlier in the summer, Murray had marked his victories by looking up and pointing his fingers skywards, a celebration which he had declined to explain, preferring to keep it private; here it was again. There were a few tears, but most didn't notice them, because he didn't sob again; one big, weepy catharsis was presumably enough for one summer. He was sorry, he later said, if he didn't look that happy on the outside, because he was very happy on the inside. And he wasn't about to change his behaviour, and turn up the dial from looking 'shocked and pleased' to 'ecstatic' just because that's what America was expecting of him. In a way, there was something quite appealing about Murray's under-stated reaction, and in the next issue of *Private Eye*, a British satirical magazine, they published a small item on 'The Many Faces of Andy Murray'. The same image was repeated four times, with four different captions: defeat, disappointment, frustration, triumph.

For Murray, this was about relief as much as it was about joy. Never again would he be asked 'that stupid question' about whether he could emulate Fred Perry by winning a slam. It was a 'stupid question' that Murray had been asking himself just hours before as he had sat in the locker-room waiting for the final to begin. 'It's something I've been asked most weeks of my life since I was twenty-one. It had really started to get to me earlier in the year. It wasn't just the media. It was everyone. A lot of people had been coming up to me and saying, "Don't worry, you'll win the next one." That had almost made it worse,' Murray would later say. 'I'm just glad I can move on.'

When Murray looked over at his box, he didn't seek out eye contact with one person in particular. His support group were bouncing. Everyone's hugging everybody, Murray thought. Apart from Ivan Lendl, all the other members of Murray's staff had been there for years, and the Scot was thrilled that he could finally share with them the excitement and satisfaction of winning a grand slam. The professional photographers would take thousands of images, but Kim Sears, using a phone with a Union flag case, wanted to capture the moment herself.

But Murray's first minutes as a grand slam champion brought confusion and panic. Roger Federer is so used to slipping on a Rolex for the trophy presentation after a grand slam final that he probably doesn't even realise he is doing it, but wearing a watch for a prize-giving ceremony was still very new for Murray, having become an ambassador for Rado only a couple of weeks before Wimbledon. Indeed, he had forgotten to put his watch on after the Wimbledon final, and that was making him even more anxious now; he was in danger of standing there after another slam final with a bare wrist.

'I don't have it, I don't have it,' Murray called over at his entourage, and he then hobbled over to ask: 'Do you have my watch? I don't have it.' The stadium disc jockey had his carefully chosen party tunes, 'Start Me Up' by the Rolling Stones, and 'Chariots of Fire', which had been played to death during the London Olympics, but Murray was fretting about the wristwatch. It was Sears who told him to have another fish around in his bag; the crisis was averted, and he could prepare for holding up the silver trophy.

Ivan Lendl wasn't about to dance on the furniture either. But Murray did think that he had seen a smile on his coach's face. The player and coach – or as the *New York Times* magazine had called them, 'tennis's odd couple' – had a hug backstage, though that was interrupted when assistant coach and hitting-partner Dani Vallverdu hosed both of them down with champagne. Lendl started swearing and the hug was over. There simply wasn't the chance that night for Murray and Lendl to have a proper debrief.

Murray's victory was a validation of the decision to employ Lendl, a move which had not been without risk. Boris Becker went further than most when he argued that, without Lendl, Murray would not have won the Olympics and the US Open. 'I didn't come here to have a good time,' Lendl said. 'I came here to help Andy win and he did just that. So it's job done.' Except that, in Lendl's head, this was a very long way from being 'job done'. Already, Lendl was thinking to the future, to what might happen next for the Scot. Lendl didn't need to be reminded of what had happened to him after he won his first grand slam title on his fifth appearance in the final of a major; he then lost his sixth and his seventh, so in American sporting parlance that left him at 1-6 for finals. Lendl wanted Murray to avoid that fate.

And, just because Murray was now a grand slam champion, Lendl wasn't going to give any secrets away. 'Andy still has a career to go, we are going to be playing more and more matches against those guys, and if I tell you what we've worked on, if I dissect these matches, I'm giving away stuff. You see how small the margins are. For me to tell the media this would be suicidal.'

Murray's former coaches were also celebrating his 7-6, 7-5, 2-6, 3-6, 6-2 victory. Commentating on the match for Sky Sports, Mark Petchey cried out: 'History has been made.' Brad

Gilbert was perhaps even more emotional. 'I am not ashamed to admit I was a little choked up as I watched Andy Murray win the US Open final, mainly because I was so pleased for him and a bit due to some personal involvement in the whole journey,' the American wrote in the *Daily Mail*. 'There were always going to be bumps and bruises along the way, but I always thought the probability was that he would get to a grand slam title in the end, and it was like watching some sort of completion.'

Djokovic's coach, Marian Vajda, is a decent man, and he was gracious in defeat, arguing that Murray and Djokovic 'are the future guys who will rule tennis. I say it openly and I believe in it: this is the next future. Because I don't see so many players coming in. For ten years it has been Federer–Nadal and now it's Novak and Murray. It will be more often this way. I respect Roger and Rafa and the rest of the top ten, but we're going to keep on seeing these guys at the end.'

'Yippee,' read the one-word text message which Murray's mother, Judy, sent to her parents Roy and Shirley Erskine, who had been following the final from Dunblane. For Judy Murray, watching her youngest son play is never better than a mixture of 'nausea and heart-attack', but this had been worse, bordering on mental and psychological 'torture'. 'The momentum was all with Novak going into the final set but I just had this feeling,' she said. 'I could see in Andy's face and tell from his mannerisms that he wasn't going to let it get away from him.'

Throughout the five-setter, Shirley had felt like 'a rag-doll', and, at the moment of victory, she hadn't been quite sure how to react, so she did nothing. For a while she just sat there on her armchair. Shirley had always teased Murray for being 'Britain's last hope' and now all that hope, as well as a great deal of expectation, angst and agony, had amounted to something. Something 'absolutely wonderful'. 'I just sat there, and then I said, "He's done it, he's done it!" It was such a funny feeling. You've wanted this for so long and then suddenly it's there and you can't take it all in.' Her husband, who had been 'cursing and swearing' at the television for five sets and almost five hours, no longer had to shout at pictures of his grandson to tell him what he was doing wrong and how he could win the match; Murray was a grand slam champion now. Murray's father, Willie, who watched every ball of the match, celebrated too.

Now both of Willie and Judy's sons were grand slam champions. Jamie, the mixed doubles champion from Wimbledon 2007, had followed the match from a hotel room in Luxembourg. Though Jamie had thought that Andy hadn't played his best tennis on the way to the final, he had believed that it was his younger brother's 'time', and an opportunity to get some 'peace of mind' on court. It was 3am local time in the Grand Duchy when Andy completed his victory, 'so quite late'; Jamie didn't shout, scream or use the bed as a trampoline, he just went to bed as he had a match the next day.

Most of Murray's post-match interviews took place in the media centre or in television studios. But one had a better setting. Throughout the tournament, he had been doing a series of interviews with the *New York Times*, and the last of these

'Conversations With Murray' was conducted back in the now-empty Arthur Ashe Stadium. Murray thought back to the last shot of the match, that service return which Djokovic had hit hard and just long. 'I'll remember that bit of court for a while.'

By the time Andy Murray arrived at Hakasan, a Chinese restaurant in midtown Manhattan, his friends and family were light-headed from a combination of the night's events and 'zesty martinis', other cocktails and bottles of Louis Roederer champagne. Murray would later say that everyone else was so drunk that there was no point even trying to catch up. But Murray probably never had any intention of doing so; winning a grand slam title was no reason to break his teetotal regime. To wash down the truffle-roasted duck, stir-fried Brazilian lobster tail and roasted silver cod, he drank nothing stronger than a six-dollar lemon soda.

Judy Murray, who has rarely needed an excuse to have one pudding, thought the occasion warranted a second dessert, so she ordered a chocolate mousse with black cherries and blackcurrant sorbet. The one person missing from the celebrations – the party got through $5,040 of food and $1,408 of alcohol – was Ivan Lendl, who had told Murray how 'dead' he was after the final, which drew this response: 'Tired? He just sat there. I'm the one who has just played for five hours.'

But Lendl, who would wake early the next day to play golf, had undoubtedly been right when he had told Murray that winning a grand slam means better treatment in restaurants, as Hakasan waived the bill for the food and drink, saying that the

US Open champion had to pay only the service charge of $1,290 (we know all of this because, as a sign of Murray's new stardom, a photograph of the bill appeared online and in newspapers). Some of Murray's party went on to a club; he returned to his hotel room around 3am, and that was the best bit; lying there on his bed and taking it all in. In his words, this was about trying to find calmness, and 'a return to neutral'. As Murray would later remember it, he 'wasn't bouncing off the walls or anything', but he didn't fall asleep until 5am.

Then, at 6.30am, he climbed out of bed to begin his 'media blitz' of New York's talk shows. Ordinarily, Murray would have been in a vile mood after just an hour and a half's sleep, but this Tuesday morning was different. 'I woke up and jumped out of bed, which wasn't like me.. I was very excited.' As Murray went from studio to studio, in the company of his silver trophy, it soon became plain that he hadn't changed since becoming a grand slam champion. So, on the set of *CBS This Morning*, he said how he was 'very shy, very self-conscious' and then, when the hosts said they were about to show a clip of his grandparents sitting in their armchairs at home in Dunblane, he cringed: 'Oh, do we have to?'

Appearances on NBC's *Today* and *Live with Kelly and Michael* followed; at the second of those he met the *Friends* actor Matthew Perry and gave him the thrill of holding the trophy. Long gone are the days when a grand slam champion's media commitments finished just minutes after the match with one press conference and maybe a couple of broadcast interviews; there was much more to come for Murray. Just in case anyone had missed him on one of those three shows, he also popped in to the filming of *Late Night with Jimmy Fallon*, where the house band The Roots played a song in his honour. There were other interviews, and a photo-shoot in Central Park's Sheep Meadow where he sat down on the grass to pose with his prize.

It was 11 September, 11 years on from the terrorist attacks on New York, so not the day you would usually choose to throw a party in the city, but no one thought that the celebrations organised for Murray were in any way insensitive or inappropriate. When Murray arrived for the reception held in his honour at the British Consul-General's residence on East 51st Street, there was a piper in tartan playing 'Scotland the Brave'. For all the guests, there were sausage rolls, cucumber sandwiches, balloons and mini-flags. For Murray, there was a hamper full of British junk-food: Hob-Nobs, salt and vinegar Hula Hoops, Winegums and Maltesers.

Murray reached first for a bottle of Irn-Bru, the bright orange fizzy drink (someone said the drink was 'good for hangovers', but of course the Scot didn't have one of those). The party included another interview, this time with a group of print journalists. As Murray had said to Lendl, he had been concerned about how winning a slam would change his life. Still, the day was very much a one-off. He knew that. 'You can treat your life as you want, and I want to keep mine the same.' For Murray, the worst thing that could possible happen after winning a grand slam title would be to change as a person.

Reading the international press coverage, it seemed that the rest of the world's media had almost been as pleased for Murray as the British had. 'It's tempting to declare this a shameful day for English sport,' said the *Sydney Morning Herald*. 'To claim that, 76 years after that country produced its last male grand slam winner, even cross-border rival Scotland has one ... Besides, Murray's groundbreaking victory deserves far greater respect and acclaim. To carry the doubts created by his four previous grand slam final defeats – not to mention the expectations of a success-starved tennis nation – into a fifth set, and emerge with the trophy, is a monumental achievement of the body and the mind.' Reuters news agency declared: 'The nation that invented modern tennis finally has a champion for the new age. The jokes about wooden rackets and men playing tennis in long, white trousers have lost their punchline and Perry can now rest in peace.'

For American writers, Murray's victory had been nothing less than epic. 'Fred Perry, you have company,' noted *Sports Illustrated*'s Jon Wertheim. 'Murray picked a heck of a way to win his long-elusive first major. The win over Djokovic was epic in the truest sense, a wild, five-set odyssey that featured swings of momentum, obstacles, acts of God, redemption and, finally, triumph.' The *New York Times* was thrilled for the Scot: 'Epic is an overused word in tennis, particularly in this era of extraordinary defence when rallies and finals routinely extend to tremendous lengths. But this mettle detector of a US Open final was worthy of the term as was Murray's own personal quest for possession of one of the trophies that continue to define tennis careers.' The paper observed how 'the Big Three is finally and undeniably the Big Four – after years of chasing the lead group of Federer, Nadal and Djokovic, Murray joined their golden-age club in earnest . . . He did it by trumping his own perfectionist streak and the negativity that has long accompanied it: letting a few groans and oaths escape his Scottish lips but never allowing himself to exit this monumental match emotionally or mentally.'

All day, Murray had been receiving messages from friends teasing him about the possibility of becoming Sir Andy (he thought that premature, saying that no one should be knighted for just one good tournament), as well as reading messages from film stars, comedians, sportsmen and politicians. The actor Russell Crowe, the footballer Rio Ferdinand and the cricketer Graeme Swann were among those who logged on to Twitter to congratulate Murray. Sir Sean Connery, the great tartan warrior, was telling everyone to stop saying Murray is British, as 'he's Scottish, and this is great for Scotland'. While Sir Alex Ferguson spoke of his pride after what had been 'the real test of a champion', and the third of Murray's trio of New York celebrity cheerleaders, the actor Kevin Spacey, said he had never previously wanted something so badly for someone else: 'And I'm sure it's going nuts in Britain now.' The former Prime Minister Gordon Brown and the rock star Mick Jagger had both contacted Murray's manager Simon Fuller asking him to personally pass on their congratulations to Murray.

The messages kept coming. Fred Perry's children, daughter Penny and son David, said how happy they were that their father was no longer Britain's last male grand slam champion. There was one note which meant more to Murray than the others. It was from Rafa Nadal. 'Rafa messaged me and said: "Just enjoy it. I'm very happy for you. You deserved it." I got a lot of congratulations but, when you get it from someone you're competing against, and from one of the best players ever, it means a little bit more.'

As Murray walked through arrivals at Heathrow's Terminal Five, tired but happy after a flight from New York's John F.Kennedy Airport, and with a small entourage of air-stewardesses, he would have started to fully appreciate the impact that his victory had had on Britain. The night before, when the Scottish football team had played at Glasgow's Hampden Park, supporters had chanted, 'There's only one Andy Murray.'

Up and down the British Isles, Murray's victory had also had the effect of extending the great Olympic summer. Murray hadn't been able to make the parade of medallists through London on Monday, but he had had a good reason for his absence: winning a slam. 'Just when it seemed that the glorious sporting summer of 2012 was coming to a natural end, an epilogue is provided from New York,' said the leading article in *The Times*, which finished like this: 'At the risk of reimposing the pressure there is at least one more thing to ask of Andy Murray. By next summer, it will be 77 years since Fred Perry won Wimbledon.'

The editorial in the *Daily Telegraph* praised Murray for his graft: 'In sport, we tend to privilege genius over graft. Yet effort can have a nobility of its own. Despite his talent, this triumph did not fall into his lap: he did it the hard way, taking years to hone his game, his approach and his support team. Defeat at Wimbledon this summer – making him the only man save his coach, Ivan Lendl, to have played and lost his first four major finals – could have broken him. Instead, he fought back, dismissing Roger Federer in the Olympics and then breaking Novak Djokovic's resistance in as brutal and wearying a match as ever has been played.'

Sections of the British public hadn't even liked Murray until he had cried on Wimbledon's Centre Court, and then won a gold medal on the same patch of grass; his victory in America asked them to consider their feelings once again. Was that affection? Perhaps even adoration? In *The Times*, Matthew Syed argued: 'It is time to stop fretting about his voice, his hair, his tantrums and his relationship with his mother and to embrace him without inhibition.'

Murray and Kim Sears were also greeted with front-page and inside-page speculation about their relationship, with a number of papers suggesting that he was to keep the party going by proposing. 'Wedding Smasher,' said the *Daily Mirror*, which reported: 'Andy Murray may have sealed his place in history, but he is already planning for the next big match – his wedding.' There was also much conjecture about what Murray's victory would mean financially. The *Sun* tied the all-important bathroom break and the possible riches into one front-page headline: '1 Pee to £100 million.'

*

For three or four days after returning from New York, Andy Murray had hardly left his house in Surrey, only getting out to walk the dogs. That time was spent sleeping, 'chilling' and sitting on the sofa with his girlfriend Kim Sears thinking: 'Did that summer really just happen?' 'Neither of us,' Murray said, 'could quite process the summer.' Murray had been too tired to appear in the parade of Scottish Olympics in Glasgow, which had been held just a couple of days after he flew back into Britain. So Murray's first public appearance in Britain since turning his tennis life around would be in Dunblane.

'There will be bagpipes blowing all over Scotland,' Mary Carillo of CBS had ventured in the moments after Murray's victory. Of course, that was pushing the stereotype too far, but it was impossible to overstate the pleasure that Murray took, on the first Sunday after winning the US Open, when he returned on an open-top bus to Dunblane, to what Monty Python's Flying Circus had described as the worst tennis nation on earth. No one in the little cathedral city cared that it was raining; in fact, it added to the occasion. The only thing more unexpected than a Scottish tennis player winning a grand slam singles title would be for that same Scot to be celebrating his victory under sunshine and Hollywood-blue skies.

It had been a week of celebrations in Dunblane, back where Murray's tennis life had started with swingball in his back garden and then on the artificial grass of the Sports Club. The morning after Murray's victory, people had gathered around the postbox which had been painted gold by the Royal Mail to commemorate his victory at the Olympics, and newspaper front pages had been stuck on the inside of shop windows.

Some 20,000 people, more than the population of Dunblane, were there to see Murray ride the open-top bus and walk around greeting his public. At some points on Murray's route, the crowd was ten deep. Thousands of fans had stood in the drizzle and the downpours for hours as they waited for Murray. A long wait and rain; this was a very British homecoming for a new grand slam champion. There were women in their seventies and eighties who called themselves 'Andy's groupies', there were old school friends, old neighbours, old fans and new fans who had travelled from across Scotland to be there when the US Open champion returned home. Murray was nervous beforehand, if not quite as apprehensive as he had been when preparing to play Novak Djokovic.

Murray signed hundreds, perhaps even thousands, of autographs, he posed for pictures, he was introduced to someone's Jack Russell terrier pup, he accepted hugs from strangers, he chatted and smiled, and he hit a few balls in the rain with children at his first tennis club. About halfway through his walkabout, everything became a bit of a blur for Murray, but he carried on smiling, posing, signing and waving. If Murray didn't kiss any babies, he came close, having his photograph taken with one infant. This was also a celebration of his success at the Olympics, and he handed his singles gold medal and mixed doubles silver medal to children so they could take a closer look. Had you told Murray, as he left the All England Club after the Wimbledon final, that it would end up being the best summer of his life, he probably would have burst into tears again, thinking you were being cruel. Who would have thought that Murray would recover from the disappointment of losing to Roger Federer to win both the Olympics and the US Open? Or that his management company would need to find and hire an open-top bus?

Murray's walkabout lasted for the best part of five hours, so almost as long as it had taken him to fend off Djokovic. Suddenly everyone in Dunblane was a tennis expert, discussing Murray's place in the sport and his future. There was a good case for Murray being seen as the player of the year. The majors had been shared out equally during the 2012 grand slam year, with each of the top four winning one each. Djokovic had won the Australian Open with two remarkable performances, taking almost five hours to beat Murray and then close to six hours to defeat Nadal. With his victory at Roland Garros, Nadal won a record seventh title at the French Open and confirmed that he was the finest clay-courter of all time. Federer's triumph at Wimbledon put him level with Pete Sampras with a record seven titles at the All England Club. And now Murray was the King of New York. So why give Murray the honour? Because of the historical baggage of Britain's 76-year wait for a slam, as well as the personal baggage of having lost his first four slam finals, and his victory at the Olympics. As Lendl put it, Murray had won two 'big ones' in 2012, even if one was bigger than the other.

People spoke about Murray becoming Britain's first world number one as if it was almost an inevitability, while others argued that the first grand slam was always going to be the hardest, and now he had won that, he would play with greater freedom. And Murray hadn't escaped Fred Perry just yet; could he go on to become Britain's first male Wimbledon champion since Perry in 1936?

Jamie Murray had undoubtedly been right when he imagined that winning a slam would give his brother 'peace of mind'. Going back to the practice court after the US Open would be easy for Andy Murray; he wouldn't have to wonder, as he did after his four previous defeats, whether he was the hardest-working failure the sport had ever seen. In the weeks after winning the slam, Murray also felt as though he was going to have a new on-court approach. No longer would he view almost every defeat, even at small tournaments, in such apocalyptic terms; he could be more measured with his thinking. Put simply, Murray was at ease with himself, his tennis, his achievements and his place in the sport. Murray's pre-match nerves in New York had demonstrated that his Olympics victory hadn't done what he thought it had: taking away self-doubt. For that to happen, for Murray to really feel as though he belonged in tennis's golden age, he had to win a grand slam.

Only winning the US Open put the idea of tennis having a Big Four beyond dispute. 'I'm very happy to have been part of this era. Playing against them has made me improve so much. I always said that if I had played in another era, maybe I would have won more, but I wouldn't have been as good a tennis player,' Murray said. 'I think that's how you should be judged at the end of your career, not just on how much you're winning but on the people you're competing against and how good a player you actually were. The guys I've been playing against are some of the best of all time.'

If injury or illness had forced Murray into retirement on the morning after winning the US Open, he would have been happy with his lot, as he would have gone into the tennis afterlife with a slam. But, since he didn't have to retire, Murray wanted more slams. Twenty-five wasn't young for a first-time grand slam champion, but it wasn't desperately old either. He was in his prime, and still thought that he had another five, six or possibly even more years challenging for the sport's biggest prizes.

'I hope,' Murray said, 'that this isn't the conclusion of a dream, but the start of something.'

Acknowledgements

I'm indebted to my fellow tennis writers for their help with this project, and in particular to Simon Cambers of The Tennis Space, the *Independent*'s Paul Newman, and Stuart Fraser. My thanks to Ian Marshall, Kyle McEnery and the rest of the brilliant team at Simon & Schuster, and to David Luxton of David Luxton Associates.

Andy Murray's Career Record

Grand slam record

2005 Wimbledon:
First round: Beat George Bastl (Switzerland) in straight sets
Second round: Beat Radek Stepanek (Czech Republic) in straight sets
Third round: Lost to David Nalbandian (Argentina) in five sets

2005 US Open:
Murray won three rounds of qualifying to reach the main draw
First round: Beat Andrei Pavel (Romania) in five sets
Second round: Lost to Arnaud Clement (France) in five sets

2006 Australian Open:
First round: Lost to Juan Ignacio Chela (Argentina) in straight sets

2006 French Open:
First round: Lost to Gael Monfils (France) in straight sets

2006 Wimbledon:
First round: Beat Nicolas Massu (Chile) in straight sets
Second round: Beat Julien Benneteau (France) in four sets
Third round: Beat Andy Roddick (USA) in straight sets
Fourth round: Lost to Marcos Baghdatis (Cyprus) in three sets

2006 US Open:
First round: Beat Robert Kendrick (USA) in four sets
Second round: Beat Alessio Di Mauro (Italy) in straight sets
Third round: Beat Fernando Gonzalez (Chile) in five sets
Fourth round: Lost to Nikolay Davydenko (Russia) in four sets

Andy Murray's Career Record

2007 Australian Open:
First round: Beat Alberto Martin (Spain) in straight sets
Second round: Beat Fernando Verdasco (Spain) in straight sets
Third round: Beat Juan Ignacio Chela (Argentina) in straight sets
Fourth round: Lost to Rafa Nadal (Spain) in five sets

Murray missed the 2007 French Open and Wimbledon because of a wrist injury.

2007 US Open:
First round: Beat Pablo Cuevas (Uruguay) in straight sets
Second round: Beat Jonas Bjorkman (Sweden) in five sets
Third round: Lost to Hyung-Taik Lee (Korea) in four sets

2008 Australian Open:
First round: Lost to Jo-Wilfried Tsonga (France) in four sets

2008 French Open:
First round: Beat Jonathan Eysseric (France) in five sets
Second round: Beat Jose Acasuso (Argentina) in straight sets
Third round: Lost to Nicolas Almagro (Spain) in four sets

2008 Wimbledon:
First round: Beat Fabrice Santoro (France) in straight sets
Second round: Beat Xavier Malisse (Belgium) in straight sets
Third round: Beat Tommy Haas (Germany) in four sets
Fourth round: Beat Richard Gasquet (France) in five sets
Quarter-final: Lost to Rafa Nadal (Spain) in straight sets

2008 US Open:
First round: Beat Sergio Roitman (Argentina) in straight sets
Second round: Beat Michael Llodra (France) in four sets
Third round: Beat Jurgen Melzer (Austria) in five sets
Fourth round: Beat Stanislas Wawrinka (Switzerland) in straight sets
Quarter-final: Beat Juan Martin del Potro (Argentina) in four sets
Semi-final: Beat Rafa Nadal (Spain) in four sets
Final: Lost to Roger Federer (Switzerland) in straight sets

2009 Australian Open:
First round: Beat Andrei Pavel (Romania) after a retirement in the second set
Second round: Beat Marcel Granollers (Spain) in straight sets
Third round: Beat Jurgen Melzer (Austria) in straight sets
Fourth round: Lost to Fernando Verdasco (Spain) in five sets

2009 French Open:
First round: Beat Juan Ignacio Chela (Argentina) in straight sets
Second round: Beat Potito Starace (Italy) in four sets
Third round: Beat Janko Tipsarevic (Serbia) after a retirement in the second set
Fourth round: Beat Marin Cilic (Croatia) in straight sets
Quarter-final: Lost to Fernando Gonzalez (Chile) in four sets

Andy Murray: Champion

2009 Wimbledon:
First round: Beat Robert Kendrick (USA) in four sets
Second round: Beat Ernests Gulbis (Latvia) in straight sets
Third round: Beat Viktor Troicki (Serbia) in straight sets
Fourth round: Beat Stanislas Wawrinka (Switzerland) in five sets
Quarter-final: Beat Juan Carlos Ferrero (Spain) in straight sets
Semi-final: Lost to Andy Roddick (USA) in four sets

2009 US Open:
First round: Beat Ernests Gulbis (Latvia) in straight sets
Second round: Beat Paul Capdeville (Chile) in four sets
Third round: Beat Taylor Dent (USA) in straight sets
Fourth round: Lost to Marin Cilic (Croatia) in straight sets

2010 Australian Open:
First round: Beat Kevin Anderson (South Africa) in straight sets
Second round: Beat Marc Gicquel (France) in straight sets
Third round: Beat Florent Serra (France) in straight sets
Fourth round: Beat John Isner (USA) in straight sets
Quarter-final: Beat Rafa Nadal (Spain) after a retirement in the third set
Semi-final: Beat Marin Cilic (Croatia) in four sets
Final: Lost to Roger Federer (Switzerland) in straight sets

2010 French Open:
First round: Beat Richard Gasquet (France) in five sets
Second round: Beat Juan Ignacio Chela (Argentina) in four sets
Third round: Beat Marcos Baghdatis (Cyprus) in four sets
Fourth round: Lost to Tomas Berdych (Czech Republic) in straight sets

2010 Wimbledon:
First round: Beat Jan Hajek (Czech Republic) in straight sets
Second round: Beat Jarkko Nieminen (Finland) in straight sets
Third round: Beat Gilles Simon (France) in straight sets
Fourth round: Beat Sam Querrey (USA) in straight sets
Quarter-final: Beat Jo-Wilfried Tsonga (France) in four sets
Semi-final: Lost to Rafa Nadal (Spain) in straight sets

2010 US Open:
First round: Beat Lukas Lacko (Slovakia) in straight sets
Second round: Beat Dustin Brown (Germany) in straight sets
Third round: Lost to Stanislas Wawrinka (Switzerland) in four sets

2011 Australian Open:
First round: Beat Karol Beck (Slovakia) after a retirement in the third set
Second round: Beat Illya Marchenko (Ukraine) in straight sets
Third round: Beat Guillermo Garcia-Lopez (Spain) in straight sets
Fourth round: Beat Jurgen Melzer (Austria) in straight sets
Quarter-final: Beat Alexandr Dolgopolov (Ukraine) in four sets

Andy Murray's Career Record

Semi-final: Beat David Ferrer (Spain) in four sets
Final: Lost to Novak Djokovic (Serbia) in straight sets

2011 French Open:
First round: Beat Eric Prodon (France) in straight sets
Second round: Beat Simone Bolelli (Italy) in straight sets
Third round: Beat Michael Berrer (Germany) in straight sets
Fourth round: Beat Viktor Troicki (Serbia) in five sets
Quarter-final: Beat Juan Ignacio Chela (Argentina) in straight sets
Semi-final: Lost to Rafa Nadal (Spain) in straight sets

2011 Wimbledon:
First round: Beat Daniel Gimeno-Traver (Spain) in four sets
Second round: Beat Tobias Kamke (Germany) in straight sets
Third round: Beat Ivan Ljubicic (Croatia) in four sets
Fourth round: Beat Richard Gasquet (France) in straight sets
Quarter-final: Beat Feliciano Lopez (Spain) in straight sets
Semi-final: Lost to Rafa Nadal (Spain) in four sets

2011 US Open:
First round: Beat Somdev Devvarman (India) in straight sets
Second round: Beat Robin Haase (Netherlands) in five sets
Third round: Beat Feliciano Lopez (Spain) in straight sets
Fourth round: Beat Donald Young (USA) in straight sets
Quarter-final: Beat John Isner (USA) in four sets
Semi-final: Lost to Rafa Nadal (Spain) in four sets

2012 Australian Open:
First round: Beat Ryan Harrison (USA) in four sets
Second round: Beat Edouard Roger-Vasselin (France) in straight sets
Third round: Beat Michael Llodra (France) in straight sets
Fourth round: Beat Mikhail Kukushkin (Kazakhstan) after a retirement in the third set
Quarter-final: Beat Kei Nishikori (Japan) in straight sets
Semi-final: Lost to Novak Djokovic (Serbia) in five sets

2012 French Open:
First round: Beat Tatsuma Ito (Japan) in straight sets
Second round: Beat Jarkko Nieminen (Finland) in four sets
Third round: Beat Santiago Giraldo (Colombia) in straight sets
Fourth round: Beat Richard Gasquet (France) in four sets
Quarter-final: Lost to David Ferrer (Spain) in four sets

2012 Wimbledon:
First round: Beat Nikolay Davydenko (Russia) in straight sets
Second round: Beat Ivo Karlovic (Croatia) in four sets
Third round: Beat Marcos Baghdatis (Cyprus) in four sets
Fourth round: Beat Marin Cilic (Croatia) in straight sets
Quarter-final: Beat David Ferrer (Spain) in four sets

Andy Murray: Champion

Semi-final: Beat Jo-Wilfried Tsonga (France) in four sets
Final: Lost to Roger Federer (Switzerland) in four sets

2012 US Open:
First round: Beat Alex Bogomolov Junior (Russia) in straight sets
Second round: Beat Ivan Dodig (Croatia) in straight sets
Third round: Beat Feliciano Lopez (Spain) in four sets
Fourth round: Beat Milos Raonic (Canada) in straight sets
Quarter-final: Beat Marin Cilic (Croatia) in four sets
Semi-final: Beat Tomas Berdych (Czech Republic) in four sets
Final: Beat Novak Djokovic (Serbia) in five sets

Other career highlights

First final on the ATP Tour:
In Bangkok in 2005

First title on the ATP Tour
In San Jose in 2006

Year-end ranking:
2003: 546
2004: 51
2005: 6
2006: 17
2007: 11
2008: 4
2009: 4
2010: 4
2011: 4

****

2012 Olympic Games singles (best of three sets apart from the final, which was the best of five sets):
First round: Beat Stanislas Wawrinka (Switzerland) in straight sets
Second round: Beat Jarkko Nieminen (Finland) in straight sets
Third round: Beat Marcos Baghdatis (Cyprus) in three sets
Quarter-final: Beat Nicolas Almagro (Spain) in straight sets
Semi-final: Beat Novak Djokovic (Serbia) in straight sets
Final: Beat Roger Federer (Switzerland) in straight sets

Murray also won a silver medal in the Olympic mixed doubles tournament, with Laura Robson.